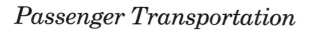

Passenger Transportation

Passenger

Transportation

Martin T. Farris
Arizona State University

Forrest E. Harding
California State University, Long Beach

PRENTICE-HALL, INC., ENGLEWOOD CLIFFS, NEW JERSEY

Library of Congress Cataloging in Publication Data

FARRIS, MARTIN T.   (date)
     Passenger transportation.

     Includes bibliographies and index.
     1. Transportation—Passenger traffic.   I. Harding, Forrest E., (date), joint author.
     II. Title.
     HE151.F23   380.5'2   75-35709
     ISBN 0-13-652750-7

©1976 by Prentice-Hall, Inc.,
Englewood Cliffs, New Jersey 07632

Printed in the United States of America.

10   9   8   7   6   5   4   3   2   1

Prentice-Hall International, Inc., *London*
Prentice-Hall of Australia, Pty. Ltd., *Sydney*
Prentice-Hall of Canada, Ltd., *Toronto*
Prentice-Hall of India Private Limited, *New Delhi*
Prentice-Hall of Japan, Inc., *Tokyo*
Prentice-Hall of Southeast Asia Pte., Ltd., *Singapore*

To Rhoda and Linda
whose patience, help and devotion
made this book possible.

Contents

Preface

Society suffers from many problems. A considerable number of these problems share one common characteristic: the movement of people. Passenger transportation probably affects more parts of society than does any other single problem. It is an important part of urban problems, national problems, and international problems.

For example, there are these considerations:

1. Passenger transportation is an important part of the overall transportation problem of the nation and affects in some way nearly all aspects of transportation in general. To illustrate this point we would cite: the coming of AMTRAK and its attempts to solve intercity-rail passenger transportation problems; the dilemma of urban transportation, with buses, the private automobile, parking difficulties, subways and transit problems; attempts to update transportation systems with acts providing for urban mass transit aid, highway aid, and airport/airway improvement legislation; the problem of the intercity transportation interface with urban transportation; the problem of airline fares and earnings coupled with performance problems resulting in delays and passenger frustrations; the decline of ocean passenger transportation, subsidization of ships, and the lack of maritime policy.

2. Passenger transportation is an important part of society's ecological problem. Air pollution, noise pollution, highway and street congestion, airway congestion, and water pollution are directly or indirectly related to the movement of people.

3. Passenger transportation is an important part of the sociological problems of society. Mobility—or the lack of it—affects social groups; interaction between groups is in direct ratio to the means of transporting people; the character and structure of neighborhoods and regions are affected by the quality of transportation.

4. Passenger transportation is an integral part of the energy crisis, with transportation consuming over 53 percent of all petroleum sources of energy domestically and 24 percent of total energy from all sources going into transportation.

5. Passenger transportation provides one of the limits to planning and urban-regional development. At the same time, it is one of the prime candidates for development and is considered part of the "social overhead capital" necessary for growth.

6. Finally, passenger transportation provides one of the major challenges to the engineer and city planner, one of the limiting factors to the public administrator, and one of the stated parameters to the geographer. In a phrase, the common thread among many disciplines and professions, among many social problems, is the movement of people.

STUDY OF PASSENGER TRANSPORTATION

From an academic viewpoint, material on and study of passenger transportation appears in at least seven academic areas. Courses that are based at least in part on passenger transportation can be found in the areas of Business and Economics, Civil Engineering, Public Administration, Sociology, Geography, Technology or Aeronautics, and Architecture. It should be emphasized that these courses vary in their treatment of the problem of passenger transportation but all are concerned with passenger transportation in some way.

To the best of our knowledge, no comprehensive treatment of passenger transportation now exists. There is today no one book, text or otherwise, that adequately treats this subject. Small parts of the subject are included in several places and in several types of books but no single treatment of passenger transportation exists.

GENESIS

The authors were faced with a lack of textual material when they taught a course called "Passenger Transportation" at the University of Hawaii. Similarly, both have been faced with the problem of choosing textual material for a course called "Air Transportation" at their respective institutions. Further, our colleagues in both engineering and geography tell us that material considering the economic, social and business aspects of the movements of people are notably lacking in textual material on transportation engineering, urban geography, city planning, regional planning, and so on, even though material exists on the engineering, geographical, and planning aspects.

In view of this situation, we resolved to write a book that (a) could be used as a text to set the tone and present an approach to passenger transportation as a separate subject, and (b) could be used as a supplemental resource in those many courses that consider passenger transportation primarily from an engineering, geographical, or planning viewpoint.

APPROACH

The subject of passenger transportation is so broad in scope and affects so many aspects of modern life that a single book comprehensively treating the subject would be practically impossible. Accordingly, we asked ourselves "What is common to all these approaches to the movement of people?" The answer is that passenger transportation is basically a series of interrelated "systems"—physical, economic, pricing, and regulatory. Out of these systems flows a series of interrelated "problems"—a marketing problem, an urban problem, an ecological problem, a policy-making problem, and the problem of managing change. Hence, we cast our approach in a "systems and problems" framework.

A second innovation of this project has been to adopt a functional framework. Instead of considering the movement of people from a modal viewpoint (for example, air transportation, highway systems), and instead of considering transportation from a spatial view (for example, urban transportation, regional planning), we consider it from the view of the function produced: passenger transportation.

Third, since the subject is so broad and comprehensive, we cannot hope to offer a complete and well-rounded discussion of even the underlying systems and related problems of passenger transportation. We can, however, offer a series of short chapters designed to provide an approach or a framework within which the subject of passenger transportation can be more fully developed.

It is hoped that these three innovations—a systems-problems approach, a functional orientation, and an overall framework—will assist both the students and the professor in understanding the intriguing subject of passenger transportation.

Finally, we wish to express gratitude to all of our colleagues who have encouraged us in this task, especially to Professor H. David Bess, University of Hawaii, who made valuable early contributions to our thinking on the subject; Professor Donald E. Cleveland, University of Michigan, who read the manuscript and made valuable suggestions; Professors Norman Daniel and Douglas Cochran, Arizona State University; G. L. Gifford, University of Arizona; and Roy J. Sampson, University of Oregon, who graciously used the manuscript in classes in Air Transportation, Passenger Transportation, and Problems of Transportation, in a semifinished form; and students in these classes, as well as our own, who helpfully assisted us with their comments and evaluations. We are, of course, responsible for any errors of omission or commission.

Martin T. Farris
Arizona State University

Forrest E. Harding
California State University,
Long Beach

1

THE IMPORTANCE OF PASSENGER TRANSPORTATION

There's something about transportation that is inherently appealing to most people. Authors have been enthralled by the subject for many years. If one looks at the typical collection of transportation books in most libraries, chances are very good that a number of them deal with the role of transportation in history. Historians are fond of connecting transportation with the development of countries and regions. Writers of screen stories often find transportation a perfect setting for mysteries, adventure, and intrigue—formerly it was a train rocketing through small European countries on its way to Istanbul or some other "romantic" eastern destination, but nowadays it may well be an airplane journey or a motorcycle experience. Ballad writers use transportation as their setting—the hero or anti-hero is returning to or leaving from a familiar place or venturing into the unknown. Even love songs celebrate transportation—in the sense that someone is coming back, going away, or separated temporarily only to return. The adventure of the open road is no new feeling confined to today's youth. Truly, the "romance of transportation" has many meanings.

Mankind has always traveled. While one might be wise to avoid searching for the motive, it may often be Thorstein Veblen's celebrated "idle curiosity." Of course, many journeys are made with a specific purpose in mind—work, trips to the store, travel to class, to visit relatives. However, the propensity to travel—to experience the unknown, to see new places and new things—seems to be built in.

Passenger transportation, or "people travel," has usually led the way, and the transportation of things or goods has normally followed. Freight transportation is extremely important from an economic, engineering, political, military, or business viewpoint, but typically it has been passenger transportation that has pioneered the routes, led to the development of technology and procedures, and sometimes even provided the equipment by which goods have later been moved.

Much of what we call civilization is based on transportation. In fact, Kipling once wrote: "Transportation *is* civilization." In the spread of ideas, the interchange of cultures, the knowledge of new and previously unknown peoples, customs, and tribes, passenger transportation is indeed the pivotal ingredient. In his interesting little book *Transportation and Politics,* Roy J. Wolfe details civilization after civilization that has either prospered or fallen due to its transportation policies and the existence of geographic "barriers and corridors." It is indeed interesting that civilization has developed most notably in areas where transportation presented fewer problems than elsewhere—as in most of Europe, parts of Asia, and throughout North America—and that it has been held back where transportation was difficult—as in many parts of South America, much of Africa (particularly tropical Africa), and the highlands of Asia.

Cultural advance is based on new ideas. New ideas come from man's travels. Alexander spread Greek culture, knowledge, and customs by military might originally, but it was the travels and commercial activities that followed that established those concepts we now call "Western Civilization." The Phoenicians were great sailors, travelers, and traders whose horizons were almost unlimited. While their power, state, and culture have long passed, their alphabet lives on as a reminder of the importance of travel. Marco Polo brought the ideas of the then well developed East to a backward and isolated West. Many of these ideas contributed to the reawakening in Europe that historians call the Renaissance. So, too, the Crusades exposed many to the concepts and ideas of the Middle East. While the cost was high, Europe was the better for it. The point is, cultural interaction is based on passenger transportation and communication.

Passenger transportation has also played a major role in the location of cities. There are few urban centers in America of over 100,000 population not located on a river, body of water, or stream—water transportation being originally the cheapest and easiest way for men to move. Many European and Asian cities are located where trails and streams meet. London, Marseilles, Paris, Venice, Vienna, Rotterdam, Antwerp, Singapore, Shanghai—the list of major cities tied to natural transportation is inexhaustible.

The importance of transportation to the military has been detailed many times. The Roman Empire was based on superior roads and a superb system of military highways, the most famous of which was the Appian Way. These roads were laid out with an eye to moving troops—it was passenger transportation, not freight transportation that was important. The great ancient empire of the Incas was supported by a superior system of roads used for passenger travel. Unfortunately, foot transportation was the only type known to these people, and so their roads were of little military significance against mounted men with guns. Bismarck used railroads to unite the quarreling states of Germany and central Europe. England controlled the huge subcontinent of India by owning and controlling railroads—and locating them primarily for political and military purposes (passenger transportation) rather than economic purposes (freight transportation). Russia consolidated its control over Siberia and its eastern provinces by railroads. Indeed, the Trans-Siberian Railroad was used as an instrument of expansion against parts of China. Hitler saw the need for the autobahn to move people rapidly for military purposes and based the blitzkrieg on rapid transportation. Hannibal crossing the Alps on elephants to assault the back door of Rome, Genghis Khan sweeping out of the Mongolian uplands on horseback to conquer huge areas of Asia—the examples of the importance of passenger transportation to military might, conquest, and defense are legion.

Within a region or territory, passenger transportation provides the unifying force—literally the "tie that binds." Communications and interchange are as necessary for politics as they are for business and economic action. To be a unified whole, a region must have effective transportation. This truism led to the use of the railroad in the past as a method of holding a country together. Examples of unification by rail include the western expansion of railroads in the United States and the construction of transcontinental railroads in Canada. It is sometimes said that the Union triumphed over the Confederacy in the Civil War because its transportation system was superior, connecting all of the states of the north with an east-west orientation. The southern states had less rail mileage, all units or states were not connected to all others by rail, and unfortunately (from a military and political viewpoint), rail lines were predominantly north-south oriented. No effective transportation link existed as a unifying force for the region. For a region to be a separate entity, government and business must have an effective transportation link to all areas. Cultural and economic interchange between people is the unifying force of all regions.

Passenger transportation is also an important unifying force in regional alliances, where the association of nations is more often than not based on transportation links. Internationally, countries are linked by transportation. It is no accident that all the countries of the European Economic Community (the Common Market) are well connected by transportation, that the North Atlantic Treaty Organization exists among countries interconnected by several transportation modes, or that the Communist bloc alliances are based on closely knit transportation.

Passenger transportation is a very large user of natural resources, particularly energy sources. The energy crisis of the 1970s has graphically called attention to the predominant role of the automobile, the unusual frequency of air service between cities, need for more effective public passenger transportation, and the emerging renaissance of intercity rail transportation. It is expected that energy shortages will continue for many years, which is another reason to be cognizant of passenger transportation as a major force in our society in the last quarter of the twentieth century.

Passenger transportation is of major importance to cities also. Once more the unifying force seems to be the transportation linkages and systems. The suburbs are bound to the central business district by effective transportation. The interaction of one suburb with a neighboring suburb is often much less significant than the interaction between the central business district and each suburb. Even the more recent development of regional shopping centers and the corresponding decline of the central business district is based on passenger transportation. As the automobile and the street system reduce dependence on public passenger transportation, the central business district begins to decline and regional concentrations of business grow up where parking is available and goods and services are conveniently located. The German historical school long ago developed a theory of development of cities based on the transportation linkages between the hinterlands and the city.

Given this importance of passenger transportation, it is not surprising to find that urban development has followed public transportation systems. It is often pointed out that in areas like Greater New York City, one of the most densely populated places in the U.S., pockets and corridors of relatively sparse population exist because of lack of public transportation. While the automobile has changed the development pattern somewhat, cities are still laid out along the trolley lines of the past—the subways, bus lines, and rapid transit transportation corridors of the present.

A most interesting phenomenon is evidenced in tracing the development of urban centers. People tend to both congregate and live near means of rapid and public transportation. Public transportation, on the other hand, can exist only where people concentrate and where sufficient points of origin and destination justify the investment in transportation facilities. Which comes first—the transportation? Well, no—the demand must exist to make transportation economically justifiable. Then do people come first only to be followed by transportation? No, people locate where transportation is convenient. The answer to the paradox is that both develop together: Concentrations of people and transportation are closely interconnected and mutually interdependent in their growth and development.

This mutual interdependence is not confined solely to development but pervades much of passenger transportation. Take, for example, today's multiplicity of social, urban, and environmental problems. Passenger transportation is at once both a cause and an effect. Many of these problems are due to the urbanization and suburbanization, the development, and the centralization of the population in the city. These developments come about because of effective passenger transportation. Yet congestion, smog, pollution, depressed neighborhoods, urban blight—these problems are also caused by or contributed to by passenger transportation. Passenger transportation thus becomes both cause and effect—a perplexing and ever present problem.

This two-way relationship will probably become even more intense in the future. The most recent census discloses that in the U.S. the population is becoming increasingly concentrated in urban centers. In 1970, 58 percent of the population occupied exactly 1 percent of the land area; in 1960, 54 percent of the population was living in urban locations. The general population of the U.S. grew 13 percent between 1960 and 1970 but population in urban places grew 19 percent during the same period. It is estimated that about two-thirds of the population now lives on less than 1 percent of our land area.

However, at the same time that the urbanization phenomenon is taking place, so is the phenomenon of suburbanization. That is to say, the central business districts (usually referred to as "CBD") are on the decline and the population growth of the city proper has often decreased. This phenomenon is the direct result of better transportation for both people and freight. Many firms have left the CBD to locate on the periphery of the urban area, where land is cheaper, congestion less, and conditions more pleasant. With a well-developed street and highway system, workers and executives can readily reach these new locations. Likewise, the delivery and pickup of goods produced and the supplying of parts and materials are facilitated by these same passenger transportation systems. In many types of economic undertaking, plants no longer need to be located on a rail line or near a waterway. Further, with a well-developed passenger transportation system, workers are attracted, for they understandably prefer to avoid the problems of the CBD. They likewise locate on the edge of the city, thereby causing urban sprawl, congestion, pollution, and the problems of suburbia. Once more the mutual interdependency effect takes place—effective passenger transportation causes people and firms to move to suburbia, the move to suburbia causes a demand for more effective passenger transportation and a myriad of sociological and ecological problems.

This is to explain briefly that which is known, felt, and experienced by every reader of this book—the U.S. is becoming an urban nation. It also points up the importance of passenger transportation in two ways. First, urbanization and suburbanization both rest on passenger transportation. Without it, urbanization cannot take place and the suburbs cannot grow. Second, passenger transportation between these urban and suburban concentrations becomes even more important. As population concentrates, passenger transportation between concentration—we call it intercity passenger transportation—takes up more time, effort, and economic resources—indeed becomes the "tie that binds" the nation into a whole or the society into one.

One final demographic characteristic is worth mentioning relative to the importance of passenger transportation: The age composition of our population has shifted dramatically. For many years little attention was paid to the subject except by demographic experts and those interested in the changes in long-term population. The "gravity center" of our population was around age 40 due to infant mortality, the normally high percentage of older people, and a fairly low birth rate. Then in the late 1940s and up to the mid-1950s, a tremendous "baby boom" took place. This postwar bulge in birth rates was followed by a drop in birth rates in the 1960s and some further decline in the 1970s, but even so its effect has been to shift the gravity

center of population away from the 40 age group to a younger one—
the so-called "young adults" of today.

This change in population composition has had dramatic effects
on our economy. In the 1960s, the most populous age in the labor
force suddenly shifted from 40 to 16-17. For a decade, up until 1972,
the largest group in the labor force each year was 16-17. This was the
"bulge" of the baby boom of 1945 to 1955 entering the labor force.
Given the level of medical knowledge, we can anticipate this population bulge will yearly progress throughout time into the future.
Perhaps it will cause another "bulge" as families are formed during
the 20-30 group and another delayed bulge will become apparent in
the labor force data in the 1985-1995 period.

Given the level of affluence in our society plus the behavior
pattern of people, this changed population composition is having and
will continue to have profound effects on passenger transportation
just as it has had profound effects on retailing, housing, demand for
baby food and children's toys, and so forth. Young people are curious
and restless. They long to see the unknown and to broaden their
horizons. Even after settling down to their chosen work, they remain
flexible and anxious and able to travel. A young population is a
mobile population. In the late 1960s, society experienced a new era
in which youth travel was the "in" thing to do. Never were more
students in Europe and abroad. Never had we seen quite the number
of young people on our highways and byways involved in apparently
aimless moving from place to place. Witness the "youth fares" and
"youth plans" of our carriers as they began slowly to appreciate the
potential of this market.

The automobile remains not only the most flexible means of
transportation but a conspicuous status symbol. Young adults demand
cars and have the means to acquire and maintain them. The effects
on the streets and highways is only beginning to be felt—as the baby
bulge continues to enter the workforce and acquire the means of
purchasing even more cars, we shall see even more congestion, pollution, and ecological problems.

Further, the younger generation learned to travel early. In the
past, it was not uncommon to find that a large majority of the population had traveled less than a few hundred miles from where they
were born and raised. Today, the means, both physical and economic,
are available for the travel experience. Few of today's young adults
have not already traveled distances that would have been unheard of

a generation ago. These travel experiences will certainly be reflected in behavior in the years ahead as young adults graduate into middle age and finally old age. One can confidently predict that population mobility will be exaggerated and be with our society for many years to come.

All of this means simply that passenger transportation is now and will continue to be more important than in the past. People have always traveled and much of the world's civilization, culture, advancement, and structure has been affected by this fact. In the future, people will travel even more. This is particularly true for the youth-oriented, modern world of the 1970s.

Passenger transportation, then, becomes not only more important to our society but also more of a problem. The manner in which people move, the whole structure of passenger transportation, and the effects of movement become problems for study and consideration.

We do not conceive of passenger transportation in terms of "things" such as vehicles, roadways, airways, railways, status symbols, places to spend money—but rather in terms of a series of "systems" and "problems." A "system" is an organized whole made up of components that are integrated, interactive, and adaptive. The relationships between the components tie the system together. The systems approach stresses the examination of these components individually, in relation to each other, and to the system as a whole. To us, passenger transportation is made up of four interconnected and interacting systems: the physical system, the economic system, the pricing system, and the regulatory system of passenger transportation.

Out of these four "systems" flow five interconnected and interacting problems: the marketing problem, the urban transportation problem, the problem of social cost vs. benefits (the ecological problem), a gigantic public policy problem, and finally, the problem of managing or living with change. Rather than merely describing passenger transportation and its many facets, we cast our approach in terms of parallel and interacting "systems" and "problems." The chapters that follow reflect this innovative systems and problems approach. It is, we hope, a more rational and effective way to comment on one of the more important aspects of our society: passenger transportation.

ADDITIONAL READINGS

BRAY, N. P., *Transport and Communication* (London: Weidenfeld & Nicolson, Ltd., 1969), 145 pp.

FROMM, GARY, ed., *Transport Investment and Economic Development* (Washington, D.C.: The Brookings Institution, 1965), 314 pp.

GILMORE, HARLAN W., *Transportation and the Growth of Cities* (Glencoe, Illinois: The Free Press, 1953), 170 pp.

HAEFELE, EDWIN T., ed., *Transport and National Goals* (Washington, D.C.: The Brookings Institution, 1969), 201 pp.

LEE, NORMAN E., *Travel and Transport through the Ages,* 2d ed. (Cambridge: The Cambridge University Press, 1958), 187 pp.

MACGILL, CAROLINE E., *History of Transportation in the United States before 1860* (Washington, D.C.: Carnegie Institution of Washington, 1948), 677 pp.

OWEN, WILFRED, *Cities in the Motor Age* (New York: Cooper Square Publishers, 1970), 176 pp.

——, *Strategy for Mobility* (Washington, D.C.: The Brookings Institution, 1964), 249 pp.

——, *The Accessible City* (Washington, D.C.: The Brookings Institution, 1972), 152 pp.

RAE, JOHN B., *The Road and the Car in American Life* (Cambridge, Mass.: The M.I.T. Press, 1971), 390 pp.

RINGWALT, J. L., *Development of Transportation Systems in the United States* (Philadelphia: 1888, Johnson Reprint Co. Ltd., 1966), 398 pp.

WOLFE, ROY I., *Transportation and Politics* (New York: D. Van Nostrand Company, Inc., 1963), 136 pp.

PART ONE

Systems
Of
Passenger
Transportation

We have referred to the "systems" concept as our approach to passenger transportation. Perhaps a further analogy will prove helpful in illustrating systems thinking. Visualize, if you will, a black box that performs a given function utilizing inputs at one end and outputs at the other. Let us call it a "system." In seeking to understand how this system works and how it performs its function, we discover that our black box has a cover. When we lift the cover, we should be able to see the components of the black box, or the system.

But upon lifting the cover, we find inside another series of somewhat smaller black boxes! Each of these is also a system (let us call them component systems) and they are all working together and interrelating and interacting on one another as they use the inputs and contribute in various ways to the output of the overall system. Each of these black boxes must also be analyzed if we are to understand its role or function in the whole system. We discover that each of these black boxes (component systems) has a cover. When we lift these covers, we should be able to see the working parts of each.

But upon doing so, we find inside still another series of black boxes! Each of these, smaller still, is likewise a system (let us call them subsystems). They, too, are all working together and interrelating and interacting on one another to perform their particular task.

The analogy of a black box full of component systems which are also black boxes and full of subsystems could go on and on. Enough has been said for the reader to understand that systems have parts that are also systems—and that these parts have more parts that are themselves systems, and so forth. Our task is not to continue to trace down each black box and analyze each part back to its foundation (ultimately we would arrive at a man with a body, a mind, and a personality doing a job—and this is the greatest system of all!). Rather, our task is to understand as best we can how each component system interacts with and relates to all other component systems to make up the whole, and, how each component system is made up of interacting and interrelated subsystems.

One final analogy may be useful in explaining the systems concept. The human body may be thought of as a system—it has input, outputs, and performs functions. But the body is made up of many component systems such as the circulatory system, respiratory system, nervous system, digestive system, vascular-muscular system, and so forth. In turn, each of these component systems, say the circulatory system, is made up of yet other systems—in this case, veins and arteries. To understand the way the body functions, it is well to know something about the component systems and how each component system relates to other component systems. Also, one should appreciate that each component system is itself a system. But to understand how the body functions, in running, say, one does not need to know all there is to know about the veins—only that they exist, that they are necessary for the function to be produced, and that they are both a system themselves and also part of a larger system.

Our understanding of passenger transportation can rest on the same approach. We can break down the function of moving people into component systems (opening the first black box and finding a series of black boxes). Each component system is also a system (the series of second black boxes) and so forth.

Basically, we conceive of passenger transportation as composed of four interrelated component systems: the physical, the economic, the pricing, and the regulatory. Each is also a system, and as we analyze each component, some of the subsystems will be apparent. But to understand passenger transportation, one does not have to be an expert on concrete structures (a part of the subsystem of the "way" which is in turn a part of the component part "physical system"). It is enough to know that a system of the "way" exists without analyzing its subsystems in depth.

And so our task in Part One will be to discuss in general each component system, to look at its properties, and perhaps even to examine briefly its subsystems. We leave to others the important analysis of each of the subsystems and concern ourselves here mainly with the whole system of passenger transportation and its component system-parts.

2

ECONOMIC AND PHYSICAL SYSTEMS

Now that the "systems concept" has been established, our task is to turn to specific systems components of passenger transportation. Two of the most important of these are the physical and the economic.

It will be noted that we are analyzing two components at the same time—literally looking at two black boxes at once. The reason for this is because of the very close interrelationship of the physical and the economic aspects of passenger transportation. While it is much easier and much more meaningful to discuss both aspects together, we do hope the reader realizes that he may consider each as either a separate system or as part of the overall system.

VARIOUS ECONOMIC AND PHYSICAL MEANINGS OF THE TERM "SYSTEM"

While it is fairly common practice to use the term "system" when referring to physical passenger transportation, it actually has three meanings or uses. Many for-hire firms refer to themselves as a system: The Greyhound Bus system, the Pan American Airline system, the Penn Central Railroad system are examples. The use of "system" in this context refers to only a small part of the overall physical system of passenger transportation. A second, somewhat broader, use of "system" is found when industry groups publish statistics or other data about "the highway system," the "rail system," the "airline system," and so forth. Obviously, a "system" here refers to a collection of firms or components of similar and sometimes competing types of physical passenger transportation operations. A third and still more comprehensive use of the term "system" occurs when one considers all modes (with their individual firms or components) providing the total physical function of moving people. Here the physical system of passenger transportation becomes broad, intermodal, multiple-firm and multiple-unit, nongeographic, and all-inclusive. It is in this third, and broad, context, that we will approach the physical system of passenger transportation.

Additionally, it must be recognized that there is a concurrent "economic system" of passenger transportation. Once more this economic aspect also exists at the previously noted three levels. Hence, a for-hire firm has such economic characteristics as revenues, costs, investment, and rate of return. Private components, such as the private automobile, have the same economic characteristics although they are less well known and less frequently quoted. Similarly, economic statistics for the highway system, airline system, and bus system are common. Typically, these are an aggregation of the economic data of the firms involved in this particular industry. Finally, reference to the economic characteristics of the whole passenger transportation system noted above is somewhat less common. Typically, this is found when comparing broad sectors of the economy—for example, manufacturing vs. transportation, or retailing-wholesaling vs. transportation. Another broad economic meaning of "system" is found when the passenger transportation portion of the Gross National Product is noted, or when the passenger transportation portion of total U.S. investment both private and public is analyzed, or when passenger transportation as an end use of resources is compared to all resource use, and so forth.

We shall make use of the term "system" in all three of these contexts but we shall also try to give emphasis to the broad definition of a physical and economic system of passenger transportation. Data limitations will force us to consider various firms and various modes, but our objective will be to aggregate the modal and firm data in such a way as to help the reader appreciate the overall physical and economic system of passenger transportation.

THE PERFORMANCE OF THE PASSENGER TRANSPORTATION SYSTEM

One measure of the overall physical and economic characteristic of the passenger transportation system is the amount expended nationally on it. Another measure is the number and distribution of passenger-miles produced and the use of the system as measured by vehicle-miles. Further insight can be had by considering the number of passengers carried, the average fare on a passenger-mile basis, and, total overall fares per journey. All six measures of the physical and economic characteristics of the passenger transportation system will be used here.

The National Passenger Transportation Bill

By estimating expenditures, it is possible to arrive at an approximation of the total "bill" for passenger transportation in a given year for the entire economy. The Transportation Association of America has made available such estimated data for many years and provides some idea of the physical and economic characteristics of the passenger transportation system. This material is contained in Table 1.

Both 1962 and 1972 are included in Table 1 so that some idea of change is possible. It will be noted that in 1962, the total passenger

TABLE 1

The Nation's Estimated Passenter Transportation Bill, 1962 and 1972
(IN MILLIONS OF DOLLARS)

	1962	1972
PRIVATE TRANSPORTATION		
Automobiles		
New and Used Cars	22,093	46,389
Tires, Tubes, and Accessories	3,008	8,320
Gasoline and Oil	15,186	30,027
Tolls	385	720
Insurance	2,398	5,366
Interest on Debt	2,913	6,485
Auto Registration Fees	931	1,800
Operator's Permit Fees	120	251
Repair, Greasing, Washing, Parking, etc.	6,118	12,278
	53,152	111,636
Air		
Aircraft	182	743
Operating Cost	834	2,992
	1,016	3,735
Total Private	54,168	115,371

TABLE 1 (continued)

	1962	1972
FOR-HIRE TRANSPORTATION		
Local		
Bus and Transit	1,333	1,651
Taxi	828	1,580
Rail Commutation	127	177
School Bus	576	1,547
	2,864	4,955
Intercity		
Air	2,385	8,227
Bus	616	838
Rail	597	330
Water	16	14
	3,614	9,409
International		
Air	723	2,592
Water	267	268
	990	2,860
Total For-Hire	7,468	17,224
GRAND TOTAL	61,636	132,595
Gross National Product (billions)	560.3	1,158.0
Passenger Transportation as Percentage of GNP	10.5	10.9

Source: Transportation Association of America, *Transportation: Facts and Trends,* 11th edition, December 1974, p. 5.

bill was about $62 billion and that by 1971 this estimate had grown to almost $133 billion. In order to place these figures in some perspective, the Gross National Product for both years is also noted, as is the amount expended on passenger transportation as a percentage of GNP. From these data, one may say that approximately one out of every ten dollars expended in the economy goes to providing passenger transportation—a truly prodigious sum.

From the point of view of expenditures, private passenger transportation—principally the private automobile—dominates overwhelmingly. This same predominance will appear in passenger-miles produced and in other statistical measures. In spite of this predominance, the for-hire sector of passenger transportation is of considerable importance as the basic underlying foundation of the nation's passenger transportation system. Private passenger transportation by automobile is characterized by sporadic use, convenience travel, seasonal and temporal variability, and high user cost. For-hire transportation, on the other hand, provides the basic day-to-day, hour-to-hour, regularly scheduled, convenient, and inexpensive service upon which the movement of people in the economy rests.

Passenger Transportation Produced

Some of the different physical and economic characteristics of the system of passenger transportation can be seen by considering the total passenger-miles produced. The measurement unit "passenger-miles" is just what it says: one passenger carried one mile. While there are some shortcomings to the term, it is a uniformly accepted measure of use. Passenger-mile data are found in Table 2.

TABLE 2

Total Passenger-Miles Produced, 1973
(IN MILLIONS)

Private Carriers		1,184.7
Automobile	1,174.0	
Air	10.7	
Motorcycles and Bicycles	N/A	
Public Carriers		172.1
Air	132.4	
Bus	26.4	
Rail	9.3	
Water	4.0	
Local Transit	N/A	
GRAND TOTAL		1,356.8

Source: Transportation Association of America, *Transportation: Facts and Trends,* 11th edition, December 1974, p. 18.

Once more it is apparent that the private automobile predominates in the production of passenger transportation. This predominance is readily seen in Fig. 1. More than 86 percent of all passenger-miles were produced by the private automobile in 1973.

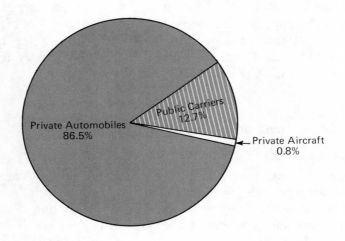

Figure 1.   Percentage of Intercity Passenger-miles By All Modes, 1973. (Source: *Transportation Association of America,* Transportation: Facts and Trends, *11th edition, December 1974, p. 18.)*

On the other hand, we noted above that the public or for-hire passenger transportation sector provided the basic foundation of travel. Fig. 2 compares the relative shares of passenger-miles produced in the public carrier sector in 1973. It will be noted here that the leading producer of intercity passenger-miles is the commercial airline.

One further dimension of intercity passenger transportation is the effect of distance traveled on the mode of passenger transportation utilized. As distance traveled over 100 miles becomes greater, the share of trips taken by automobile decreases—as noted in Fig. 3. It will be seen that over 40 percent of all person trips are for under 400 miles and that 97 percent of these are by private automobile. However, for the 19 percent of person trips that fall in the "over 1000 miles" category, private carriers (principally automobiles) provide 63 percent and public carriers 37 percent. However, the reader

Bus 15.3%
Rail 5.4%
Water 2.3%
Air 76.9%

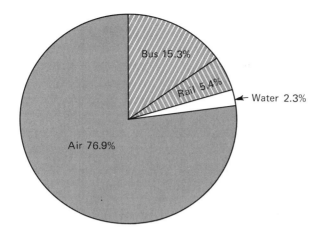

Figure 2. Percentage of Intercity Passenger-miles By Public Carriers, 1973. (Source: *Transportation Association of America,* Transportation: Facts and Trends, *11th edition, December 1974, p. 18.)*

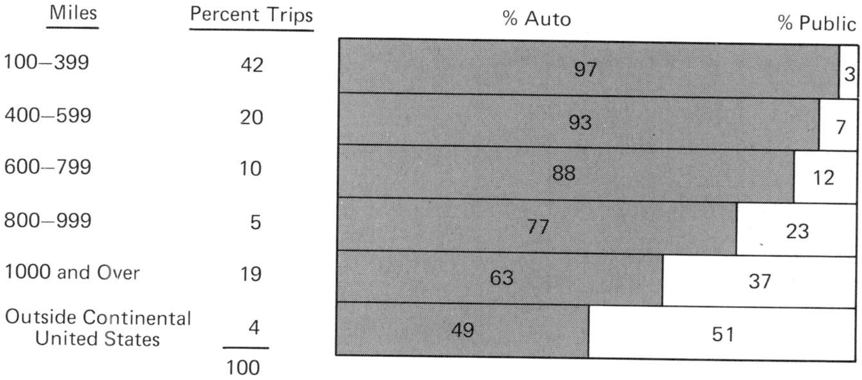

Miles
Percent Trips
% Auto
% Public
100–399
42
97
3
400–599
20
93
7
600–799
10
88
12
800–999
5
77
23
1000 and Over
19
63
37
Outside Continental United States
4
49
51
100

Person-trip: trip by one person to a destination 100 miles away from home and return.

Figure 3. Intercity Person-trips By Distance of Trip, 1972 - Percent by automobile and by public transportation. (Source: *Transportation Association of America,* Transportation: Facts and Trends, *11th edition, December 1974, p. 20.)*

should note that with the exception of travel outside the continental United States, the automobile predominates in every distance category.

To a considerable degree, passenger-miles will depend on the "load factor," or number of passengers in a vehicle. If the vehicle carries 200 passengers, many more passenger-miles per mile are produced than is the case if the vehicle has only two passengers.

Passenger-mile data are not reported for local transit, unfortunately. Additionally, only intercity travel is noted in our tables and figures presented up to now. Consideration of vehicle-miles produced partly overcomes these shortcomings. These data are presented in Table 3.

TABLE 3

Total Vehicle-Miles Produced, 1970
(IN MILLIONS)

Private automobile and other		900,992
Passenger Car	890,844	
Motorcycle	10,148	
Bicycle	N/A	
Buses		5,043
Intercity	2,943	
School	2,100	
Local Transit		1,883
Motor Busses	1,409	
Trolley Coach	33	
Surface Rail	33	
Subway & Elevated	407	
Rail (passenger only)		93
Air[1]		
Domestic[2]		2,099
International[2]		534
		910,644

[1] Excludes General Aviation.
[2] Includes Supplementary air carriers.

Source: Department of Transportation: *Summary of National Transportation Statistics,* November 1972, p.8.

On a vehicle-mile-produced basis, the private automobile once more predominates. This predominance appears even greater (roughly 98 percent of the vehicle-miles) due to the fact that the typical journey by private automobile has a much smaller load factor than in the for-hire sector.

Both passenger-miles and vehicle-miles are valid measures of the physical characteristics of passenger transportation. Each emphasizes a different aspect but both point up the predominance of the private automobile in passenger transportation. Additionally, both point up the immensity of passenger transportation, with over 1.3 trillion passenger-miles produced in 1973 and over 910 billion vehicle-miles produced in 1970.

Economic Dimension of Passenger Transportation

Turning now to greater emphasis on the for-hire sector of passenger transportation, we can gain some idea of the physical and economic characteristics by considering the number of passengers involved, the average fare charged per passenger-mile, and the total average fare per journey on for-hire carriers.

Table 4 shows the total number of revenue passengers in 1973. Unfortunately, no good estimate exists of the number of private automobile, motorcycle, or bicycle passengers or operators. The reader should note that from a passengers-carried viewpoint, local transit predominates. Of course, these passengers do not travel many miles, and hence the number of passenger-miles would be a much smaller proportion. Intercity bus carries the second largest number of passengers, rail is third, domestic air transportation fourth.

TABLE 4

Number of Revenue Passengers, 1973
(IN MILLIONS)

Local Transit		5,293.9
Motor Bus	3,652.8	
Rail	1,567.2	
Trolley	73.6	
Bus (intercity)		385.0

TABLE 4 (continued)

Rail (Class I)		254.1
Commuter	182.6	
Other	54.6	
AMTRAK	16.9	
Air (Domestic)		185.4
Automobile and other		N/A
GRAND TOTAL		6,118.4

Sources: Local Transit: American Public Transit Association, *'74-'75 Transit Fact Book,* p. 17; Bus and Air: Transportation Association of America, *Transportation: Facts and Trends,* 11th edition, 1974, p. 19; Rail: *Statistics of Railroads of Class I in the United States,* 58th Summary (August 1974), pp. 7, 16.

Turning to the fares charged, we see that Table 5 indicates the cost to the passenger of using for-hire transportation by noting the average revenue per passenger-mile. Once more, the widely accepted passenger-mile measure is used. Unfortunately, local transit data are not reported on a passenger-mile basis, but the average fare per passenger was 31.5¢.

TABLE 5

Average Passenger Revenue Per Passenger-Mile, 1973
(IN CENTS)

Air		6.63
First Class	8.93	
Coach and Economy	6.11	
Rail		5.19
Motorbus[1]		4.05
Local Transit[2]		N/A

[1] Class I only.
[2] Average revenue per passenger: 31.50¢

Source: Transportation Association of America, *Transportation: Facts and Trends,* 11th edition, December 1974, p. 7; American Public Transit Association, *Transit Fact Book,* 1973-1974, p. 11.

In order to get a rough comparison, it should be noted that studies prior to the energy crisis show the cost of operating a private automobile as 15.8¢ per mile. This was based on the assumption of a standard-size sedan driven 100,000 miles over ten years.[1] Obviously, the passenger-mile costs are cut in half if two persons ride in the car, by two-thirds if three people ride, and so forth. Once more, the load factor becomes important.

Looking at revenue from another view, Table 6 considers the total average fare per journey by the for-hire carriers. Here the factor of miles or distance is involved in all but local transit.[2] That is, since air travel is typically over a considerably greater distance than, say, intercity bus, the total average fare per journey will be ten times as great by air even though the passenger-mile revenue is less than twice as great. Also note that Table 5 was in cents per passenger-mile whereas Table 6 is stated in dollars.

TABLE 6

Average Total Fares, 1970
(IN DOLLARS)

Air[1]		40.71
Bus[2]		3.48
Rail, Intercity		3.19
Rail, Commutation		.84
Local Transit		.28
Motorbus	.29	
Trolley Coach	.24	
Surface rail	.27	
Subway and elevated	.23	

[1] Certificated domestic scheduled service only.
[2] Class I only.

Source: Department of Transportation, *Summary of National Transportation Statistics,* November 1972, p. 39.

[1] U.S. Department of Transportation, Federal Highway Administration, *Cost of Operating An Automobile* (Office of Highway Planning, Highway Statistics Division, April 1974), p. 9. With increases in gasoline prices since 1974, these costs are obviously higher.

[2] Where zone fares are used, mileage will be partially reflected.

Once more a general picture of the physical and economic characteristics of the various modes emerges. At this point, we can draw a rough summary of each mode of passenger transportation.

The private automobile is obviously the dominant mode, with an annual 1972 cost of $111 billion, producing 1.2 trillion passenger-miles (86.5 percent of all passenger-miles) in 1973, 890 billion vehicle-miles in 1970 at an estimated cost of 15.80¢ per mile. Air transportation accounts for the next largest annual cost, approximately $14.4 billion in both domestic and foreign passenger transportation. It produced 143 billion passenger-miles and 2.5 billion vehicle-miles, carried 185 million passengers (domestically) at an average per-passenger-mile fare of 6.63¢ and a total fare per journey of approximately $40.71. Air passenger transportation is obviously used for long mileage at relatively high rates (though less than half the per-passenger-mile cost of the automobile with a single passenger) with many passengers per vehicle.

Local transit displays different characteristics. At an estimated 1970 annual cost of $1.6 billion, it carried an astounding 5.3 billion passengers 1.9 billion vehicle-miles at an average fare of 31.5¢. The intercity bus passenger transportation cost $838 million and produced the second largest for-hire number of passenger-miles (next to air). It produced 26.4 billion passenger-miles from 5 billion vehicle-miles and carried 385 million passengers at a passenger-mile fare of 4.05¢ and an average total fare per journey of approximately $3.48. Intercity bus travel can be characterized by intermediate distances at low fares. Finally, rail passenger transportation cost the economy $330 million and produced over 9 billion passenger-miles from 93 million vehicle-miles. It carried the third largest number of passengers (254 million) at an average passenger-mile fare of 5.19¢ and with average total fares per journey of approximately $3.19 intercity and 84¢ commuter travel. Rail passenger transportation is used for both intermediate and short distance at relatively low fares and serves a substantial portion of the passenger transportation demand.

Each mode has its unique characteristics. Each fills a particular need and plays a special role in the total passenger transportation system. Finally, each operates under a special and separate set of institutional arrangements and different physical and economic characteristics—as will be apparent as we continue our analysis into the components of a passenger transportation system.

COMPONENTS OF THE PASSENGER
TRANSPORTATION SYSTEM

Irrespective of the level of analysis or use of the term "system," a transportation system is really composed of four interacting component parts. These are the "way," the "terminal," the "vehicle," and the "carriers" (both for-hire and private). These four parts combine to produce an astounding amount of physical and economic activity. Our next task will be to consider the physical and economic characteristics of each of these component parts of the system.

The Way

One approach to the physical characteristics of passenger transportation is to consider the way. Hence, the highways and streets, the railways, the airways, and the waterways and seas all have distinctive physical characteristics even though their function is the same—providing the glide path for passenger transportation. They are also an economic consideration, involving ownership and financial support. While we are generally not used to thinking of the "way" as a separate entity, it is a handy classification when analyzing the physical and economic characteristics of passenger transportation. We will consider the way from three viewpoints: extent, provision, and financial support.

Extent of the Way

If we limit ourselves to domestic transportation, there are approximately 4.3 million miles of way in the United States. The breakdown by types of way appears in Table 7.

If one takes a somewhat broader definition of the way, the mileage data in Table 7 for both airways and waterways would be considerably larger. That is, if one thinks of the whole sky as the airway instead of merely controlled routes or the whole sea as a waterway (Table 7 lists only inland waterways), the mileage would be infinite. Likewise, if one considers passenger transportation from the point of view of walking or hiking, the whole land mass of the world

TABLE 7

Miles of Way in United States Passenger Transportation, 1970

Highways[1]		3,730,082
Rural	3,169,412	
Municipal	560,670	
Airways[2]		278,822
Low Altitude	170,651	
Jet Routes	108,171	
Railways[3]		206,265
Local Transit[4]		53,248
Motor Bus	52,176	
Subway & Elevated	419	
Surface Rail	366	
Trolley Coach	287	
Waterways[5]		25,543
Bikepaths[6]		25,000
TOTAL		4,318,960

[1] U.S. Department of Transportation: *Summary of National Transportation Statistics* (November 1972), p. 19.
[2] Federal Aviation Administration: *Statistical Handbook of Aviation*, 1970, Table 2.1, p. 11.
[3] D.O.T. *Summary*, p. 31. Miles of line only. Miles of track (including yards, double track, switching track, etc.) in 1970 was 336,332. American Association of Railroads, *Yearbook of Railroad Facts*, 1970, p. 46.
[4] D.O.T. *Summary*, p. 27. Miles of line only. Mileage of routes is substantially higher. American Transit Association: *Transit Fact Book*, 1970, p. 2.
[5] Mileage of commercially navigable inland channels only. D.O.T. *Summary*, p. 29.
[6] Estimate only: Michael Everett, "Commuter Demand for Bicycle Transportation in the U.S.," *Traffic Quarterly* (October 1974), p. 586.

would be a way. However, we are referring to controlled or actual glidepaths or physical foundations upon which passenger transportation is produced or takes place. Even with this more limited definition, the extent of the way is enormous.

Naturally there are considerable variations in the physical condition or degree of improvement of the way. Some highways, for instance, are unimproved and little more than rough trails; others are multiple-lane concrete divided roadways with a width of 25 or more feet per direction. To some considerable degree, the physical condition of the way will depend on which agency provides the way and the manner in which it is provided.

Provision of the Way

The way is provided in one of two patterns: It is man-made or it is nature-made. Likewise, the ownership and responsibility for the way can be considered from two viewpoints: either privately owned, operated, and maintained or publicly owned, operated, and maintained. The variety of ownership and responsibility for the way will be quite important since it affects the cost of the particular carrier (private or for-hire) using the way and hence the prices, fares, or rates charged, or the operating costs absorbed by that carrier. Since nature-made ways are typically publicly owned, operated, and maintained, we therefore find three combinations of characteristics in the provision of the way: nature-made publicly owned, operated and maintained;[3] man-made publicly owned, operated and maintained; and, man-made privately owned, operated and maintained.

Two examples of a nature-made publicly owned, operated, and maintained way are, respectively, the waterways and seas, and the airways. By conscious social policy, the nation has assumed ownership of these two natural ways, and as we shall see directly, expended considerable sums on their improvement and operation. The major example of a man-made publicly owned, operated, and maintained way is the street and highway system of the nation. Practically all roads and streets are publicly owned and "free" in that sense. Although a few private roads do exist, most of them are short and in the form of driveways, access roads, forest logging roads, roads in industrial plants, and so forth. Moreover, all of them are dependent on the publicly owned highway and street system for connection and almost without exception, they would not be economically viable without a connection with a publicly owned road or street. The extent of public ownership of the streets and highways is so great

---

[3]Quite obviously most of the nature-made way has been improved by man or physically controlled in some way to assist in the provision of transportation or for other social reasons, that is, waterways are controlled physically by dams, dredging, and levies for both transportation purposes and flood control; harbors are dredged, and nature-made waterways are harnessed for man's use.

that we are startled to find the sign "private road—no trespassing" and indeed a substantial portion of the population regularly ignores such signs, as any owner of a private road will readily attest.

The major example of a man-made privately owned, operated, and maintained way is the railway system of the nation and a portion of the local transit system. Partly due to historic accident and partly to conscious social policy, railways are provided by the railroad or transit firm. Subways and elevated local transit systems were originally provided by the carrier, or, if the public streets were used, the carrier provided the tracks for street cars and trolleys. In a later period, much of this trackage came to be publicly owned. The inter-city railway system of the nation has traditionally been privately owned, operated, and maintained, and provides the best modern-day example of the third combination: privately owned way.[4]

Finally, the factor of level of government complicates the combination of man-made publicly owned way and nature-made way. For example, to refer back to Table 7, all waterways and coastal seas are federally owned, maintained, and operated, as are all airways. A small portion of the highway system is also federally owned and controlled. A considerably larger portion of the highway, street, and bikeway system is state provided, operated, and maintained, but by far the greater portion is provided, operated, and maintained by local governments. Ownership of the way is an important factor in the financial support of the way.

Financial Support of the Way

While we will have considerably more to say in a later chapter about the subject of financial support of the way and its ramifications, it is sufficient for now to develop in outline various patterns of support for the way. Accordingly, the reader should realize that definite patterns of financial support do exist and that these do affect the operation and the cost of passenger transportation. Likewise, patterns have varied historically and have changed over time. It is also possible to say that all means of passenger transportation have received public support at some time or other historically. Gener-

---

[4]Even this may be changed as Congress considers public ownership of a portion of the railway one alternative solution to the bankrupt situation of the northeast railroads in the early 1970s.

ally these patterns may be categorized as, (1) means of support, (2) sources of funds, and (3) reimbursement plans. Table 8 gives a diagrammatic summary of these categories by mode.

Railroads.   The railroads were aided in their development by massive land grants, gifts, subsidies in the form of bonds, stocks, and the foregiveness of property taxes, and in outright cash payments. All levels of government were involved and most of this support took place between the 1850s and 1870s, although some federal land grants were not exercised until a later date, when the railways were built. The exact value of the lands granted plus other aid in the construction of the railway system vary, depending on the assumed value of the public lands given. In all, there were 75 federal land grants of approximately 179 million acres (including state land grants) during this period. Some railroads sold their land immediately, others held it for a time, and still others continue to hold some today. Net proceeds from land sales was somewhere between $434 and $440 million. The total value of these benefits is more difficult to estimate since land values vary, but the principal source of funds was land.[5]

As to reimbursement, the railroads agreed to haul government passengers and freight at reduced rates, and since most railroads wished to participate in government hauling, practically all rail carriers granted this reduction even though all railroads had not received land grants. This reimbursement provision did not end until 1945, almost 100 years after the first land grants. The value of this reduction of rates and fares was estimated to be a total of $580 million over the years. This became a particularly valuable provision for government during both World War I and World War II.

Historically, public aid in the building of the railways was justified on a passenger transportation basis. That is, one of the major rationalizations for the federal land grant program was the need to "settle the West." The social benefits of mobility and good communication "tying the nation together," were stressed. That the railroads today are more carriers of freight than passengers does not detract from the fact that "passenger transportation came first" and greatly aided the development of the major example of man-made, privately owned way.

[5]See Roy J. Sampson and Martin T. Farris, *Domestic Transportation: Practice, Theory and Policy*, 3rd ed. (Boston: Houghton Mifflin Co., 1975), pp. 443-444 for more detailed discussion. Much of the general material for this section on the way is drawn from this source.

Highways.   As noted above, highways, streets, and bikepaths are the major examples of man-made publicly owned way. From the very first, highways have been provided by the public treasury of different governmental levels.

Highways and streets have historically received aid in many ways. Local governments build, improve, maintain and operate the majority of the mileage as noted above. State governments have jurisdiction over, and hence support, the majority of the remaining mileage in the country, and significantly, are involved mainly with the highly improved highways. The mileage under direct federal ownership, control, and maintenance is small, existing principally in national parks and monuments, military installations, and the like. The means of support is typically by annual appropriation. Bikepaths, a recent development, are provided by local governments in conjunction with streets.

When considering sources of financial support, the situation is more complicated. For many years, the federal government has provided substantial funds as "aid" to support highway construction by state and local government. The federal government itself undertook a massive highway improvement program early in our nation's history with the "National Pike" or Cumberland Road Project. Authorized in 1797 and constructed between 1806 and 1838 at a cost of $6.8 million, this project was the major direct federal involvement in road-building. The matter of "internal improvements" became controversial and after the election of President Andrew Jackson and the rise of the "States Rights" movement, the federal government ceased its direct involvement in providing highways. Since that time, the usual device has been "grants-in-aid" for highways.

In the typical pattern of federal aid programs, the national government provides a portion of the financial support but the state government owns, operates, and maintains the highways. The first federal aid program began with the Highway Act of 1916. Since that time, several federal aid systems have been established. Accordingly, today we have a Federal-Aid Primary System, Federal-Aid Secondary System, Federal-Aid Urban System, and the well-known "National System of Interstate and Defense Highways," otherwise known as the "Interstate System." The amount of federal aid varies from 50 percent to 90 percent (on the Interstate System) with the state government "matching" or otherwise providing the remaining sum of money. It should be understood that each of these "systems" is limited as to mileage; for instance, the Interstate System is approximately 42,000 miles, the primary system approximately 240,000 miles, the secondary system approximately 580,000 miles, and the urban system approximately 21,000 miles. Obviously, this means that the vast majority of the mileage remains as local streets and roads or as state roads not directly aided by the federal government.

Until 1956, the source of funds for federal aid programs was by Congressional appropriation. Periodically, a highway bill would be enacted that appropriated funds for a limited period of time and provided the federal share of matching funds. While various means of revenue raising existed, such as a federal gasoline tax, there was little connection between the amount of funds raised and the amount appropriated. With the advent of the Interstate System in 1956, "linkage" took place and a "trust fund" arrangement was instituted. In order to finance the massive crash program of the Interstate (originally to be 40,000 miles constructed to highest standard on the most intensively used roads in a short period between 1956 and 1972) specific taxes were enacted and the revenues therefrom earmarked exclusively for highway improvement. Specifically, these were taxes on tread rubber, tires, and tubes, a vehicle-use tax (graduated by weight) and the big revenue producer: a 4¢-per-gallon federal tax on gasoline and motor fuels.[6] These revenues have been considerable, amounting to over $5.5 billion annually in the early 1970s. In toto, it is estimated that the federal government expended over $88 billion for highways from 1921 to 1974.[7]

For its share, state government has raised funds for the provision of the way from numerous sources. On some occasions, state borrowing has been used. This has been a particularly important source of funds for toll roads and bridges. Property taxes have also been used, as have registration fees and license fees. However, beginning with Oregon in 1919, every state has enacted a gasoline and fuel tax and this has proven to be the major revenue source for the states just as it has for the federal government. Local governments (municipalities, townships, and counties) have depended primarily on the property tax as a source of highway, street and bikepath

[6]"Highways—the Years Beyond 1972," *Modern Transportation: Selected Readings*, Martin T. Farris and Paul T. McElhiney, eds. (Boston: Houghton Mifflin Co., 1967), p. 67.

[7]Association of American Railroads, Government *Expenditures for Highways, Waterways, and Air Facilities and Private Expenditures for Railroad Facilities* (May, 1974), Table 5.

funds. The amount of funds expended by state and local governments has been considerable and exceeded $16 billion annually in the early 1970s. Over the years, the majority of the funds have come from state and local governments and it is estimated that over $312 billion were expended for streets and roads by these agencies from 1920 to 1974.[8]

Depending as it does on user taxes, particularly the gas tax, highway financial support has a built-in reimbursement plan for most of the federal aid funds and for a large portion of the state expenditures. As the highway user buys more fuel, he pays more for the use of the highway and provides funds for more highway improvements.

It should be noted that his user charge plan does not cover all the costs of providing the highways and streets (due to limited mileage in the "aid systems" noted above) and is not available to all levels of government since its use is limited primarily to state and federal government. Local governments are reimbursed for street expenditures, if they are reimbursed at all, through higher property taxes. The theory is that property served by streets and roads should be more valuable because of the access provided by the streets or highways and hence its owners should pay higher taxes. Additionally, a portion of state gasoline taxes may be distributed to the lower units of government. These reimbursement plans are far less direct and considerably less automatic than a direct highway-user tax. Finally, it should be noted that the funds raised by user taxes typically go into the improvement and construction of new streets and highways and not for repayment for past highway investment.

In summary, it should be noted that the streets, highways, and bikepath system provides the way for several means of passenger transportation. That is, the private automobile, motorcycles, bicycles, pedestrians, and hitchhikers all use the streets and highways in the private sector of passenger transportation. In the for-hire sector, transit and intercity buses use the streets and highways. Whereas the railways, airways, waterways and seas are primarily used by a single means of passenger transportation, the streets and highways are used by several means.[9] This is a unique feature of highways and streets.

[8]*Ibid.* Total expenditures 1921 to 1973 are estimated at $400.8 billion—$312.8 billion from state and local sources, $88 billion from the federal government.

[9]In the case of private airplanes and private boats and ships, a dual means of passenger transportation exists on airways and waterways to a limited extent.

Airways.   As noted above, airways and waterways are the two major examples of ways that are nature-made publicly owned, operated, and maintained. Both are also federally owned, as distinct from highways, where provision and support of the way are split between various governmental levels. However, since each have somewhat separate characteristics, each will be summarized separately.

Air transportation is the only means of passenger transportation that is solely a twentieth century development. As such, it reflects the existence of a more complex economy and particularly a domestic society in which the national or federal government has assumed a dominant and major role. The provision and operation of the airways by the federal government is but one aspect of the close connection of the two. The federal government also has been involved with the research and development of aircraft, helping provide terminals (which shall be considered directly), payment of a portion of the carriers' operating costs (via direct subsidies and concealed subsidies in air mail contracts and the like), training of personnel and other aids and promotions. As the "last" (or at least the latest) means of transportation, air transportation has benefited more from federal action in the field of transportation than any other mode.[10]

Prior to the Air Commerce Act of 1926, two federal agencies, the Army and the Post Office, were pivotal in the development of the airway. The Army pioneered in aerial map making and in early air mail experiments in connection with Post Office activities. A chain of radio stations at airports was completed in the 1920s and night flying techniques were developed with congressional appropriations in 1924. The noted author John Frederick has stated: "The completion of a night airway system from coast to coast before the end of 1926 was one of the Post Office Department's greatest contributions to commercial air transportation."[11]

With the passage of the Air Commerce Act of 1926, Congress gave responsibility to the Department of Commerce to "foster air transportation, developing and establishing safeguards for such commerce, and encouraging the establishment of airports, civil airways and other air navigation facilities." Control of the airways was trans-

---

[10]Consult Sampson and Farris, *Domestic Transportation,* Chap. 27, for a discussion of the nature of the problem of promotions and aids, its goals, methods, and effects.

[11]John H. Frederick, *Commercial Air Transportation,* 5th ed. (Homewood, Illinois: Richard D. Irwin, Inc., 1961), p. 69.

ferred from the Post Office to the Department of Commerce, and the Weather Bureau (then in the Department of Agriculture) was directed to cooperate and work with the Department of Commerce to the fullest extent.[12] While the Post Office remained important (from an economic viewpoint), the development and operation of the airways became primarily the responsibility of the Department of Commerce.

From 1926 until 1958, the airways were built and operated by the Department of Commerce. With the passage of the Civil Aeronautics Act of 1938, responsibility for development and operation of the airways was assigned first to the Administrator of Civil Aeronautics, then, in 1940, to the Civil Aeronautics Authority. With the adoption of the Federal Aviation Act in 1958, this portion of the Department of Commerce became an independent regulatory commission (similar to the independent regulatory commissions of the Interstate Commerce Commission and the Civil Aeronautics Board) and was known as the Federal Aviation Agency (F.A.A.). Finally, the F.A.A. was transferred to the Department of Transportation in 1966 when the latter was created, and was renamed the Federal Aviation Administration (the letters F.A.A. remained the same). Thus, after eight years as an independent regulatory commission, the F.A.A. once more became a portion of the executive branch of the federal government. Development and operation of the airways has been financed by congressional appropriation throughout all these organizational changes.

The federal airways have increased from slightly over 3,000 miles in 1926 to the 278,822 miles noted in Table 7. But far more important than the miles in the airway system is the fact that a program of periodically upgrading the physical condition of the airways has been the responsibility of the federal government.

Of even greater importance, it should be noted that by annual appropriation the federal government administers, maintains, and operates the airways—a major item of federal expense. In 1975, some $1,362,029,000 was expended for this task and over 52,000 people were employed by the F.A.A.[13] The amount of annual congressional appropriation for this function exceeded $1 billion for the first time

---

[12]*Ibid.*, p. 41.

[13]F.A.A. appropriation for fiscal 1975 was $2.12 billion, from which trust funds have been deducted to arrive at this figure. *The Budget of the United States Government* (Fiscal Year, 1974), p. 680.

in 1970 and it has been estimated that from 1925 to 1974, almost $16.5 billion was expended on the construction, operation and maintenance of the federal airways.[14]

With the passage of the 1970 Airport and Airway Improvement Act (Public Law 91-258), a type of reimbursement plan was instituted for the first time in air transportation. More will be said of this important legislation in the next section on terminals, but it will suffice to indicate here that a portion of the revenues from the Airport and Airway Trust Fund established in that act are expended on the upgrading of the airway control system. It should be emphasized, however, that the funds under this act are for *improvement* of the airways and are not to be expended for either the operation of the airways nor the repayment of past federal investment in the airways.

Obviously, the example of the airways has its own distinguishing characteristics. Not only is it nature-made and publicly owned, improved, operated, and maintained at considerable cost, but it is controlled by a separate federal organization and its future improvement has some reimbursable features in the Aviation Trust Fund.

Waterways, Harbors, and Seaways.   The second major example of nature-made publicly owned, operated, and maintained way is the waterways, harbors, and seaways. Once more, distinctive physical and economic characteristics are involved.

As noted above, waterways, harbors, and seaways have historically been owned and controlled by the federal government. Water transportation literally "came first" in the carriage of both passengers and freight. Historically, the nations with seacoasts were the explorers, discoverers, and traders of the world. Rivers and lakes were exploited as a means of travel early in man's history and constituted man's most convenient means of communication. Because of this, it was an easy step to consider waterways "free" and "public" once men began setting up governments.

When improvements were to be made, it was also natural for them to be made collectively or as part of the "public obligation" in practically all nations. All persons in a society gain by better communication, by improved ways to travel and to trade. While specific improvements, such as docks and wharfage, might be private (as we

---

[14]*Government Expenditures for Highways, Waterways and Air Facilities* (May, 1974), Table 2. Research on the "civil supersonic aircraft" (SST) was included in that figure since 1962.

shall see under the discussion of terminals), the source of capital for waterways, seaways, and harbor improvements has historically been a total social or public obligation.

In our nation, waterways, river and harbor improvements, and seaways have been controlled by the federal government from the very earliest times, and appropriations for improvements have historically come from the federal government. No small amount of funds has been expended in these undertakings over the years. One of the very earliest acts of Congress was a "Harbors Bill" in 1789. By 1823, periodic "Rivers and Harbors" acts were passed and since 1866, Congress has annually appropriated funds for rivers and harbors.

State and local governments have also expended moneys on waterway improvements. Historically, the states were of major importance in the development of canals. Indeed, beginning with the famous Erie Canal, constructed by the State of New York in 1825 for $7 million, the nation experienced a short period in which massive expenditures were made by practically all states. This is known as the "canal era"; it lasted from 1825 to 1840. There are conflicting estimates of the amount of expenditures, but we do know that over $200 million in public debt was incurred by the states during that period.[15]

Since the canal era, states have sporadically expended money on waterway improvements. During the early part of this century, New York spent over $100 million to convert the old Erie Canal into the New York Barge Canal. Other projects by states were also considerable. However, it has basically been the federal government with its annual rivers and harbors appropriation that has provided the majority of the funds for waterways and harbor improvements. It has been estimated that over $10.5 billion had been expended on rivers and harbors up to 1974.[16] State and local expenditures, estimated at $7.9 billion since 1947, have gone to both waterways and the terminal facilities thereon.[17]

Additionally, massive amounts have been expended for navigational aids and facilities relative to the seaways and the harbors of the nation. The U.S. Coast Guard has actively been involved over the years, as has the U.S. Navy. While it is difficult to separate the

[15]See Sampson and Farris, *Domestic Transportation*, pp. 23-25 for a summary of this era.

[16]*Government Expenditures for Highways, Waterways and Air Facilities* (May, 1974), Table 6.

[17]*Ibid.*

defense aspects of expenditures for the Coast Guard from those aspects that promote and aid transportation, more than $12 billion had been expended by the federal government via the Coast Guard up to 1974.[18]

Of course, it is impossible to separate that portion of these expenditures which have been applied to passenger transportation from that portion applied to freight transportation. Both functions are often carried out at the same time and sometimes by the same vessel. Also, some of these expenditures have to do with terminals and are not exclusively for the "way." Even so, it is possible to say that massive expenditures of funds, principally by the federal government in modern times, have gone toward providing a "way" for waterborne transportation.

Finally, considering reimbursement plans, it should be noted that no direct reimbursement is generally involved. While states may charge tolls and there may be small charges for specific services such as pilotage, in general these federal and state expenditures are considered an obligation of the whole of society. The nation is said to benefit by better communication and increased trade and commerce. No "user charges" are made for waterway use and no "trust fund" or any such reimbursement arrangement has been established. Indeed, the inland waterway carriers are fond of saying that the Constitution and U.S. history guarantee that the waterways will be "forever free"—although there is a substantial group that challenges that reasoning. However, the slogan "forever free" does epitomize the reimbursement plan for waterways.

Summary on the Characteristics of the Way

The physical and economic characteristics of the way are obviously one of the most important components of the system of passenger transportation. The way has been considered from the point of view of the extent of the 4.3 million miles of way, its physical condition, whether it is nature-made or man-made, privately provided or publicly provided, the various governments involved in financing, operating, and maintaining the way, the manner in which the way has been provided and financially supported, and the existence or lack of existence of a reimbursement system. Reference should be

[18] *Ibid.,* Table 9.

made once more to Table 8, where these various patterns are summarized, but the overall conclusion must be that the way possesses many distinctive physical and economic characteristics, each of which in some manner vitally effects the passenger transportation system.

TABLE 8

Summary of Financial Support of the Way

	OWNERSHIP	SUPPORT	SOURCE OF FUNDS	REIMBURSEMENT
Railways	Private	Historically all govt. levels	Federal land grants, various state and local aids and gifts	Reduced fares and rates to federal govt. 1850s to 1945
Highways, Streets and Bikepaths	Public	Construction, operation, and maintenance by state and local govt. Aid by federal govt.	Annual congressional appropriation, trust fund, annual property taxes, govt. borrowing	Partly by user fees since 1920s to states; federal since 1930s
Airways	Public	Construction, operation, and maintenance by federal govt.	Congressional annual appropriation and trust fund	Partly by user fees since 1970
Waterways and Seas	Public	Construction, operation, and maintenance by federal govt.	Congressional annual appropriations	None
Local Transit	Public and private	Historically local govt. only, recent matching fed. funds	Property taxes and borrowing; fed. grants	None

The Terminal

Although the way is of pivotal importance, there are other components of the physical and economic system of passenger transportation. The second component, the terminal, is sometimes thought of as part of the way even though it is indeed a separate component. Terminals can be situated along the way, at the beginning and end of the way, or even separate from the way itself. But irrespective of its location, the terminal becomes an integral part of the passenger transportation system.

Functions of the Terminal

The terminal can be thought of as providing five functions: concentration, dispersion, passenger service, vehicle service, and interchange. Each is important and should be briefly noted as a part of the physical and economic system of passenger transportation.

Concentration.   People are brought together at terminals and concentrated or grouped into unit loads for specific destinations. Hence, the plane for New York or the train for Chicago or the transcontinental bus to California leaves from a terminal with its load of passengers. While it is entirely possible that other passengers may be boarded en route, this process typically takes place at other terminals and is a repeat of the concentration function. Even in private transportation, the garage or carport or street may be thought of as a terminal where people are concentrated or grouped for a journey.

Dispersion.   Once the journey has ended, the terminal serves as a point of dispersion. Journeys "terminate" at terminals and people go their various and diverse ways *from* a terminal as well as *to* a terminal. The dispersion function, or "from" function, is as important as the "to" function, and they are carried on simultaneously.

Passenger Service.   In for-hire passenger transportation, the terminal provides the place where passenger service takes place. The process of ticketing, the handling of luggage and personal belongings, the inspection of passengers (a new phenomenon in air transportation), the feeding and entertaining of passengers and catering to their various needs (through gift shops, coffee shops, bars, insurance counters, travel-aid desks, telephone booths, and so forth)—all take place within the terminal. One of the important functions of a terminal is obviously passenger service.

Vehicle Service.   Terminals typically provide a location for vehicle service as well. Maintenance and repairs, as well as the fueling, cleaning, and storing of vehicles, will typically take place as part of the terminal operation.

Interchange.   Finally, terminals will provide the function of interchange both intramodally and intermodally. Intramodal interchange occurs where transfer from one route to another is accomplished (connecting flights or transfer on a transit line) or where transfer is made from one carrier to another carrier of the same mode (for example, changing from TWA to American Airlines at O'Hare in Chicago). Intermodal interchange occurs where the passenger transfers from one mode to another, as for example, at the airport when the air traveler leaves the airplane and transfers to a limousine or a taxi or a private automobile to complete his journey. It is perhaps the interchange function that we most often associate with a terminal but the other functions—concentration, dispersion, passenger service, and vehicle service—are equally important.

Provision and Ownership of the Terminal

The previous classification of the way as man-made privately owned, man-made publicly owned, and nature-made publicly owned, prevails only to a small degree in terminals. The majority of the terminals are man-made. A more useful classification may be to relate the terminal ownership and provision to the characteristics of the way. Once more, a modal approach will be useful.

Railroads.   Terminals here traditionally have been privately owned and provided and the private property of the carriers. Sometimes several railroads have joined together in the ownership of a terminal for passenger service, sometimes they have even formed a separate company jointly owned and operated as a "Union" terminal. In most cases, however, the terminal is owned and provided by a single carrier. Irrespective of the arrangement, the terminal in railroad transportation follows closely the ownership pattern of the way and is private. Costs are recouped in the price of the ticket.

Local Transit.   The pattern of total ownership becomes important in this case too. When the local transit system is publicly owned (as it is in the vast majority of cases) the terminal is publicly owned; when ownership is private, terminal provision and ownership is private even where the operation is over a public way. Privately owned "car barns" as places of vehicle service were once common and still exist today, as do privately owned "stations," or points of interchange. Generally, however, local transit terminals are publicly owned, typically by local governments, and costs are either included as a portion of the passenger fare or absorbed as part of public support of local transit.

Intercity Bus.   Private ownership of terminals, or at least that part of a facility providing one of the functions of a terminal, such as vehicle service, is common. Sometimes terminals are publicly owned and leased by the intercity bus operator, sometimes some part of the terminal function, such as ticketing, will take place in an agency relationship when a store or service station sells tickets and fulfills the role of passenger service in a small community. At major points, however, the terminal is usually owned by the carrier and considerable private investment is involved in terminal facilities. In the case of the bus, the ownership pattern of the way is not repeated in the terminal component (as it is in rail and local transit). The way is publicly owned, the terminal is typically privately owned. Costs of the terminal function obviously become a portion of the passenger fare.

Private Automobile.   Another example of publicly owned way but privately owned terminals is the case of the private automobile. The terminal here would be the private garage or carport and the parking lot or parking garage in the place of destination (perhaps the parking lot in the shopping center). Parking garages and parking lots are privately owned and rented, or provided "free" to their users, or publicly owned and "free"; private garages at homes are by definition privately owned.

Some cities have found it necessary to provide "public parking" in order to facilitate traffic, stimulate business, and serve their social function. Tied in with "public facilities," which are really an extention of the public street system, are the for-hire parking lots. Where on-street parking is permitted, a portion of the public way may be thought of as a type of terminal fulfilling the storage function. Vehicle service, however, is almost always privately owned. Thus the pattern in private automobile transportation is variable, with the way always being publicly owned and provided, the terminal being provided and owned both publicly and privately, and in various combinations. Parking fees and property taxes on the owner's facilities are the manner in which costs are recouped. Where the public provides the terminal (such as in free off-street parking) the costs are normally recouped in higher property taxes, based on more valuable business property.

Airports.   Airports provide an example of publicly owned terminal and publicly owned way, but with different levels of government involved. Typically, the airport is owned by the local government or by a combination of local governments operating through a "port authority," while the airway is federally owned and operated, as noted previously.

The Air Commerce Act of 1926 specifically prohibited the federal government from building airports and reserved this area of activity for the local governmental units. Notwithstanding, large expenditures of federal funds were made during the 1930s for airport improvements. Airport construction and improvements were an important part of the Public Works Administration and Works Progress Administration programs to stimulate the economy. Finally, with the passage of the Civil Aeronautics Act of 1938, Congress ordered the Civil Aeronautics Authority to draw up a plan of airport development and make recommendations on the desirability of federal aid to airports. The plan involved a matching provision whereby local governments generally provided 50 percent of the cost, and federal funds the remaining 50 percent with funds allocated among the states generally on a formula based on population and area.[19]

After World War II, airport aid and development accelerated. The federal government played a more active role in its National Airport Development Plan, and the degree of expenditures increased. Between 1947 and 1969 almost $2.5 billion was expended on airports—$1.2 billion from federal sources and $1.3 billion from state and local sources—on 2,319 approved airports.[20]

Even with these massive expenditures, airports and airways lagged behind the development of air commerce. An attempt to catch up was made with the passage of the Airport and Airways Improvement Act of 1970 (Public Law 91-258), mentioned above. This act included both a development plan and, importantly, a revenue source. An aviation "trust fund," patterned after the High-

[19] Frederick, *Commercial Air Transportation.*

[20] Department of Transportation, Federal Aviation Administration, *FAA Statistical Handbook of Aviation* (Washington, D.C., U.S. Government Printing Office, 1972), p. 55.

way Trust Fund, was established and special user taxes were levied. These were an 8 percent tax on domestic airfares, a $3 surcharge on international air tickets, a 7¢-per-gallon fuel tax on noncommercial aviation, a 5 percent air-freight waybill tax, and a graduated weight tax on noncommercial aircraft. The previous allocation formula (75 percent of which was based on population and area, 25 percent discretionary) was revised so that the funds are allocated one-third on population and area, one third on passenger enplanements, and one-third at the discretion of the Secretary of Transportation. Matching airport aid by local sources continues. A minimum of $250 million a year was earmarked for modernization of the airway with the rest going to airport improvement. The plan is to last ten years and, depending on traffic projections, the trust fund will handle between $11 and $12 billion between 1970 and 1980.[21] Compared to the $2.5 billion expended in the 22 years from 1947 to 1969 ($1.2 billion federal) noted above, the $11 to $12 billion of federal funds with almost equal amounts of local funds in a ten-year period must be characterized as both a "massive" and a "crash" program.

Finally, the total expenditures on airports by both federal and local sources over the years have not been small. Through 1970, it has been estimated, $11.8 billion had been spent over the years on airports ($2.9 billion federal and $8.7 billion state and local).[22] While these figures can be challenged in that military contributions are included, and while they include estimates of acquisition costs of all airports and not just expenditures for improvements, the fact remains that massive amounts have been spent by various levels of government to provide the airports of the nation.

The matter of the sources of these funds is interesting. Obviously, prior to 1970, the source of federal aid to airports was congressional appropriation; and, after 1970, the Aviation Trust Fund. Local governments attempt to recoup their airport operating costs from fees and charges levied against the airport user. These are in the form of landing fees, concession charges, rents, and the like. Many airports recoup all their operating costs, some do not. Some airports also recoup a portion of the capital costs involved in their matching funds. Some do not. On many occasions, local governments issue

[21]Department of Transportation, *Fourth Annual Report* (Fiscal Year, 1970), pp. 65-68.

[22]*Government Expenditures for Highways, Waterways and Air Facilities* (May, 1974), Table 3.

bonds for airport improvement and repay the bonds from revenues gained from airport users. Sometimes local governments are happy to have airports recoup only operating costs, being willing to subsidize airport improvements on the theory that an improved airport stimulates business. Generalizations are difficult and cases vary, yet it is probable that the provision of airports by local governments has some degree of social subsidy involved in it, at least historically. But, given the many competing uses of public funds, plus the new 1970 act, future costs of airports will be assessed directly and indirectly to the airport user.

Seaports and Harbors.   An analogy can be made between seaports and airports. In both, several levels of governments are involved. In both, the role of the federal government in providing the way becomes commingled with providing the terminal. In both, combinations of local government are involved—indeed, in some cases, such as that of the Port of New York Authority or the Port of San Diego Authority, seaports and airports are administered by the same group.

Basically, port facilities are provided by local governments or combinations of local governments in the form of port authorities.[23] Sometimes private ownership prevails in docks, wharfs, and seaport facilities, but more often they are publicly provided and leased to private operators. The general feeling that port facilities are a part of the social obligation of the local government is quite strong.

Some port maintenance, such as dredging, is carried on as an obligation of the federal government as part of the provision of the way. The line between the way (waterway, river, or harbor) and the terminal is most difficult to draw in water transportation. As noted before, while practice does vary, generally the federal government has assumed the obligation of providing the way in water transportation, and generally local government or private ownership provides the dock, wharf, and facilities. Total local and state expenditures from 1947 to 1974 have been estimated at almost $8 billion mostly for terminal facilities.[24] Though it is difficult to assess the exact costs, the amount is considerable.

[23]Some history and background of the port authorities movement can be found in Marvin L. Fair, "Port Authorities in the United States," *Law and Contemporary Problems* (Autumn, 1961), pp. 703-14.

[24]*Government Expenditures for Highways, Waterways and Air Facilities* (May, 1974), Table 6.

Of course, state and local governments recoup a portion of these costs from wharfage charges or from leases. Some of the capital invested has come from borrowing, and revenues are used to repay bonds. An unknown portion also is from the general social obligation of the local government involved. A large part of these expenditures deal with freight transportation, of course, and no good estimates are available of the port costs for passenger transportation.

Summary of the Characteristics of the Terminal

The terminal is the second component of the physical and economic system of passenger transportation. It serves the five functions of concentration, dispersion, passenger service, vehicle service, and interchange. Provision and ownership of terminals varies. Sometimes the arrangement follows the pattern of ownership of the way (examples: railway ownership is private, terminal ownership is private, local transit ownership is public, terminal ownership is public). Sometimes ownership of the way and the terminal are diverse (intercity buses use the public way but typically own their own terminals, private automobile use publicly owned ways but typically own their garages or pay parking fees to privately owned terminals—the exception being on-street parking and "free" public parking). Sometimes combinations of governments are involved (such as port authorities in air and seaports); sometimes different governmental levels are involved (local governments provide airports in conjunction with federally owned airways); and sometimes it is difficult to separate the terminal from the way (as in seaports). The provision of air terminals is perhaps the most interesting and most highly developed economically of the various ownership patterns and plans for recouping the cost of the terminal.

The Vehicle

The third component of the physical and economic system of passenger transportation is the vehicle. The vehicle traverses the way (our first component) between terminals (our second component).

Some idea of the total number of vehicles operated in the United States is gained from Table 9. The almost complete domination of the private automobile, 89 million of the 92 million vehicles, is quickly apparent.

TABLE 9

Total Vehicles Operated in the United States in Passenger Transportation, 1970

Private Sector		92,094,594
Passenger Cars and Taxis	89,279,864	
Motorcycles	2,814,730	
Aircraft	N/A	
Bicycle	N/A	
For-Hire Sector		98,317
Airline Carriers (Domestic & International)		2,690
Certificated	2,564	
Supplemental	195	
Intercity Bus		23,100
Railway[1]		11,177
Local Transit		61,350
Motorbus	49,700	
Subway & Elevated	9,338	
Surface Rail	1,262	
Trolley Coach	1,050	
GRAND TOTAL		92,192,911

[1] Passenger and Pullman cars only.

Source: U.S. Department of Transportation, *Summary of National Transportation Statistics* (November 1972), p. 11.

Reference should be made once more to the discussion of passenger-miles and vehicle-miles noted above and the obvious importance of the load factor. For example, while the number of vehicles in air transportation is the smallest of all the classifications, these 2,690 vehicles produce the second largest number of passenger-miles (the largest amount of passenger-miles in the for-hire sector), as noted in Table 2, and the third largest number of vehicle-miles, as noted in Table 3. The reason the smallest number of vehicles produces such large amounts of both passenger-miles and vehicle-miles is that the vehicle has a capacity in terms of hundreds (as compared to a very few for each passenger automobile), the vehicle is intensively used many hours a day (as compared to a few hours a day for the passenger automobile), and the vehicle has such great speed that it rapidly adds up miles per passenger (as compared to other means). In spite of this, the private automobile still leads the airplane in both total passenger-miles and vehicle-miles. The reader may wish to compare passenger-miles transportation to the number of vehicles noted in Fig. 4. However, there is no escaping the conclusion that the private automobile is the predominant type of vehicle in passenger transportation.

Some idea of the growth in numbers of private automobiles is found in Fig. 4. It will be noted that the number of private passenger automobiles and taxis more than doubled in the 20 years from 1950 to 1970. Some scholars, extending this rate of growth in number of vehicles into the future, predict dire consequences for the world—a subject we will discuss more fully in Chap. 7, where we deal with social costs and social benefits.

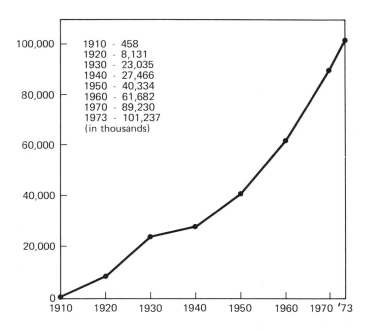

Figure 4.   Passenger Car and Taxi Registrations, 1910-1973 – In thousands. (Source: *U.S. Department of Commerce,* Statistical Abstract of the United States, *1974, p. 556.)*

A further appreciation of the importance of the private automobile is gained when one realizes that in 1973 there were 118,414,000 drivers registered in the United States. It should be noted that this exceeds the 101 million passenger cars and taxis. Of the 65.1 million family units in the country in 1971, 83 percent owned automobiles with 55 percent owning one car and 28 percent owning two cars or more. Of these cars, 11 percent were less than two years old, 25 percent were two to three years old, 40 percent were four to seven years old, and 24 percent were eight years old or more in 1971. This ownership pattern is one reason that air pollution abatement devices as required on new cars produced in the 1970s have such a delayed impact on the problem of air pollution. A final dimension is that in 1970, there were 19.8 million cars purchased; 8.3 million were new, and sold for an average price of $3,690, and 11.5 million were used, and sold for an average price of $1,170.[25] The total cost of operating these vehicles in 1972 was $111 billion, as noted in Table 1, and at a per-mile cost averaging 15.80¢ in 1974, as also noted previously. The reader should once again refer to the earlier section of this chapter for the statistics on total cost and per-passenger-mile cost on the for-hire sector of passenger transportation.

While we will have more to say about it later, it should be mentioned that the efforts to aid local transit may well considerably increase the number of vehicles in this category in the future. Various aid programs in the form of federal grants to local transit operations began in the 1960s. With increased concern over the social problems of congestion and pollution, increased funds were appropriated for such grants in the late 1960s and early 1970s. Generally, these grants were for "demonstration projects" and were limited to capital expenditures based on a formula of 80 percent federal and 20 percent local matching funds. In 1973, Congress allowed local governments more flexibility in the use of federal-aid money and a portion could be used for local transit, bikepaths, and other local transportation needs.

The energy crisis of 1974 added further urgency to the need to help local transit become a viable alternative means of passenger transportation. Accordingly, in late 1974, Congress enacted a six-year crash program of massive federal aid ($11.8 billion) for mass transit.

---

[25]Data taken from United States Department of Commerce, *Statistical Abstract of the U.S.* (1972), pp. 546-47.

The majority ($7.8 billion) of these funds continue to be allocated to capital improvements on an 80-20 basis but a portion ($4 billion) is available for operating subsidies on a 50-50 matching basis or capital improvements at the option of the cities involved. While a portion of these funds will probably be spent on the way and on terminals in local transit, the vast majority will undoubtedly be used to update old equipment and acquire new vehicles in local transit.

In summary, the vehicle that operates on the way and between terminals is the third component of the physical and economic system of passenger transportation. The private automobile overwhelmingly predominates in number of vehicles as well as in passenger-miles and vehicle-miles, although a small number of vehicles in the for-hire sector produce astounding numbers of passenger-miles and vehicle-miles due to their larger capacities plus more intensive use and sometimes speed. The number of private automobiles has grown amazingly in the U.S. over time and ownership of the private automobile is not only widespread but has various economic characteristics such as age of vehicles, number and cost of new and used vehicles purchased, and total dollars expended on private passenger transportation.

The Carrier

The fourth and final component of the physical and economic system of passenger transportation is the carrier. We are using the term "carrier" here to mean both private and for-hire carriers. Literally, each of the 118,414,000 registered drivers of the 101 million registered private automobiles noted above is a "carrier" when he provides his own transportation. The same is true for motorcycles, bicycles and other privately owned vehicles. Obviously, if the passenger uses for-hire transportation, a firm called a "carrier" supplies this service. Hence, "carrier" here means anyone or any organization supplying passenger transportation.

Turning to the for-hire sector, we find that Table 10 indicates the number of firms involved in passenger transportation. It should be noted, however, that beginning in May 1971, AMTRAK (National Railroad Passenger Corporation) assumed operation of all intercity rail passenger service except for that of three railroads and existing commuter services. Therefore, the number of rail firms would be somewhat reduced after 1971.

TABLE 10

Number of Firms in For-Hire Passenger Transportation, 1970

Airlines (Domestic & International)		43
Certificated	39	
Supplemental	14	
Buses (intercity)		1,000
Railway [1]		71
Local Transit		1,096
Subways & Elevated [2]	15	
Motorbus	1,075	
Trolley Coach	6	
Water [3]		100
Inland & Coastal	81	
Maritime	19	
Taxis		N/A
GRAND TOTAL		2,310

[1] All Class I Railroads did not operate passenger service in 1970. Beginning in May, 1971, AMTRAK assumed operation of almost all intercity rail passenger services except commuter service.

[2] Includes surface rail.

[3] No indication of how many carry passengers.

Source: U.S. Department of Transportation, *Summary of National Transportation Statistics* (November 1972), pp. 15, 22, 26, 29.

Due to continued deficits and long-standing economic problems with intercity rail passenger service, the AMTRAK experiment was authorized by Congress in late 1970. A semipublic corporation was created and assumed operation of rail passenger service (excluding distances of less than 50 miles) from participating railroads. Railroads choosing not to participate (three) were required to continue their passenger service for a limited period; railroads choosing to participate entered into a contract with AMTRAK to allow passenger trains operated by AMTRAK to use their roadbed and facilities on a fee basis. AMTRAK received an original federal grant of funds plus guarantees, as well as cash contributions from the participating railroads based on the amount of their prior revenue losses from passenger service. The Secretary of Transportation designated as "essential," rail routes between a limited number of major cities (14 originally) and abandoned all rail passenger service on other routes. The idea was to decrease the routes and points served and upgrade the remaining service as an essential part of the passenger transportation system. The number of trains was drastically reduced and commendable efforts were made to upgrade the remaining trains.

Actually, the smaller number of routes and cities is somewhat deceiving. In its first year of operation, AMTRAK operated 1,500 trains a week over 24,000 miles of track and reached 440 cities and towns in the United States. This was, however, considerably less rail service than had previously been provided. The early years of AMTRAK have not been profitable and annual deficits prevail as AMTRAK attempts to lure passengers back to the rails with public relations, better services, lower prices, and publicity.

While it is still too early to evaluate the AMTRAK experiment, there are several interesting aspects worthy of mention. First, the traditional pattern of publicly provided way and privately owned means (firms or vehicles) operated on that way has been completely reversed in the AMTRAK operation. That is, the way remains privately owned but the carrier is public. Second, a "rescue" type of public undertaking was authorized in recognition of the obvious fact that a viable passenger transportation system cannot exist without all possible means of movement. Thus Congress, representing public sentiment, was not willing to see rail passenger service cease nor was it willing to continue to saddle the rail carriers with an unprofitable service. This point will be further discussed in Chap. 8, which deals with public policy problems. Finally, of immediate interest, the number of rail carriers has now decreased to those few continuing to serve commuter traffic and a single interstate rail passenger carrier— namely, AMTRAK.

A second dimension of the carrier component of the physical and economic system of passenger transportation is the operating revenues of the carriers. This information is contained in Table 11. While it is often difficult to separate passenger operating revenues from freight operating revenues, the passenger figure does exceed $11½ billion in 1970 and does give some idea of the relative dollar importance of the various for-hire carriers.

A final dimension of the carrier component is the number of employees involved in carrier passenger transportation service. This

TABLE 11

Operating Revenue of Passenger Transportation Carriers, 1970
(IN MILLIONS)

Air Carriers		$ 8,237
Certificated	6,359	
Supplemental	248	
International	1,630	
Intercity Bus		901
Rail Carriers		420
Intercity	248	
Commuter	172	
Local Transit		1,707
Motorbus	1,236	
Subway & Elevated	384	
Surface Rail	55	
Trolley Coach	31	
Water Carriers		288
Domestic	13	
International	275	
GRAND TOTAL		$11,553

Source: U.S. Department of Transportation, *Summary of National Transportation Statistics* (November 1972), p. 7.

material is contained in Table 12. Once more difficulty exists in separating employees in freight service from employees in passenger service. For air transportation, all employees are noted since passenger transportation is the major service involved. For rail and water transportation, however, freight transportation is the major service and so no attempt to estimate the employees involved solely with passenger transportation has been made. In spite of the incompleteness of the data, the number of employees does give another view of the carrier component of the physical and economic characteristics of the passenger transportation system.

In summary, the fourth component of the physical and economic system is the carrier. Carriers may be conceived of quite broadly and thus the term includes all the 118,414,000 registered drivers of the 101 million registered private vehicles. It also includes the 2,310 for-hire firms, with over $11.5 billion operating revenues

TABLE 12

Number of Employees in Passenger Transportation, 1970

Taxis		111,300
Airlines[1]		304,630
Certificated	246,687	
Supplemental	4,755	
International	53,188	
Intercity Bus		49,600
Local Transit		138,040
Subway & Elevated	36,442	
Surface[2]	101,598	
Rail[3]		N/A
Water[4]		N/A
GRAND TOTAL		603,570

[1] Excludes international supplemental.
[2] Includes motorbus, surface rail, and trolley coach.
[3] Total of Class I rail employees in 1970 was 566,282 with no breakdown as between freight and passenger.
[4] A 1970 total of 14,845 employees in maritime service and 7,811 employees in inland water transportation service is not divided as between freight and passenger.

Source: U.S. Department of Transportation, *Summary of National Transportation Statistics* (May, 1972), pp. 15, 20, 22, 26, and 31.

and employing over 600,000 persons. Special attention must be given to the AMTRAK experiment because of its uniqueness, its policy implications, and its potential as a force in future passenger transportation.

SUMMARY OF PHYSICAL AND ECONOMIC CHARACTERISTICS OF THE PASSENGER TRANSPORTATION SYSTEM

One way to consider passenger transportation is to look at the physical and economic characteristics of the system. This can be accomplished by considering the role of passenger transportation from the viewpoint of the National Passenger Transportation Bill; the amount of passenger transportation produced as measured by passenger-miles and vehicle-miles; the economic dimension of passenger transportation as measured by the total number of revenue passengers, the average passenger revenue per passenger and the cost per mile of operating a private automobile, and the total average fare per journey charged. Another useful approach is to analyze the four interacting components of the system: the way, the terminal, the vehicle, and the carrier. Each of these has separate characteristics. The way is important from the viewpoint of extent and the manner in which it is provided, owned, and financially supported. The terminal is important from the point of view of its functions and its ownership, provision, and financial support. The number of vehicles operating on the way to their terminal, and their characteristics are the third component. Finally, analysis of the carriers, whether private or public, their number, operating revenues, and number of employees, completes the picture of the four component parts of the physical and economic system of passenger transportation.

Our next task will be to consider another aspect, the pricing system used in passenger transportation.

ADDITIONAL READINGS

AMERICAN TRUCKING ASSOCIATION, "Highways to 1985," *Modern Transportation: Selected Readings*, 2nd ed., Martin T. Farris and Paul T. McElhiney, editors (Boston: Houghton Mifflin Co., 1973), pp. 76-83.

FAIR, MARVIN L. and ERNEST W. WILLIAMS, JR., *Economics of Transportation and Logistics* (Dallas, Texas: Business Publications, Inc., 1975).
    Chap. 1:   "The Transportation System of the United States: Its Importance, the Saga of Its Developments, Its Competition," pp. 3-18.
    Chap. 3:   "Transport and Sociopolitical Development," pp. 33-47.
    Chap. 7:   "Intercity Passenger Logistics," pp. 103-122.
    Chap. 8:   "Urban Logistics: Human and Goods," pp. 123-142.
    Chap. 25: "Government Provision of Transportation Facilities," pp. 495-517.

FREDERICK, JOHN H., *Commercial Air Transportation*, 5th ed. (Homewood, Illinois: Richard D. Irwin, Inc., 1969).
    Chap. 2:   "Airports and Airways," pp. 38-67.

LOCKLIN, D. PHILIP, *Economics of Transportation,*   7th ed. (Homewood, Illinois: Richard D. Irwin, Inc., 1972).

    Chap. 1:   "Economic Significance of Transportation," pp. 1-18.

    Chap. 2:   "The Transportation System of the United States," pp. 9-48.

    Chap. 27:   "Highway Finance," pp. 622-641.

    Chap. 28:   "Highway Transportation," pp. 642-665.

    Chap. 33:   "Air Transportation," pp. 770-796.

NORTON, HUGH S., *Modern Transportation Economics,* 2nd ed. (Columbus, Ohio: Charles E. Merrill Publishing Co., 1971).

    Chap. 1:   "Transportation: An Economic, Social and Political Function," pp. 3-17.

    Chap. 2:   "Railroads, Motor Carriers, and Air Carriers," pp. 18-55.

NORTON, HUGH S., *National Transportation Policy* (Berkeley, California: McCutchan Publishing Corp., 1966).

    Chap. 3:   "Federal Promotion Policies," pp. 36-49.

PEGRUM, DUDLEY F., *Transportation: Economics and Public Policy,* 3rd ed. (Homewood, Illinois: Richard D. Irwin, Inc., 1973).

    Chap. 1:   "Transportation and the Economy," pp. 3-21.

    Chap. 2:   "Elements of a Modern Transport System," pp. 22-45.

    Chap. 3:   "Development of Transportation in the U.S.," pp. 46-70.

    Chap. 19:   "Financing Transportation," pp. 441-473.

    Chap. 22:   "Transport Terminals," pp. 513-533.

SAMPSON, ROY J. and MARTIN T. FARRIS, *Domestic Transportation: Practice, Theory and Policy,* 3rd ed. (Boston: Houghton Mifflin Co., 1975).

    Chap. 1:   "The Significance of Transportation," pp. 3-15.

    Chap. 2:   "The Development of Transportation," pp. 17-38.

    Chap. 8:   "Terminals and Special Line-Haul Services," pp. 123-134.

    Chap. 27:   "Public Aids and Promotions in Transportation," pp. 437-453.

TAFF, CHARLES A., *Commercial Motor Transportation,* 4th ed. (Homewood, Illinois: Richard D. Irwin, Inc., 1961).

    Chap. 2:   "Highways," pp. 12-50.

    Chap. 3:   "Highway Financing," pp. 52-90.

    Chap. 19:   "Intercity Passenger Operations," pp. 429-455.

    Chap. 20:   "Urban Mass Transit," pp. 456-477.

3

PRICING
SYSTEMS

As previously noted, passenger transportation may be thought of as a series of systems. The physical and economic systems have been discussed, and so our task in this chapter is to analyze the pricing system.

It is possible to think of pricing in two contexts. The first is to consider the establishment of a single price for a single commodity at a given period of time. Here the market forces of supply and demand are traditionally thought to balance one another in an equilibrium that creates the price that clears the market. For such a complex area as passenger transportation, this view is much too narrow. A broader and more comprehensive approach is preferable.

The second context is to think of pricing as a "system"—that is, as a combination of interacting factors and circumstances. Rather than be concerned solely with an individual price that clears the market for a single commodity at a given time, this pricing system approach looks at all the multiple forces that come to play on the matter of providing the service. Price is not thought of as an independent variable determined by the impersonal factors of supply and demand, but rather as a dependent variable that is affected by supply and demand factors but that in turn affects them. Actual prices (or fares in for-hire passenger transportation) are but one facet of the pricing system. While prices may be the end result, to be sure, our concern with the whole pricing system calls for analysis of all the interacting and interconnected factors affecting the supply of and the demand for passenger transportation.

The pricing system is very complex and has many facets. We will concern ourselves in this chapter primarily with the economic aspects affecting price and affected by price, which will be a helpful simplifying assumption. Furthermore, we shall adopt the approach of considering one factor at a time. This will allow us to give consideration to a particular factor in some depth. However, it should be kept in mind that the approach is intended to simplify and that in actual practice many aspects other than economics come to bear, and that even within the economic aspect, many factors interact and are involved in the pricing system. Our simplifying assumptions are merely reasoning devices to assist in analysis.

As all students already know, prices are established by the interaction of supply and demand. But this truism is too generalized and too simplified. As the sophisticated reader also must know, it's what's behind the supply and the demand that really counts.

Another way of saying "what's behind supply and demand" is to note the economic characteristics of each. That is, what is distinctive or different about each side of the pricing equation? Once these peculiarities or differences have been analyzed, the pricing function can be more easily understood. An added task is to note the market structure within which the pricing system operates and, finally, the manner in which the pricing decision manifests itself.

Therefore, our task will be to analyze the demand side of price, then the supply side of price, then equate the two and note the market structure within which price operates. Ultimately, it will be to consider the pricing decision itself.

DEMAND CHARACTERISTICS

There are eight separate demand characteristics that must be taken into consideration in passenger transportation pricing. These are instantaneous demand, extreme variability of demand, multiplicity of demand, intermodal competition and elasticity, intramodal competition and elasticity, intraclass substitutability and elasticity, dollar competition and income elasticity, and emphasis on conditions of service and nonprice competition. Each will be discussed in detail.

Instantaneous Demand

One of the characteristics of many service industries is that the demand is immediate and instantaneous. While it is true that for certain portions of the passenger transportation market (analyzed in

Part Two) such as pleasure cruises, long air flights, and rail trips by Pullman car, reservations will often be made in advance, much passenger movement is made without either reservations or prior knowledge by the carrier as to who will travel. People want to get on a bus, train, plane, subway, or taxi, or get in their car or on their motorcycle or bike and go.

Many manufacturing firms with a long production cycle, a shortage of capacity to produce, or a very popular product will have a large "backlog" of orders. Demand in such circumstances already exists and can be counted on to produce revenues. Likewise, many firms have a long marketing channel or "pipeline" of goods, which provides a basically constant demand for the product in order to keep the pipeline full. But passenger transportation is by and large demanded without such devices as backlogs, back orders, inventories, and channel pipelines. The demand is instantaneous.

It is obvious that instantaneous demand causes a problem for the firm or agency supplying the service. How much passenger transportation needs to be available at a given time on a given route by a given carrier? The degree of uncertainty here is considerably greater than for many other types of business. Naturally, experience is important in predicting demand, and a firm can use past trends and past usage of facilities in its planning process. Yet there is no certainty that the present and future will follow the trend of the past. Passenger transportation firms sometimes find themselves providing capacity to fulfill an anticipated demand after such a demand has shifted or changed. And since demand is instantaneous, it may well have shifted or changed for the very reason that capacity was not available where and when it was desired. A cumulative effect is often noted in the problem of meeting instantaneous demand: Where demand exceeds supply, potential customers become unhappy. By the time capacity has been adjusted to meet the new demand, the customers may have chosen alternative means of movement.

Faced with this uncertainty, there is a natural tendency for management to provide more capacity than is needed "just to be sure." This tendency is reinforced by other demand factors (such as variability, to be discussed directly). It is not uncommon for public transportation firms to have more vehicles and capacity in the way and in terminals than is necessary to handle most of their customers most of the time. In Chapter 2 we noted the load factors of various modes of passenger transportation; these can be thought of as a measure of the overcapacity of passenger transportation produced.

The same overcapacity is true for private transportation. The family car usually runs with excess seating capacity partly because there are limits to the choices of seat configuration and partly in case a friend might be invited along for a ride at the last minute. It is a rare situation when all of the capacity available to move passengers is utilized in a single mode or in passenger transportation in general. Overcapacity is a way of life in passenger transportation and is partly the result of the characteristic of instantaneous demand and partly the result of the next characteristic: variability of demand.

Extreme Variability of Demand

Not only is the demand instantaneous, but it is extremely variable. Almost all modes of passenger transportation suffer from the "peaks and valleys" of demand. Both the demand for and the need for passenger transportation vary over the hours of the day, days of the week, time of the month, and seasons of the year. Capacity to handle the peak load or demand must be available, but it may be unutilized or underutilized during other periods. The result is that much of passenger transportation is supplied with excess capacity (empty seats) much of the time.

Variability of demand not only causes excess capital to be invested, with resultant underutilization much of the time, but it may also cause underutilization of the other factors of production. Labor is one of these. Crews must be available to handle peak demands and may not be fully utilized during nonpeak periods. The urban passenger transportation demand provides the best example of this variability problem. In most cities, the peak demand occurs in the hours between 6 and 9 A.M. and again between 4 and 7 P.M. Subways, buses, taxis, and commuter trains are packed during the rush hour. The labor force that serves this demand (as well as the capital in vehicles, ways, terminals, and so forth) may be extremely taxed for this short period of time. For the rest of the time, they may be underutilized. In the case of labor various laws confining working time to eight hours cause a further problem. It should be noted that the two peak periods in our example are more than eight hours apart. This may mean two complete sets of labor inputs will have to be used even though labor will be efficiently utilized for only a three-hour period or less (with five hours of underutilization).

Variability of demand causes a further problem in pricing. Investment and labor must be paid for out of revenues. How should the peak demand be charged for this service and how should the off-peak demand be charged? Revenue must be great enough to cover costs overall and the tendency has been to charge the peak user no more than the off-peak user. In effect, a type of cross-subsidization is involved here. The capital facilities, labor, and other costs are geared to covering the peak demand yet the charges are designed on an average use basis. Many analysts have suggested that peak-period users should be charged more; off-peak users less. The rationale for this approach is that the capabilities to move people are designed almost entirely around the necessity of covering the peak demand. The extra capacity in capital and labor to cover the peak demand should be paid for by the peak user. This is the so-called "peak-load pricing" solution and is part of the "marginal-cost pricing" argument (users should be charged the marginal costs of the service).

In fact, fares in the for-hire transportation area use an average-cost pricing approach. Some attempts to lower price for the off-peak user can be noted but there have been few attempts to raise the price charged to the peak user. In effect, temporal cross-subsidization is a fact of life in passenger transportation.

There has been very little use of price to stimulate off-peak use of facilities or to counteract the variability of demand in passenger transportation. Some off-season pricing is found in the airlines and occasionally in passenger trains but rarely is this fully developed. Nor is it widely found in all means of moving people. The lower midweek and night air fare is well known but similar arrangements are rarely found in other passenger transportation modes. We will return to these approaches farther along in our analysis but for now it is sufficient to note that one characteristic of demand in passenger transportation is its extreme variability by hour, day, month, and season.

Multiplicity of Demand

Another important complicating characteristic is that there is not one demand for passenger transportation but several demands. Demand must be "segmented" into its parts and analyzed separately as to its motivation, its responses to price, its frequency, and the like.

Several segmentations of demand are possible. Perhaps the

simplest is to consider demand as either business demand or pleasure demand. These two demands have different motivations, frequencies, and responses to price. Business demand can be thought of as the demand for travel for purposes of conducting business or travel to work. Travel by salesmen, executives, engineers, and various specialists are examples that quickly come to mind—as does the familiar commuting. Pleasure demands, on the other hand, are involved with vacation, visiting, touring. Certainly the motivation and response to price and frequency of these two will be different.

Another somewhat allied segmentation of demand is into the categories of primary and derived. In fact, the two are not easily separable. Yet some passenger transportation demands involve more derived elements than others. A good example of primary demand would be the tourist whose demand for travel is the pleasure of the travel itself. Some people just like to travel and the very fact of movement is an end in itself, enough of an experience to constitute a separate demand. The idea of "let's go somewhere"—and it doesn't particularly matter "where"—illustrates this primary demand.

Far and away the largest segment of passenger transportation demand, however, is of a derived nature. By this we mean that the demand to travel is derived from the demand for something else. An executive traveling on business to a distant city creates a demand primarily because of the necessity to reach his destination for business purposes. His demand is derived from the demand for the product or service of his business. Should he take his wife along either because she has nothing else to do or simply likes to travel, her demand will be primary and his derived. The person traveling to work by automobile, subway, commuter train, or bus will have a demand derived from his particular type of work plus the physical separation of his place of residence from his work; the person accompanying him "just for the ride" has a primary demand. Most demands are derived from some reason other than simply the pleasure of travel itself.

This distinction can be very important for the pricing system. Derived demand may respond more to forces quite outside the passenger transportation industry than primary demand. A change of fares will affect primary demand but may not affect derived demand. If business conditions in a particular industry are poor, demand for travel may also be poor even though fares and the conditions of service remain good or even improve. This complex interrelationship involved in derived demand will be further analyzed but for now it should be realized that no single demand exists; rather there is a multiplicity of varied demands.

Finally, demand may also be segmented by distance. The demand for short-distance passenger transportation is quite different from the demand for long-distance travel. Intermediate distance variations are also possible. Many other segmentations of demand are possible and the list here is not exhaustive. But the point is: It is a mistake to think solely in terms of one demand in passenger transportation; various demands must be considered, and this is an extremely complicating problem.

Intermodal Competition and Elasticity

A further characteristic of demand for passenger transportation that must be noted is the considerable opportunity for substituting one mode of transportation for another. Demand can readily shift, for example, from train to bus to automobile. All modes of passenger transportation are competitive (within obvious limits) with all other modes of transportation. Therefore, the people behind the demand for a given means of transportation will be highly sensitive to the price and service of a competitive means of travel.

The economist uses the term "elasticity" to indicate this sensitivity. Strictly applied, he considers price elasticity and income elasticity to refer to the sensitivity of the quantity demanded to changes in price or changes in income. Specific quantifiable derivations of elasticity are possible with this approach. Thus, demand for air travel may be considered as having a coefficient or price elasticity of -1.3, for example. This would mean roughly that a 10 percent change in price would cause a 13 percent change in the quantity demanded.

We will use the term "elasticity" here in the more general context of substitutability. Hence an elastic demand is one that is sensitive to substitutability; an inelastic demand is one with less potential substitutability. For the exact measure of this substitutability, the reader should refer to some of the important econometric studies of demand elasticity of passenger transportation.

The degree of elasticity of demand will depend on many things. As noted above, when demand is segmented, the potential competition on a given segment of demand will be an important factor in elasticity.

Potential water carrier substitutability on demand for the journey to work in suburban to urban travel is slight in general (although the use of ferries in the San Francisco Bay area is being promoted for this very demand). Air transportation is not ordinarily considered a substitute for short-distance travel, but transportation for long-distance travel, or automobiles for intercontinental travel. But within a given segment of demand (travel from A to B) several means of travel or modes of transportation are regularly available and potential substitutes for one another. We use the term "intermodal competition and elasticity" for this phenomenon.

Several factors will be important as determinants of this elasticity. Price has traditionally been thought of by economists as the most important. We shall consider other elasticity of substitutability determinants shortly, but for now emphasis on price is worthwhile.

The price of one service relative to the price of the substitute service on a given segment of demand may be an important factor. All too often managers of passenger transportation services tend to overlook it. Some demands are price-elastic. Pleasure travel is generally thought to have a higher degree of price elasticity than business travel. Rarely will a business trip be canceled in response to a price rise, but this is often the case in terms of a vacation. Primary demand may be much more price-elastic than derived demand. The price of movement from place of residency to place of work, while an expense to the traveler, is generally thought of as part of the costs of employment. Although it occasionally happens, one rarely finds a person who changed jobs because the price of travel to work increased. But in primary demand, people may avoid travel simply because it's "not worth it." In economic terms they may mean that the utility or satisfaction derived from the journey is not equal to the disutility or price of the movement.

An allied intermodal competition and price elasticity exists between private carriage and various for-hire carriers. While a price is not usually charged for the use of the private automobile or bicycle (unless you are renting it), there is a consumer's cost which could be considered as a price and could play the role of price in elasticity. Unfortunately, few consumers know the cost of owning and operating a private automobile (as we noted in the previous chapter: 15.8¢ per mile based on 100,000 miles of use in 10 years of a $4,000 car in 1973 prices) so comparisons on a price basis are infrequently made. Some business firms make such comparisons, however, and may use

for-hire modes of transportation where possible due to price considerations (either where auto expense is an expense-account allowance or
company cars are furnished certain employees). Of course, other
factors, such as availability of alternative modes on a given route
segment of demand, convenience, and hours of travel are also involved. Even so, price comparisons between for-hire and private
carriage can be made even though they are not as easily seen as between alternative for-hire modes.

Various studies have been conducted on the effect of price on
intermodal competition and substitution (usually called modal-split
studies). Almost always other factors are involved—as prestige, comfort, speed, convenience. But the point here is that price remains a
factor; its importance will vary with the particular segment of the
demand considered and the other factors involved, but it continues as
a factor and must always be considered. Substitutability is always
possible and price is one of the reasons for it.

Intramodal Competition and Elasticity

Not only is there a competition between such modes as air, rail,
bus, private automobile, and ship, but there is a competition within
a given mode between carriers. This competition among firms of a
given mode of passenger transportation, such as competition between
airline companies or bus companies or railroads or steamship companies, is what we mean by "intramodal competition." For-hire
passenger transportation firms do compete where their route patterns
are duplicative, and substitutability between firms is just as possible
as substitutability between modes.

The potential substitutability among transportation firms may
not be as responsive to price as it is to conditions of service. Generally
prices or fares are similar if not identical between competing firms.
Part of the reason for this comes out of transportation regulation,
which we shall discuss in the next chapter. Of course, where regulation is uneven or where all competitors are not regulated in the same
way (as with scheduled airlines as compared to supplemental air
carriers) price comparisons among firms is possible and becomes a
very real factor in elasticity or substitutability.

Intramodal competition does seem to be more concerned with
the conditions of service, however. By this we mean a whole series of

factors such as routes, frequency of service, type of equipment used, treatment by employees, perhaps meals, or even what "free movie" is shown on an airline. Elasticity or substitutability of one firm for another will definitely take place in response to these factors.

Many examples of this elasticity could be cited but equipment-caused substitutability in the airline industry comes readily to mind. In the postwar period, the airlines have gone through several difficult reequipment phases. Existing equipment was not worn out and still operated economically and yet a new "generation" of equipment was purchased by all airlines at about the same time at tremendous cost. Why? Simply because with intramodal competition, once one firm had decided to buy new equipment or a new type of plane, all others were forced to buy comparable new equipment or lose demand.

Therefore, the firm must always have in mind not only its own price and the conditions of service offered but also the price and conditions or service offered by its competitors of the same mode. Sometimes a very small change in price, time of departure, frequency of service, type of equipment, and so forth will either increase or lose demand for an individual firm. To some degree this explains why all the airlines schedule departures and arrivals at the most convenient times (thereby causing congestion problems at airports), why passenger transportation firms offer the traveler fewer options at night or during certain days of the week, and so forth. Clearly substitutability or elasticity exists between firms.

Intraclass Competition and Elasticity

A sixth pecularity or characteristic of demand is that most for-hire passenger transportation firms offer two or more classes of service. Once more no single demand is involved but rather a specific demand for a specific class.

By class of service, we mean such things as "tourist," "first class," and "economy" in airlines, the various classes of service in water transportation, the "Pullman" or "first class" as compared to "day coach" and "tourist" classes in rail transportation. Classes of travel are also found in subways and buses with local and express service. European railroads typically have three or more classes of service. Even in private automobiles, the concept of class of service may be found in different makes or brands of cars and is involved with prestige, comfort, speed. The concept of different classes of service is widespread in passenger transportation.

Passenger transportation is somewhat unique in this regard. Most goods and services are offered as a single homogeneous entity. One rarely finds first- and second-class steel or cigarettes or aluminum or radios. In agricultural commodities a grading will be found, but in most industrial commodities, no class exists. If an inferior or cheaper product is offered, it will typically bear a different brand name or other designation. Indeed, most manufacturers feel so strongly about the integrity of their product and its reputation that they will only offer a different class of the commodity through a subsidiary with a different brand name or by way of a private brand. Some firms feel so strongly about this matter that they go to great lengths to prevent erosion of their brand prestige and have been known to evoke fair trade laws, go to court, or actually destroy goods rather than allow them to be sold at a lower price. In passenger transportation, the opposite situation exists, and the firm offers several levels or classes of service at different prices to the consumer.

The classes of service idea leads to competition of the firm with itself, a unique demand characteristic. Determination of the boundaries of classes or the definition of a class of service becomes a difficult task. The conditions of transportation must be compared to the price and a compromise struck. How much better must the airline service in first class be in order to justify a 25 percent price differential? The matter of free drinks, seat widths, leg room, and "pitch" of seats, free entertainment (movies, piano bar, live music), number of stewardesses and their physical attractiveness—all are familiar manifestations of intraclass competition. Elasticity or substitutability exists and if the firm changes the "package" offered, it may well find its demand changed with more people electing not to pay the premium price and receive the "free" services or vice versa. One class of service does compete with another class of service by the same carrier in passenger transportation.

Dollar Competition and Income Elasticity

It is a truism that all firms and all goods and services compete for the consumer's dollar. Some firms emphasize this type of competition and even such single suppliers as a regulated telephone monopoly are fond of saying that they are really in quite a competitive business. Of course, this is true and what the economist means by "competition" (usually price competition) is not what the businessman may mean by competition. In order to distinguish what is meant here, we use the term "dollar competition," and we mean by this that there are many goods and services available at a given period of time and all sellers are in competition with all other sellers for the consumer's dollar.

Dollar competition is quite prominent in certain types of passenger transportation and is a real force to be considered in the demand for passenger transportation. Pleasure travel is particularly prone to the forces of dollar competition and substitutability. The substitutability here takes the form of what the economist calls income elasticity. Pleasure travel and some other types of passenger transportation may be quite income-elastic.

Each consumer unit has certain needs that must be fulfilled. The rent must be paid, an adequate diet provided, the utility companies satisfied. This takes varying amounts of the consumer's income. For low-income groups, these "essentials" may use up all or nearly all (sometimes even more) of the available income. For the higher income groups, some income will be left over after the essentials are purchased. This may be spent in many ways. Typically we speak of it as "discretionary income"—that is, the spending of this amount of income is at the discretion or pleasure of the individual. Some types of passenger transportation demand are in rigorous competition for the consumer's discretionary income. This situation is a special type of dollar competition and must be recognized when considering the demand for passenger transportation.

As an illustration of the importance of discretionary income to travel, the results of a 1971 Gallup Poll taken for the airline industry is of interest. In the sample of the population tested, the percentage who had flown on a scheduled airline as classed by income was as follows:

$15,000 and over	75%
10,000–14,999	61%
7,000– 9,999	46%
5,000– 6,999	42%
3,000– 4,999	33%
under 3,000	27%

Clearly air transportation is more in demand by the higher income groups, with their greater discretionary income, then by the lower income groups.

Not only is this special kind of dollar competition for discretionary income a factor, but income elasticity of substitutability may be high. For instance, as income declines, there will be a more than proportionate decline in demand for passenger transportation. Vacations are easily postponed and pleasure trips canceled. As income increases, it is typical for the family unit to take a pleasure trip or extend its vacation or demand a higher class of travel or accommodation. Pleasure travel is particularly income-elastic.

The same characteristic is involved to at least some degree in business travel. Here personal income may not be directly involved but national income or the income of the firm is. When business income and profits are up, travel budgets tend to be larger and less control is exerted on travel expenses by the firm; when business income and profits drop, one of the first items affected is the travel budget. In the face of decreasing business income, the area of expense accounts and business travel is a prime place to economize, and quite often the cost cutting in that area will be more severe than the business-income decrease. Although it is true that a good bit of business travel is essential, much of it is also discretionary and therefore subject to severe rationing in the face of poor business conditions. A type of income elasticity exists here too.

Finally, even private passenger transportation has an income elasticity effect. When family income decreases or fails to increase as much as anticipated, the tendency is to make the family car do for one more year rather than purchase a new model. When family income rises, there is a marked tendency to enter the new car market. Specialists in the economics of the automobile industry have long known that demand for automobiles is more income-elastic than price-elastic. While the effect is less pronounced and disagreement is widespread as to the meaning of "essential," in cases of decreased personal income only essential automobile trips will be undertaken. Conversely, in periods of rising income, the essentiality of automobile trips is less likely to be questioned.

All goods and services have some income-elasticity effects. In passenger transportation, however, the dollar competition for discretionary income and the income elasticity is a particularly important factor in demand.

Condition of Service and Nonprice Competition

Even though the matter of conditions of service has been repeatedly mentioned in the discussion of the first seven characteristics of demand, it is such an important factor that it constitutes the final characteristic of demand. Traditional economic theory visualizes demand as a function of several factors, sometimes in a mathematical formulation such as Quality demanded $(Qd) = f(X_1 + X_2 + X_3 \cdots X_n)$ with X_1 typically being price, X_2 income, X_3 tastes of buyers and several other factors such as stock of the goods, price of the commodity compared to substitute commodities, availability of substitutes, and complimentary goods. While no priority is necessarily applied to the various X's or parts of the function, price and income are almost always given emphasis. We have given consideration to both price and income above but in our formulation of the demand function for passenger transportation, the conditions of service would rank as X_1.

Conditions of the service can be thought of in terms of frequency; type of equipment; condition and appearance of equipment; courtesy of employees; speed; additional allowances such as drinks, meals, movies or entertainment; ease of access to boarding and egress on arrival; ease of purchase of tickets and booking reservations—in a word, the whole "package" of travel. The for-hire carriers stimulate demand or lose demand according to the condition of the services offered. No other demand factor is more important.

Finally, it will be noted that this important factor is basically a "nonprice" item. Price is a factor in demand, to be sure, just as income is a factor and the other variables noted above are factors. Basically, however, the competition for the demand for passenger transportation is of a nonprice nature. We shall return to this factor once more under market structure.

The situation noted here of nonprice competition and condition of service must be responsive to the external factors affecting the market for passenger transportation. During World War II and again during the energy crisis, the question "Is this trip necessary?" was often asked. The social policy in such situations is to restrict demand to meet available supply and the variations of demand. Obviously under such external restraints, the normal forces of supply and demand are either blunted or changed.

Summary on Demand

To summarize, the demand for passenger transportation does not resemble typical demand as noted by the economist. Eight special characteristics can be noted that tend to make passenger transportation demand both perplexing and different from other demands. These are (1) the instantaneous nature of demand with resultant uncertainity and a tendency to oversupply, (2) extreme variability of demand by hour, day, week, and season with the resultant peak problems for carriers, (3) the multiplicity of demand, which prevents analysis of a single demand and necessitates segmentation of the market, (4) intermodal competition and elasticity with potential substitutability between modes, (5) intramodal competition and elasticity with potential substitutability between firms in a given mode, (6) intraclass competition and elasticity with potential substitutability between classes of service offered by the firm, (7) dollar competition and income elasticity with emphasis on the role of discretionary income, and (8) extreme emphasis on the conditions of service and nonprice types of competition.

SUPPLY CHARACTERISTICS

Now that the unusual characteristics of demand have been noted, it is only natural to wonder if there are similar peculiarities in the supply of passenger transportation. This is indeed the case and we shall note some nine characteristics of supply that are somewhat different from the usual "supply determinants."

In traditional economic theory, supply is determined by the costs of production plus the market structure within which the firm operates, which will affect the amount of profit over cost that can be charged. We will be concerned with market structure directly, but for now, we will concentrate on costs. Supply will have to reflect the costs of production over time and these costs are typically thought of as the prices of the factors of production: resources, labor, capital, and entrepreneurship. Cost may be subdivided into fixed and variable or average and marginal. Only where special circumstances are involved does the discussion go beyond such groupings.

Just as with other industries, the supply of passenger transportation must reflect over time the prices of the factors of production, and costs can be grouped as fixed and variable or average and marginal. But it is the "special circumstances" in supply that will be of the greatest interest to us here. Some of these special circumstances are found in other industries, to be sure, but it is the particular "bundle," or combination, of these nine special circumstances or characteristics that makes passenger transportation supply complicated, unique, and perplexing.

Capital-Intensive and Fixed Costs

Transportation in general is a capital-intensive industry. Large amounts of capital are invested in the way, in equipment, and in terminals. The passenger side of transportation is no exception to the case, as was noted in Chap. 2. Even though labor costs are considerable, capital costs are often as great and, more importantly, due to their indivisibility, present a great opportunity for management to gain economies of use. If capital can be effectively used, per-unit costs may decrease with resultant increases in profit.

Having a large amount of capital committed has several important ramifications. The first of these is that much of this capital is typically borrowed and results in a high level of fixed charges or fixed costs. Interest and amortization of debt will continue even though the capital itself is idle. The tendency to overinvest in capital due to instantaneous demand and variability of demand has already been noted, that this tendency, plus the existence of fixed costs, puts pressure on the for-hire carrier to utilize invested capital if at all possible.

This pressure on management to utilize capital and meet fixed costs may result in discriminatory pricing in the sense that all passengers are not charged equally. It may also cause some odd financial results. For instance, rail-passenger deficits may have been overstated in the past due to the manner in which fixed charges were allocated between passenger and freight service. Also, the pressure of fixed costs may cause equipment to be used at less than full capacity on the theory that any revenue is better than none at all. But whether or not such reactions take place, it is a fact of transportation life that passenger transportation firms are faced with high fixed costs.

This is true not only in the case of for-hire passenger transportation but also for private passenger transportation. A personal automobile is one of the larger "fixed costs" of a household. Not only is the expenditure for a car large (second only to the expenditure for a house) but the fixed-charge nature is also considerable. Automobiles depreciate and lose value whether used or not; finance payments on automobile debt continue even when the car is in the garage. And this is true even though the householder does not finance his automobile but buys it outright. Following the economic concept of opportunity costs it is possible to think of the value of the automobile purchased outright in terms of the opportunity foregone when money is used for its purchase. Thus, if $4,000 is paid outright for an automobile, the yearly cost is the interest or alternative earnings given up on that $4,000. Once more, this is a fixed cost.

The significance of the large capital committed to both for-hire and private passenger transportation and the resultant high level of fixed cost is that they create a tendency to use the asset if at all possible. This tendency is further enforced by the second characteristic sunk cost.

Sunk Cost with Few Alternatives

The term "sunk cost" can have several meanings. Basically, it is a subcategory of fixed costs, and refers either to the existence of few alternatives for a given capital asset or the substantial capital costs involved just to start up production. In some industries it may also refer to a physical characteristic (rather than an economic one) where pipelines, water pipe, and plants are literally "sunk," or located physically in one place, so that they must be used there. Our use of the term will follow the first definition and refer to the fact that few alternative uses are available for much of the capital invested in passenger transport.

Of course, most capital investments are specialized to some degree. Yet this is particularly true in passenger transportation, for once vehicles are purchased, ways established, and terminals created, they have few other uses. A highway or a railway can be used only as a highway or a railway; most transportation terminals have few alternative applications. While it is true that vehicles can be resold (and a used market does exist); generally their use is limited entirely to transportation. From an overall viewpoint, then, transportation equipment has little alternative use.

Many industries have capital investments that permit multiple utilization. A retail food store, for example, can be used for many things. Not only can it be adapted to another line of retailing, but it may even become an office or a storefront church. Alternatives exist for even such specialized capital goods as metal-forming machinery. In general, the more specialized the capital, the fewer alternatives and the greater the sunk-cost nature of the equipment. There are few pieces of capital more specialized than a railway car, a 747 jet, or a subway tunnel. Passenger transportation depends on highly specialized capital with the resultant sunk costs.

The significance of sunk cost with few alternative uses for the pricing system is that once capital has been committed to a specialized use, the only way to recover the investment is by *use*. In other words, the existence of sunk cost puts great pressure on management to use its capital goods. By the process of use, and only by use, can the capital be converted from capital goods back to money or liquid capital. Idle capital equipment never earns money and if no alternative use for the capital exists, it must be used in its sunk capacity if at all possible.

The upshot is that transportation capital may be used in a way that does not always recover all its costs in that use. It is better to use the investment, even partially, and recover something, than not use the capital at all and still have to pay fixed charges on it. Hence, an airline would rather fly a plane (given a choice) half full than not fly at all; railroad cars half full are at least earning some revenue and would earn nothing sitting idle; buses may be dispatched with a load factor that is very low and it might make perfectly good economic sense.

Also, because of the sunk costs and the necessity to recover capital only through use, there is a marked tendency to use old equipment even though newer and more modern equipment is available. Unless the demand characteristics of intermodal and intramodal competition prevent it, sunk costs tend to mean long use of capital. We shall explore this tendency further in our next section, which deals with long cycles.

Finally, the same factor applies to private transportation to some degree. There is a subtle pressure to use the private automobile once the capital has been committed. The major capital outlay has been made, and an idle car sitting in the garage has a fixed charge (as noted above) just as great as the moving car. This whole matter of fixed charges and sunk cost for both for-hire transportation and private transportation exerts pressure to use the capital. When coupled with low incremental costs, to be considered shortly, the pressure to use becomes extreme.

Long Cycles

Before we turn to operating costs, one final factor on the capital cost side will necessarily detain us. Passenger transportation operates under the constraints of a series of three long cycles: long production cycles, long planning cycles, and long-life capital cycles. Other industries have long cycles, too, but these three seem particularly important in passenger transportation.

Even though demand is instantaneous, production is not. In order to supply passenger transportation, there must be much preparation. Vehicles must be acquired, terminals built, employees hired and trained, and sometimes ways built. Even after service has started, vehicles must be cleaned, serviced, prepared for use, and maintained. Substantial preparation and activity sometimes takes place long before the supply is furnished to the passenger. A long production cycle prevails. This is particularly true when the way must be constructed.

Likewise, planning must be done well in advance of the production of the service. The obvious factor of capital planning and acquisition is but part of the long planning cycle. Schedules of employees and vehicles are usually established well in advance of actual production. Changes in capacity take place only after a very long planning cycle involving careful consideration of where to add supply. Once a shift takes place in demand, it may be some time before capacity can be adjusted. The cumulative effect noted above in our discussion of demand is found here. Since it takes a long time to adjust supply, the change or adjustment may be too late, and demand may have once more shifted.

Finally, the capital used in passenger transportation is typically of a very long life. It is not unusual for properly-maintained equipment to last 20 years; in some areas of passenger transportation, such as railways and subways, a 35- to 50-year economic life for equipment, terminals, and ways is possible. This long-life nature of equipment and capital makes investment decisions extremely important. If a wrong decision is made in capital commitments, the firm must live with its mistakes for a very long time. Some passenger transportation firms are still living with poor capital decisions made a decade or more ago. Because of the sunks-cost nature of the industry, there is no way to erase these mistakes and start again.

In modified form, the same is true of private carriage. The private automobile lasts a long time relative to many consumer durables. It is not easy to shift it to other uses. Once purchased, the owner is under pressure to use the vehicle, and since automobiles depreciate most in their earlier years, he will often lose money or capital if he trades too early in the asset life. The buyer should be sure that the car he buys is what he really wants when he buys it, and he should be sure that he plans ahead on its use. All passenger transportation capital is involved with long production cycles, long planning cycles, and long-life capital cycles.

Small Incremental Cost of Operation

Turning now to the operating-cost side of supply, passenger transportation has unusually small incremental costs. Part of this is because of the high degree of fixed costs noted above and the sunk cost and long-cycle nature of capital, but part of it comes from the ease of adding more service up to capacity. Indeed, incremental costs may be defined as the cost of an increment or added unit of production.

Once a for-hire passenger transportation firm has acquired vehicles and terminals (and perhaps a way as well), hired labor, and set up operating schedules and procedures, the added cost of additional service is very small. Passengers can be added very cheaply until capacity is reached. The added cost of one more airline passenger, bus passenger, or rail passenger is extremely small.

Even when vehicle capacity is reached, incremental cost may be small if added system capacity exists. To put another plane on a flight that is full costs the firm only crew, operational, and preparation costs—if it has the plane anyhow. To run another bus is a small cost, and the addition of a passenger car to a train adds very little to the total costs—all assuming that the capital commitment is already made. And recalling that in our analysis of demand we noted a tendency to overinvest due to both the necessity to cover peaks in demand and the instantaneous nature of demand, it is probable that system capacity would prove a hurdle for most firms only for short periods of time.

The same principle of small incremental costs up to capacity exists for private carriage as well. It costs very little to take an extra passenger in your car. Operational costs go up very slightly. Of course, if all seats are filled, it is quite another matter to add one more passenger to a private automobile. But up to capacity, incremental costs or costs of added service are very small.

The significance of this characteristic comes mainly in pricing. Given the small incremental costs, if a decrease in price will attract added passengers, a very low fare can be offered to the incremental or marginal traveler. Until capacity is reached, the firm could add more and more customers at progressively lower rates and still show considerable profit. Of course, the reader recognizes that this is the concept behind various discount fares offered periodically by airlines, some rail passenger firms, and some bus companies. The actual pricing decision will concern us directly, but at this point it is enough to realize that one of the characteristics of supply is a low incremental cost up to capacity.

Nonstorable Supply with High Wastage Factor

The fifth characteristic of passenger transportation supply, nonstorability and high wastage, goes right along with small incremental cost. Once a vehicle is acquired, scheduled, and used, its capacity is committed. Vehicle inputs come in "capacity lumps": so many seats per model of aircraft, bus, subway car, railcar, and ship. Unless all of the capacity is used, it is wasted. Passenger seats not occupied cannot be stored for future use. There is no inventory of passenger-miles!

In a rough way this holds for automobiles also. If you drive alone in your car today, you cannot store or inventory the unoccupied seat beside you in order to carry your friend tomorrow. Once provided, passenger transportation must be used or it is lost forever.

For pricing purposes, this means, once more, pressure to use the service. Not only is the incremental cost of an additional passenger quite small but the capacity to serve is perishable. The transportation saying: "Empty seats are wasted transportation and add no revenue" illustrates this pressure to use. It is well to keep this characteristic in mind when we discuss the pricing decision.

By-Product Problem and Common Cost

To some degree, passenger transportation is a by-product of freight transportation. This is particularly true in rail passenger transportation and in ocean freighter cruises. In other cases, freight transportation is a by-product of passenger transportation. This is true of much of air, bus, private automobile, and maritime cruise ship transportation. But irrespective of which is the by-product of which passenger transportation is rarely produced alone, and this causes problems.

Two problems are involved because of this "by-product effect": the subsidy problem and the cost-allocation problem. The subsidy problem arises because the modes of transportation developed during different time periods and with different degrees of support still compete with one another. For instance, rail passenger transportation and bus transportation compete. Rail provides its own way at a considerable investment and pays taxes on this way. Buses may pay for their way in operating taxes but are spared the problem of investing in and maintaining their own way. Buses operate a package express service as a by-product of passenger transportation. Railroads charge that public expenditures for highway (part of which come from their taxes) subsidize their competition, but the bus companies charge that rail freight transportation subsidizes rail passenger service. Similarly, public aid to air transportation is "justified" on the basis of moving people and improving communication. Yet the capability to move air freight is a by-product of better air transportation. The questions remain: Which service is most heavily subsidized by public expenditures, and what should the proper cost allocation be?

To a considerable degree, the whole matter turns on the economics of "common cost." Common costs are expenditures made for the entire operation and are not easily and clearly assignable to any one function or service. All transportation has a considerable degree of common costs. Much of the cost allocation between passenger and freight service is purely arbitrary. Hence, one service may well subsidize a companion service.

Finally, the significance of this by-product effect and common cost problem is broader than just subsidy. If costs are reflected in rates or prices, then the allocation of common costs may become extremely important. For example, much of the cost of air transportation is common as between passenger and freight. If the allocation of these common costs assigns large amounts to freight, the passenger fares would be lower and the freight charges higher than they should be. It would make little difference to anyone but the stockholders except for the fact that air fares are competitive with bus and rail fares. Likewise, the share of common costs in rail that are expected to be earned by passenger service as compared to freight service is important to the competitors of rail service. No definitive answers to some of these problems are possible since common costs are arbitrarily allocated. Many firms with multiple products have these cost-allocation problems, but since passenger transportation is so competitive and possesses potential substitutability between modes, between firms, and between classes (as noted above), the problem is aggravated.

Continuity and Reliability Factors

Another pecularity of supply of passenger transportation comes from the necessity for continuity and reliability. Passenger transportation must operate 24 hours a day, 30 days a month, and 365 days a year. No 8-hour days and 40-hour weeks prevail; the services must be available continously. This necessity to supply on a continuous basis causes many problems not found in other industries.

Additionally, there can be little "inferior" production. The public expects passenger transportation at night to be as reliable as transportation during the day. Holiday services are expected to be as good or even better than services during normal times, weekend travel as easy as weekday travel, and so forth. One would hardly expect a 24-hour supermarket to give as good service at 2 A.M. as at 4 P.M. but the public expects transportation to be as reliable at 2 A.M. as at 4 P.M.! Some firms can work on a shift basis and maintain little or no service in other than business hours. Passenger transportation is expected to keep 24-hour-a-day business hours and maintain high levels of reliability.

Since passenger transportation is continuous and has a high reliability factor, there is little opportunity to cut costs or have lower pricing for a slightly inferior service at odd hours. If management should cut prices for, say night time travel, it would be as an effort to stimulate demand and utilize the "valley" in demand, not as a reflection of any cost economy. The cost to the firm to supply service is approximately the same at any time during the day.

This reliability-continuity factor applies to our expectations for our private automobiles, too. We expect our cars to start whenever we need them. We expect roads, streets, and bridges to be available at all times. Private carriage is expected to be just as continuous and reliable as for-hire services, perhaps even more so.

The significance of continuity and reliability is that they add to the total cost of the service. Because reliability and continuity are demanded and expected by the public, the cost is greater than if there were a lower level of expectation. Costs are reflected in supply and in rates or fares. Reliability and continuity must be paid for, and that cost becomes a part of the charge for transportation.

Labor and Responsibility

Because of the requirement for continuous, highly reliable production, transportation labor is different from most other labor situations. Again, no 8-hour workday and 40-hour workweek in the usual sense is found. Transportation labor has a 24-hour schedule and must be as alert and responsible at 2 A.M. as at 4 P.M. The safety of the public is involved and a high level of responsibility has been assigned to transportation labor.

So, too, the level of skill is often considerably greater than that demanded from the typical production worker. People piloting airplanes, driving buses, or operating trains and ships must be well trained and highly skilled. Since public safety is involved, various rules and regulations concerning not only level of skills but also conditions of employment have evolved. Licensing procedures that demand proof of skill are usually imposed on operators. There are also regulatory rules relative to hours of continuous work and rest periods. We shall be concerned with these in detail in the next chapter, but the point here is that transportation labor is typically well compensated in order to gain the degree of skill and responsibility necessary. The labor bill for passenger transportation firms is not small, and little opportunity exists to substitute capital for labor in the passenger transportation industry.

Public Regulation and the Supply of Passenger Transportation

Partly because of the eight preceding supply peculiarities and partly because of its history, transportation is a regulated industry. The next chapter will analyze the regulatory system within which passenger transportation operates, but from a pricing-system point of view, regulation is an important supply factor.

Public bodies decide how much transportation is offered, over which routes, and under what conditions. Passenger transportation firms cannot decide not to serve; they must serve all without discrimination or prejudice. These are the so-called "common carriage obligations" coming out of the common law, which will be considered in Chap. 4.

Because the public is often a co-user, safety and maintenance are subject to external control. The firm cannot decide to postpone maintenance or not to supply safety devices. Few other businesses work under the constraints that are imposed on transportation and management's prerogatives are limited by regulation. Funds may be spent not because they lead to profit but because regulation demands it. Due to regulation, routes must be served even though unprofitable. The whole supply of for-hire passenger transportation operates within a system of regulatory controls.

The same is partly true for private transportation supply. Safety inspections, repairs, and maintenance at minimum levels are all increasingly required by state laws. The owner might be willing to "risk it" without good lights, but public regulation demands that they function properly. Few areas have as much control exerted over them as passenger transportation, and indeed this regulatory system is of such importance that it will be the subject of the next chapter.

Summary on Supply

The supply of passenger transportation does not resemble a typical production function as defined by the economist. Nine special characteristics can be noted that tend to make passenger transportation supply both perplexing and different from other supply functions. These are: (1) the capital-intensive nature of the industry, with the resultant high level of fixed costs; (2) the sunk cost characteristic of the capital, with few alternative uses; (3) the existence of long cycles of production, planning, and capital life; (4) the small incremental cost of operating; (5) the nonstorable nature of supply with a high wastage factor; (6) the by-product effect and the problem of common cost; (7) the continuity and reliability factors; (8) the labor and responsibility characteristics; and, (9) the public-regulation aspect of the supply. All of these tend to make passenger transportation supply somewhat unique and certainly more complicated than the usual supply function.

MARKET STRUCTURE

Now that the unusual characteristics of supply and demand have been noted, our next task is to consider the market structure within which they operate. Even though this approach has been ably presented in basic economics courses a review is in order before we apply the concept to passenger transportation.

Market structure can be thought of in terms of a model or system that has predictive attributes. Hence, the economist attempts to classify various economic situations such as "pure competition," "pure monopoly," "oligopoly," and "monopolistic competition." Once the market structure is determined, we can better predict what action we would expect the firm to pursue.

Traditionally, various models of economic behavior have been developed from a theoretical viewpoint with several assumptions of behavior, and then applied to actual business situations. For example, it is predicted that a monopoly will act in a certain fashion from the logic of the pure monopoly model. If a monopoly is found, it might or might not so act in actual practice. The fact that the actual monopoly did not act as predicted would not prove the model incorrect, for numerous assumptions were made, such assumptions as "Firms attempt to maximize profit." That actual behavior of the firm varied from the predicted behavior was probably due to incorrect assumptions, not to incorrect logic on the part of the model. Even so, society is ahead because we can now say that if the assumptions are true, we can predict that a firm in a monopoly situation will react in a specific fashion. Public action can be taken to prevent or hasten such predicted behavior, and competitive firms can meet predicted action in various ways. The degree of uncertainty is considerably reduced even though the predicted action or the assumptions are not always fulfilled.

In classifying market structure, the economist has often considered three factors: number of sellers and buyers, product characteristics, and entry-exit characteristics. Various conditions for each of these factors can be assumed and defined so that any market structure can be described. For example, pure competition would have many sellers and buyers, homogeneous products, and free entry and exit. Four classifications are often used, with many subclassifications—namely, pure competition, monopolistic competition (sometimes called imperfect competition), oligopoly, and pure monopoly. For the sake of convenience, this simplified market structure approach is noted in Table 13.

TABLE 13

Market Structure Characteristics

MARKET STRUCTURE	NUMBER OF FIRMS	PRODUCT CHARACTERISTICS	ENTRY-EXIT CHARACTERISTICS
Pure Competition	Many	Homogeneous	Free
Monopolistic Competition	Many	Differentiated	Relatively Easy
Oligopoly	Few	Homogeneous, Differentiated	Relatively Difficult
Pure Monopoly	One	Indifferent	Closed

The cases of pure competition and pure monopoly are more in the nature of "limits." That is, the assumptions are so rigorous that they are rarely found in actual practice. They exist as reasoning points, benchmarks, or extremes. Actual firms fall nearer one extreme or limit than the other and hence can be said to possess more competitive than monopolistic characteristics and vice versa. Immediately a type of classification has been established.

Without going through an analysis of each of the four market-structure classifications and the three factors considered in each classification, we can ask which market structure best describes for-hire passenger transportation? (It should be added that we are here considering only the for-hire portion of passenger transportation since market structure as a concept implies sale of a good or service.) The answer is: for-hire passenger transportation seems to be a differentiated oligopoly.

The conditions for a differentiated oligopoly are: (1) few firms, (2) differentiated products, and (3) relatively difficult entry and exit. As we noted in Chap. 2, the number of firms selling for-hire passenger transportation service is few in the aggregate. If we consider passenger transportation from a "route orientation," the number of firms on a given route is even fewer. "Few" here is theoretically defined as "so few that the price actions of any one will appreciably affect the demand of any other." A similar definition of "few" refers to the "interdependency of all firms serving a given market." In absolute numbers, passenger transportation firms are few. On a given route, only a few compete. Our analysis of demand has shown intermodal and intramodal competition and potential substitutability. The actions of one firm affect all others; interdependency exists. The first condition of oligopoly is certainly fulfilled.

Turning to the entry-exit conditions: It is difficult to begin a new for-hire passenger transportation firm. This difficulty is partly due to regulatory factors, as we shall note in the next chapter, but it is also due to the capital-intensive and sunk-cost nature of the industry. Of course, the barrier to new entry of capital would vary according to the section of the industry under discussion. Thus, entry into rail passenger transportation would be more difficult than entry into bus transportation, entry into urban transit more difficult than entry into air transportation. Entry into taxi service would be the easiest of all. Also, where some of the capital required is furnished by the public, such as with highways and airways, entry might be easier than where the way is furnished by the firm.

Other factors from our discussion of supply and demand have a bearing here. The need to hire skilled and highly trained and responsible labor, the need to furnish continuous and reliable service, the need to meet peak demands with service while paying for underutilization during off-peak periods—all are factors suggesting difficulty of entry. Of course, regulations reinforce this condition by positively restricting entry to a few firms.

Finally, when we consider product characteristics, a differentiated oligopoly is the suggested answer. By differentiation we mean the attempt to make the product (service in this case) as different and distinctive as possible and still substitutable with competitive services. As noted under demand above, the conditions of service are the ultimate competitive factor in passenger transportation. Each firm attempts to make its service as distinctive as possible and still compete. The service is certainly not homogeneous (so similar that the consumer cannot distinguish one firm's output from that of another), as is the case with steel, copper, aluminum, wheat, corn, barley, and oats. The consumer can readily distinguish one airline's service from another, and airline service from bus service from rail service.

Each for-hire transportation firm attempts to make its service distinctive by as many means as possible. Some examples are: scheduling arrivals and departures to make the service different from that of competitors; equipment used and its condition; attractiveness and courtesy by employees; "free" meals, drinks, and entertainment; desirability of destination (such as a vacation in the Florida sun) and affiliated promotions. All of these are evidence of attempts to differentiate the product.

If for-hire passenger transportation is indeed a differentiated oligopoly, what action does the model predict can be expected? Due to the interdependency factor, the model predicts a minimum of price action and a maximum of action to differentiate the product. Price would tend to be "sticky" and change but slowly. Where change took place, a price leadership pattern would tend to prevail, with one firm assuming leadership on the price change either upward or downward. The price leader might be the largest firm or it might be the "barometric" firm, the one that tests market response. The role of price leader would shift from time to time and the firm leading price up at one time might not be the firm that leads price down at another.

According to modern economic theory, a "kinked" demand curve for the industry could well exist. No firm would have an individual demand curve unless the product was differentiated enough to overcome the inherent interdependency. Hence, the industry demand curve might have a "kink" in it as shown in Fig. 5. Each firm in considering its price policy would reasonably assume that a decrease in

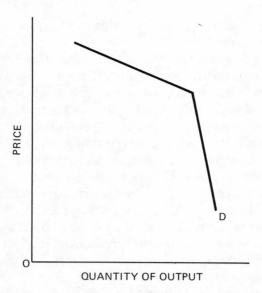

PRICE

O

QUANTITY OF OUTPUT

Figure 5.   Kinked Demand Curve of Oligopolistic Industry.

price would be matched by all its competitors. Thus, a price decrease would lead to very little increase in the share of the market. In
effect, the firm sees demand below the kink as price-inelastic. On the
other hand, the firm might believe that a price increase would not be
matched by competitors. The firm sees demand above the kink as
highly price-elastic. A price rise here would mean considerable loss of
demand as others failed to follow the increase. The upshot of a kinked
demand curve is the tendency to do nothing; that is, maintain a stable
price situation and avoid "rocking the boat." The only price change
under such circumstances takes place through all firms moving together (a price leadership situation) with concerted or identical
action of all firms at a given time.

The offsetting feature to the kinked demand curve, live-and-let-
live pricing, concerted or parallel price action with intermittent
sticky or stable prices, is product differentiation. Because firms are
competitive, this competition will take the form of product differentiation, not price competition. Every attempt will be made to make
the product as different as possible and still substitutable or competitive. As noted above, this is precisely the action found in many
parts of the passenger transportation industry. The actions predicted
by the model are very close to the actions actually found in the

passenger transportation industry. Once more, this is evidence that the market structure is one of differentiated oligopoly.

THE PRICING DECISION

The individual firm will place strong emphasis on efforts to market its service by way of product differentiation. This aspect of passenger transportation is so important that we will devote all of Chap. 5 to this subject. However, price action will sometimes be undertaken, and price is an important part of the marketing effort. Therefore, it is worthwhile to concern ourselves with the economics of the pricing decision in passenger transportation.

The economics of pricing in passenger transportation involve three interrelated concepts: "differential pricing," the "contribution theory," and the "incremental concept." In all instances, these applied economic concepts are used only as guidelines, and managerial judgment is the final decision-making factor as to price.

Differential Pricing

Beginning in a very simple manner, the oligopoly possesses considerable market power and can miximize the demand curve by creating several prices. This economic power is reinforced by legal price-making and bureau of conference rate-making, which we shall discuss in the next chapter. Given the legal power and if the firms indeed move in concert with parallel action, the industry can establish not one but several separate supply curves. Graphically, this is illustrated in Fig. 6.

Literally, three prices for three supply curves are the result. The firm here will offer three separate services at three separate prices and take advantage of a larger portion of the demand curve than a single price would permit. The firm has what is called "differential pricing," and several classes of service are supplied—each slightly different from the other and each at a separate price. This essentially is what is done when first class, tourist class, and economy class service is offered by an airline.

How are these customers classified in order to accomplish differential pricing? Many factors can be used to classify customers, but

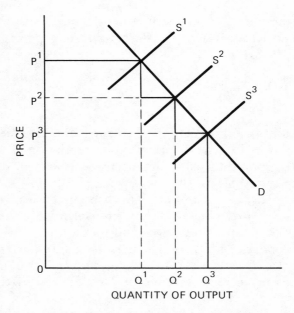

Figure 6.   Multiply Supply Curves of Oligopoly

basically they turn on the various elasticities of demand noted earlier. That is, considering factors of potential substitutability, management can establish a low price where potential substitutability is high, an intermediate price, and a high price where potential substitutability is low.

Drawing upon our demand analysis, we find that the matter becomes somewhat more complicated. Actually, as we have suggested, demand must be segmented. No single demand curve for passenger transportation exists. Likewise, the elasticities or potential substitutabilities are multiple (we noted price, income, intermodal, intramodal, intraclass, and conditions of service). Further there is a tendency to find kinked demand curves. In fact, a separate demand exists for each class and the situation would appear graphically somewhat like Fig. 7.

While Fig. 7 is nearer to reality, even more complications exist. First, there would be numerous demand curves—perhaps one for each destination. Second, several supply curves certainly would be involved. At a minimum, a supply curve for each class of service

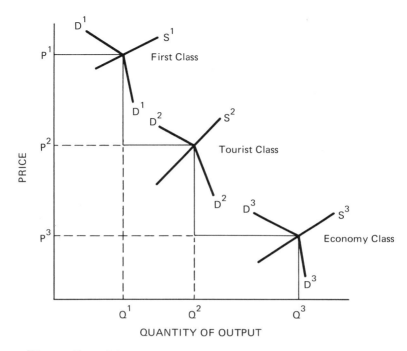

Figure 7.   Differential Pricing With Varying Degrees of Elasticity and Kinked Demand Curves.

exists. Consequently, the basic supply and demand equilibrium is involved many, many times, and for each specific differential price. All factors of demand noted in our earlier analysis would be involved, with varying degrees of importance on a given demand segment. Likewise, all supply or cost factors previously discussed would be involved with varying importance on each supply curve. But in all cases, a separate and differential price would be established on each segment.

The Contribution Theory

Bringing in the supply or cost side, what factors would be helpful in maximizing revenue in this pricing decision? Here the "contribution theory" from applied economics is helpful.

Remembering that many costs are fixed and are of a sunk-cost nature, and that incremental costs are small but that a common-costs problem exists, management should set each price or fare at such a level that it makes its greatest possible total contribution to fixed costs and still allows the traffic to move.

What this statement means basically is that each fare should cover its share of incremental costs plus as much of fixed and common costs as possible considering the elasticities of demand. Where demand is highly elastic, fares might be very low on that segment of demand. How low? No lower than incremental costs and high enough to make the greatest possible total contribution to fixed and common costs and still serve the demand. Where demand is inelastic, fares might be rather high. How high? High enough to cover incremental costs and to maximize their contribution to fixed and common costs but still serve the demand.

Obviously, in the first instance, the fare might not cover total costs as they are traditionally considered. In the second instance, the fare would more than cover total costs and substantial profit could be involved. Just as obviously, a type of "cross-subsidization" from the passengers with an inelastic demand to the passengers with an elastic demand is involved. Also, a type of price discrimination exists.

The rationalization of the use of the contribution theory is simply that fixed costs and common costs are high. It is only by arbitrary allocation decisions that total costs per passenger can be obtained anyway. Fixed costs must be covered over time with total revenue and if the high fare excluded those passengers with an elastic demand curve, the whole burden of fixed costs would fall on those with an inelastic demand curve.

As long as the differential fares cover incremental costs and make some contribution to fixed costs, all passengers will be better off. The passengers with inelastic demand will pay less than if they carried the full burden of fixed costs. The passengers with elastic demand will travel, whereas they would not have traveled at a higher price. Resources committed will have been used (remember the perishability factor) more completely and effectively.

Two absolute limits will be imposed on how high fares for the passengers with inelastic demand can go. One is demand itself. At some price and condition of service, even these passengers will refuse to travel. Two, regulation is also involved. One of the objects of regulation is to prevent "undue discrimination" in fares and prevent the firm from charging too high a fare.

The Incremental Concept

Drawing upon the differential pricing concept and the contribution theory, management must approach price setting in a very cautious manner. Considerable judgment is necessary in analyzing demand and cost factors. Estimates of potential substitutability are not easy to make; fares that are too high can easily discourage travel, while fares that are too low may not make the greatest possible total contribution to fixed and variable costs.

Each fare is a separate problem. As already noted, each segment of demand must be analyzed and all unusual characteristics of that particular segment considered. Each segment of supply will have varying cost characteristics as well. But the general pricing rule is that each fare should cover its incremental costs and make the greatest possible total contribution to fixed and common costs, and still move the traffic.

The proper process to be used in establishing a total price or fare schedule would be to follow the incremental concept. Each part of the problem should be considered separately, and after careful analysis, each fare should be separately established. The general rule of the contribution theory should be followed on each segment. As each fare is so analyzed, revenue will be maximized and so will travel on that increment of the business. As each fare is properly adjusted, a total price or fare schedule emerges. Finally, total revenue and profit will have been maximized as each segment is analyzed incrementally, total use of the resources committed will have been maximized, and total travel will have been maximized.

Actual Pricing

Finally, we must ask if differential pricing, contribution theory, and the incremental process is indeed used in the passenger transportation industry. If the theory were followed, each fare would be studied and analyzed separately. Differential pricing would reflect demand differences, as noted above, and each fare would maximize its contribution. Some fares would be lower—night time fares for example; some would be higher—such as fares during peak periods. Much effort would go into solving the "peak and valley" problem of demand and the seasonal fluctuations of demand. Some customers with elastic demands, such as the young and the elderly, would pay a low fare, while businessmen might be charged a higher one. Then too, family travel might be stimulated by price arrangements. And so it might go.

It should be obvious to even the casual observer that actual pricing only partly follows the theoretical possibilities noted in this chapter. Part of the reason is administrative. Only so many fares can be easily administered and an absolute limit imposes itself here. Part of the reason for not following the theory of price change noted here is regulatory. Public commissions do not always look with favor on price experimentation and have a tendency to want fares that remain stable. Unfortunately, many carriers have gotten into the habit of blaming many of their economic troubles on regulators. The regulatory boards are a ready scapegoat at such times. It is well to note, however, that price changes originate with the carriers and are only approved or disapproved by the regulators. No one knows how many price changes would be approved by commissions if the carrier proposed them. Blaming regulators is not a valid reason for not studying the economic situation faced by the firm and attempting enlightened action.

Probably the biggest reason that actual pricing does not more closely resemble economic pricing as noted above is simply carrier choice. To gain knowledge of all demands, analyze them, and set up different classes is time-consuming and expensive. To know all the cost characteristics and to apply them to each demand segment takes considerable analytical ability and much effort. Even though the ability to apply these principles might be present, it is easier to follow the path of least resistance and to avoid the price decision entirely.

Some carriers use economic pricing more than others. All segments of the passenger transportation industry concern themselves with some of the factors analyzed in this chapter. However, few carriers use all the concepts and some may not be completely cognizant of the full ramifications of these concepts.

Nevertheless, in actual practice it is easier to ignore price and economic considerations and concentrate on marketing and the conditions of service. This easier path is the one most often taken in the passenger transportation industry.

ADDITIONAL READINGS

CAVES, RICHARD E., *Air Transport and Its Regulators: An Industry Study* (Cambridge: Harvard University Press, 1962).
    Chap. 1:   "Seller Concentration," pp. 11-30.
    Chap. 2:   "Demand Aspects of Market Structure," pp. 31-55.
    Chap. 3:   "Cost Aspects of Market Structure," pp. 55-84.

CHERINGTON, PAUL W., *Airline Price Policy* (Boston: Division of Research, Graduate School of Business Administration, Harvard University, 1969).

DOUGLAS, GEORGE W., and JAMES C. MILLER, III, "Quality Competition, Industry Equilibrium, and Efficiency in the Price-Constrained Airline Market," *American Economic Review* (September 1974), pp. 657-669.

EADS, GEORGE C., *The Local Service Airline Experiment* (Washington, D.C.: The Brookings Institution, 1972).
    Chap. 2:   "The Demand for Short-Haul Air Service," pp. 11-30.
    Chap. 3:   "The Cost of Short-Haul Air Service," pp. 31-75.

FARRIS, MARTIN T., "Transportation Regulation and Economic Efficiency," *American Economic Review* (May 1969), pp. 244-250.

FRUHAN, WILLIAM E., JR., *The Fight for Competitive Advantage: A Study of the United States Domestic Truck Air Carriers* (Boston: Division of Research, Graduate School of Business Administration, Harvard University, 1972).
    Chap. 1:   "The Air Transportation Industry, Its Market, Financial Growth and Cost Structure," pp. 15-47.
    Chap. 2:   "A Relative Profitability Model of Air Carriers," pp. 51-68.
    Chap. 3:   "The Fight for Competitive Advantage—Fares," pp. 69-109.

HOOPER, TERRY J. and EVERETT JOHNSTON, "Marketing High Speed Ground Transportation," *High Speed Ground Transportation Journal* (Fall 1974), pp. 275-282.

JORDAN, WILLIAM A., *Airline Regulation in America: Effects and Imperfections* (Baltimore: The Johns Hopkins Press, 1970).
    Chap. 7:   "Overall Price Changes," pp. 134-143.
    Chap. 8:   "Promotional Fares," pp. 144-157.
    Chap. 9:   "Market Shares," pp. 158-177.

LANSING, JOHN B. and DWIGHT M. BLOOD, *The Changing Travel Market* (Ann Arbor, Michigan: Institute For Social Research, University of Michigan, 1964).

OI, WALTER Y. and PAUL W. SHULDINER, *An Analysis of Urban Travel Demands* (Evanston, Illinois: The Transportation Center, Northwestern University Press, 1962).
  Chap. 1:   "Introduction," pp. 3-10.
  Chap. 2:   "A Theory of Consumer Behavior in Urban Travel," pp. 10-22.
QUANDT, RICHARD E., *The Demand for Travel: Theory and Measurement* (Lexington, Massachusetts: Heath-Lexington Books, 1970).
  Chap. 1:   "Introduction to the Analysis of Travel Demand," pp. 1-17.
RICHMOND, SAMUEL B., *Regulation and Competition in Air Transportation* (New York: Columbia University Press, 1961).
  Chap. 3:   "The Concept of Competition," pp. 21-40.
SAMPSON, ROY J. and MARTIN T. FARRIS, *Domestic Transportation: Practice, Theory and Policy* (3rd ed.) (Boston: Houghton Mifflin Co., 1975).
  Chap. 28:   "Passenger Transportation Policy Problems," pp. 455-472.
SIMPSON, ROBERT W., "A Theory for Domestic Airline Economics," *Proceedings—Fifteenth Annual Meeting, Transportation Research Forum*, 1974, pp. 295-308.
SMERK, GEORGE M., ed., *Readings in Urban Transportation* (Bloomington, Indiana: Indiana University Press, 1968).
  Chap. 3:   Gilbert Ponsonby, "The Problem of the Peak, with Special reference to Road Passenger Transportation," pp. 99-116.
——, *Urban Transportation: The Federal Role* (Bloomington, Indiana: Indiana University Press, 1965).
  Chap. 9:   "The Traffic Peak and the Pricing Problem," pp. 209-234.
STRASZHEIM, MAHLON R., *The International Airline Industry* (Washington, D.C.: The Brookings Institution, 1969).
  Chap. 5:   "Costs," pp. 83-104.
  Chap. 6:   "Demand," pp. 105-130.
  Chap. 7:   "Pricing and the International Air Transport Association," pp. 131-149.
VICKREY, WILLIAM S., "Congestion Theory and Transport Investment," *American Economic Review* (May 1969), pp. 251-260.
——, "Pricing in Urban and Suburban Transport," *American Economic Review* (May 1963), pp. 452-465.

4

REGULATORY SYSTEMS

The final system within which passenger transportation operates and interacts is the regulatory. "Regulation" is a very broad term and has many meanings. We will consider regulation from three viewpoints: economic regulation, regulation of the physical aspects of transportation, and regulation by social policy.

Economic regulation in passenger transportation has three facets: control or regulation of price (rates), control of entry of new firms and economic expansion or contraction of existing firms, and control of services from an economic viewpoint. The regulation of the physical aspects of transportation refers to control over the conditions of transportation. Finally, regulation by social policy refers to the negative and positive results of aiding and supporting one means of transportation over another; to transportation as a function as compared to another economic function; to the ownership patterns allowed; to environmental restraints. Each will be analyzed in considerable detail in this chapter.

Additionally, regulation can be direct or indirect. Thus, the economic regulation of transportation is all direct—directly upon the firms supplying the transportation service. Social regulation is all indirect; it affects the economic climate within which transportation operates and the financial conditions under which passenger transportation takes place. The regulation of the physical aspects of transportation is a mixture of direct and indirect. Very often it is direct—as when such things as safety rules are imposed on carriers and private operators. Less often it is indirect—as when it involves "rule of the road" and standard operating procedures.

Finally, it should be noted that a multiplicity of agencies are involved in the regulatory system. Some are well known, others less well known, but all are organized and operated distinctively. In effect, these agencies are institutions that interact on one another and on transportation in a most complex and sometimes inconsistent manner. Transportation regulation is filled with inconsistent and conflicting rules and regulations enforced by a large group of conflicting and competing regulatory institutions. Indeed, the struggle for consistency and the resolution of conflict is found in all aspects of transportation regulation.

GOALS OF REGULATION

Before analyzing the three facets of the regulatory system, we should attempt to set forth the general goals of regulation. It is fairly easy to state them, for these goals are intended to accomplish two things: (1) the protection of the public, and (2) the promotion of the best possible system of passenger transportation.

Implementation, however, is considerably more difficult, for the goals contain inherent conflicts. To attain the best possible system of passenger transportation, the carriers and manufacturers must be strong economically. An economically marginal carrier does not produce the best possible service nor does a manufacturer losing money necessarily produce the highest quality of equipment. On the other hand, the public must not be exploited in price or in service. Conflict is apparent. So too with safety and environmental protection. The public demands that its interests be taken into consideration. But safety and environmental controls cost money and their provisions may weaken the financial health of the carrier or the manufacturer. The inherent conflict of the two-part goal is evident.

The result is conflict and countervailing powers, which must somehow be accommodated. This accommodation is usually a compromise and the conflict may be only partly resolved, with the result that the goals of regulation are probably never completely fulfilled. The public is not completely protected nor is the best possible system of passenger transportation attained. Indeed, given the inherent conflict, one could question whether these stated goals could ever be fully attained.

ECONOMIC REGULATION

As noted earlier, the economic aspect of passenger transportation regulation encompasses three devices of control: price or rate regulation, entry regulation, and regulation of transportation service.

Rate Regulation in General

Passenger transportation has long been regulated in the public interest. Even in medieval times, the cabdriver providing urban transportation was controlled by the sovereign, or by the city within which he operated. Historically, the number of suppliers of passenger transportation has usually been restricted by way of some control over entry, and the charges have been limited in some way. While we will discuss entry controls next, it is well to point out that all three devices of economic control are parts of a system that interacts and is interdependent. Historically, transportation has been organized as a monopoly or near monopoly, and has had its charges or prices controlled by society.

In modern times, in a situation with one or a few firms, the problem becomes one of how a commission or board acting as the sovereign can substitute for the forces of competition. Some administrative device is established to attempt to be a proxy for the marketplace. Society desires the benefits of restricted numbers of suppliers but wishes to protect itself from potential exploitation by the firms it has favored with this limitation. This is the age-old problem of regulation, and it turns on rate control.

In general rate regulation means the control of the prices that for-hire carriers charge. But more specifically, rate regulation encompasses both the "level of rates" and the "rate structure." The first term refers to the earnings of the carrier while the second refers to the specific prices or rates charged. This division of rate regulation has existed for a very long time and involves the two legal and economic concepts of "reasonableness" and "discrimination."

Rate Level Regulation

The level of rates is related to the reasonableness of the carriers' earnings and charges. By controlling prices, the public controls the carriers' earnings. Prices can be set too high and too low. If they are too high, the public will be exploited and pay unreasonably high prices and the firm will enjoy unusual monopoly earnings. If they are too low, the carrier may be forced to provide service at a loss and ultimately will have his property economically confiscated. The problem of the level of rates and reasonableness is a difficult one.

In the United States, rate regulation goes back to the post-Civil War period and the attempts by some states to regulate the railroad monopolies of that day. In the so-called "granger movement," states established boards to set rail rates, or legislatures set them by statute.[1] While this action was short-lived, it was determined to be a legal and constitutional exercise of state powers in the famous case of *Munn* v. *Illinois*, 1877.[2] However, the problem of rate level remained and was not legally resolved until the equally famous case of *Smyth* v. *Ames*, 1898.[3]

In this latter case, the U.S. Supreme Court stated that rates should be established for a regulated firm in such a way as to yield no more than a "fair return on a fair value" of the property committed to public use. In effect, this means that a standard was established for the determination of the level of rates deemed reasonable in all regulated firms.

The long history of the problems of defining what is meant by "fair value" and "fair rate of return" need not delay us here. Obviously, what is "fair" is a matter of judgment. More often than not a court has finally had to arbitrate what was meant by "fair return on a fair value" in a case-by-case method. Fair value can mean original cost or cost of reproduction or a combination of both. Fair return can mean earnings comparable to those of other regulated firms, earnings high enough to attract capital, earnings high enough to compensate for risk, and many other things. The long and interesting history of this problem can be found in most standard textbooks on public utility

---

[1]The most comprehensive study of this agrarian revolt is found in S.J. Buck, *The Granger Movement* (Cambridge: Harvard University Press, 1913).

[2]94 U.S. 113 (1877).

[3]169 U.S. 466 (1898).

economics and should be consulted by the interested reader.[4]

Suffice it to say at this point that the legal doctrine of fair return on a fair value is the reason that we find in passenger transportation the Interstate Commerce Commission ruling that the railroads may earn up to 6 percent on fair value or the Civil Aeronautics Board determining that airlines may earn 10 to 12 percent and that rates that yield more or less than this are "unreasonable." In effect, these institutions are acting in the ancient role of the sovereign and are determining what level of rates or earnings is fair or reasonable.

It should be noted that the determination of the rate level under the fair return or fair value criterion is theoretically a type of "target" rate level. Legally, if the firm earns over the target, rates will be decreased; if the firm earns less than the target, rates will be increased. In recent times, rather than determining a specific target of any 6 percent, a "zone of reasonableness" approach has been adopted.[5] Hence, rate levels yielding between 10 and 12 percent are not legally unreasonable in the airlines. The "target" becomes a zone of reasonable earnings levels.

It is not expected that each and every year the firms will earn the target return or even the return found in the zone of reasonableness. Further, the legal doctrine is specifically not a guarantee of any sort—it merely means that the regulated firm should have the "opportunity" to reach the target.[6] There is a tendency to apply rate-level earnings control on the "upside"—that is, to decrease rates if earnings exceed the target of reasonableness, and to disregard the target of reasonableness on the "downside"—that is, there is a hesitancy to raise rates when less than a reasonable rate of return is earned. This is not a bit surprising given the fact that in passenger transportation there is considerable competition and substitution potential, as noted previously. If regulatory authorities raised the level of rates to meet the "fair return on fair value" target, it could well mean even lower earnings for a carrier if passengers were induced to use other modes. Also, it is well to note that the legal doctrine of rate-level control is based on the historical fact of monopoly control. However, the

---

[4] See Martin T. Farris, and Roy J. Sampson, *Public Utilities: Regulation, Management, and Ownership* (Boston: Houghton Mifflin Co., 1973), Chap. 6: "Rate Regulation: Valuation," pp. 79-93, and Chap. 8: "Rate Regulation: Percentage Return," pp. 118-136.

[5] *Federal Power Commission* v. *Natural Gas Pipeline Co.*, 315 U.S. 575 (1942).

[6] *Public Service Commission of Montana* v. *Great Northern Utilities Co.*, 289 U.S. 130 (1935).

conditions of monopoly are at best only partly relevant to passenger transportation.

Finally, given the problem of determining what is a fair value and a fair return and given the degrees of competition involved in the industry, some commissions on some modes have used the "operating ratio" approach to rate-level control. The operating ratio is defined as the operating expenses over the operating revenues times 100—that is, an operating ratio of 85 would mean that 85¢ out of every dollar of revenue went for operating expenses. By determining a target operating ratio, say of 92, the commission hopes to avoid the problems inherent in the fair return on a fair value approach. This substitute has been widely used in motor transportation when the carriers are many in number and determination of fair value becomes burdensome. It should be noted that the operating ratio approach is an extremely poor substitute for an already vague level of reasonableness and has many pitfalls inherent in it as well.[7]

In summary, the regulation of the level of rates means determination of the reasonableness of prices. A legal concept has grown up over the years in which the rate level must yield a fair return on a fair value. Much difficulty exists in defining these terms where a specific problem of rates exists. The rate level approach may not act as a guarantee for the firm but is rather an ideal or target to be sought. Since it is based on monopoly control and the industry has many degrees of competition, this approach is far from perfect. The conclusion is that there is considerable difference between the legal world of regulation and the real world of passenger transportation.

Rate Structure Regulation

Turning now to the other side of rate regulation, the structure of rates is concerned with the economic and legal concept of discrimination. The concept of avoidance of discrimination has the same sort of long legal and economic history as has the concept of reasonableness. Both came out of the common-carrier obligations found in the common law, which we shall discuss directly.

Discrimination implies unequal treatment. It is possible that the schedule of passenger transportation rates could cause unequal treat-

[7]D. Philip Locklin, *Economics of Transportation*, 7th ed. (Homewood, Illinois: Richard D. Irwin, Inc., 1972); pp. 709-712 contain a good review of the argument.

ment for a given city or a given class of passengers or a given geographical point such as a port or an airport. Given the monopolistic or near monopolistic type of organization of transportation firms historically, this type of arbitrary action was to be avoided. Historically, the railroads in this country tended to lower rates to points where they competed with each other and raise rates to destinations where they possessed a monopoly. In effect, they were following the economic theory of rate-making discussed in the previous chapter under "differential pricing." While it was perfectly good economics, it was not equitable to all users and caused great public concern as to discrimination. Public outcry led to a congressional investigation,[8] and when the Supreme Court ruled that the existing state laws had no jurisdiction over discrimination in interstate commerce,[9] Congress acted to regulate interstate commerce in 1887 and prohibited discrimination in the rate structure.[10]

The term discrimination has many meanings and definitions. The legal definition is not always the economic definition, which in turn is not always the social definition, and so forth. The economist defines discrimination in terms of differences in price not reflecting difference in costs. Sometimes the legal definition of price discrimination is similar and sometimes it is not. However, because of these multiple meanings, transportation regulation typically prohibits "undue discrimination" and allows a board or a commission to determine what is "undue." Discrimination can work two ways, of course, both for and against a point or class of passengers. Hence the statutes typically prohibit "unduly preferential or unduly prejudiced rates," and let a commission determine what is meant by "undue," "preferential," and "prejudiced"—subject to judicial review, of course.[11]

It should be clearly understood that rates or price schedules are set forth initially by the carriers. While it is commonly said that the CAB or ICC "makes rates," this is really not the case. The commission or board is given the power to "approve" or "disapprove" rate

---

[8] *Report of the Senate Select Committee on Interstate Commerce,* 49th Congress, 1st Session, Senate Report No. 46, 1886; better known as the Cullom Committee Report.

[9] *Wabash, St. Louis and Pacific Railway Co.* v. *Illinois,* 118 U.S. 557 (1886).

[10] Act to Regulate Commerce 1887, later known as the Interstate Commerce Act.

[11] These terms were originally used in Sec. 3 of the Act to Regulate Commerce—or I.C. Act as it was later known—and have been used again in every statute regulating the other modes of transportation.

schedules—they do not set the prices in the first instance. If the regulatory body finds rates to be unduly discriminatory (or unreasonable when considering rate levels), they may specify what prices or rates they will approve as nondiscriminatory or reasonable. In this instance and only in this instance does the administrative commission actually set the rate.

While the distinction noted here may seem to be minor and somewhat burdened with legal niceties, it is in fact an important distinction. In spite of what the headlines say about the CAB setting rates or in spite of the oft-heard complaint by carrier personnel that the ICC sets rates too low (or too high), it is up to the carrier to set his rates as he sees fit, given the demand and cost as he perceives them. The regulatory authority then either approves or disapproves of the carrier's proposal. A great deal more innovation in pricing or rate-making might be approved if the carrier would only try or propose it. This was implied in the chapter on pricing. But, as also noted in that discussion, it is sometimes the path of least resistance on the carrier's part to compete on a basis other than price and to shift the blame to the convenient regulatory board.

In actual practice, it is more often than not a competitive carrier who resists and offers a complaint to price or rate innovation. While cities sometimes protest discrimination before regulatory groups, it is the carriers who are most alert to changes in the rate structure of their competitors.[12] If the case alleging discrimination has merit, the commission or board must specify what they consider nondiscriminatory. It is for this reason that one finds the CAB specifying that the differential between coach and first-class air fares must be at least 25 percent, concerning themselves with the degree of discount given to travelers under 25, or the degree of discount offered to travelers in the armed services, and so forth. These are examples of potential discrimination.

In summary, rate-structure regulation concerns potential preferential or prejudicial treatment. Under the law, this must be "undue discrimination" and a commission or other regulatory institution is given the authority to determine the meaning of this term subject

---

[12] For an interesting and in-depth analysis of the efforts of competitive air carriers and the role of the CAB in passenger fares up to 1969, see William E. Fruhan, Jr., *The Fight for Competitive Advantage: A Study of the United States Domestic Trunk Air Carriers* (Boston: Division of Research, Graduate School of Business Administration, Harvard University, 1972), pp. 69-109.

to judicial review. Actual prices are originally determined by the carriers and only approved or disapproved by the regulatory authorities. The parties most frequently protesting discrimination are not the passengers but rather competitive carriers. Once undue preference or prejudice has been found, the regulatory authority can specify the exact rate that removes the discrimination alleged.

Entry Regulation

The second device of economic regulation is the control of entry of new carriers and the change in the operating structure of existing carriers. This device is obviously interrelated with the other two devices of rate control and regulation of service. Indeed, historically it was the granting of monopoly or near-monopoly status that led to the need for rate structure and rate-level control.

Basically, the question involved here is: How many carriers shall be allowed to compete on a given route or in a given area? Too much competition between carriers can be just as bad as too little. The financial health of the carrier and the need of the public to be served are two sometimes conflicting criteria that must be weighed in these entry decisions.

Two regulatory devices have been used historically to control entry: the franchise, and the certificate of public convenience and necessity. The franchise has been used to control entry on the city streets, alleys, and byways and is typically issued by the city council to a bus, street-railway, or rapid transit system. While most franchises are "exclusive," that is, guaranteeing only one firm, they are not all so, and several firms sometimes have franchises to serve a given area or city. However, the number of possible firms is limited by the potential inconvenience to the public of too many vehicles on a street irrespective of potential bankruptcy due to excessive competition.

The Certificate of Public Convenience and Necessity is typically issued by a regulatory board or commission such as the ICC or CAB where intercity transportation is involved. While there are potential space limitations, and such facilities as airports, train stations, and ports can become overcrowded, it is more a matter of the economic competition that is involved. Once more the problem is balancing out the public's need for service with the need to maintain an economically sound carrier.

It is not an easy task to decide how many carriers should be allowed to serve on the city street or on an airway or highway. Under some conditions it may be necessary to decide if service should exist at all, for example in urban transportation, But once the decision as to "how many" has been made, the equally difficult decision as to "which carrier" is also involved. Because the public must be served, there is a distinct tendency to favor existing carriers over new carriers.

Further, this tendency has been reinforced by the regulatory statutes. It must be remembered that at one time almost all areas of operation were unregulated as to entry. As each geographic area or economic area (such as motor carriers or air carriers) was brought under regulation, the problem of what to do about the existing carriers had to be faced. Typically, a "grandfather clause" was used to solve this problem.

This provision allowed the existing carriers to continue to operate in the same manner as they had been operating on or near the date of regulation as "a matter of right." That is, the existing carriers were not required to show that their operation was necessary or that it served a public need. These carriers are sometimes called "grandfather carriers" and often refer to these privileges as "rights." The operating authority is, however, a privilege under the law, not a "right" such as the right to vote or right of peaceful assembly, and as a privilege can be revoked for just cause. It is common in transportation, however, to speak of "operating rights."

All new carriers and proposals for any changes in the existing carriers' operations had to show that "public convenience" would be served and that a "necessity" for the service existed. Hence the term "certificate of public convenience and necessity." Once the need was established, the entrant had to show that this need could be adequately served by proving it was "fit, willing, and able" to serve under the law. This applied to new carriers as well as to changes in the operating rights of existing carriers.[13] While the terms "fit, willing, and able" are subject to interpretation and are difficult to specifically define,

---

[13]In the case of the domestic airlines, the CAB decided early not to allow additional firms to enter the industry. Specifically they stated in the Delta Air Corporation case:

> The number of air carriers now operating appears sufficient to insure against monopoly in respect to the average new route case. . . .In the absence of particular circumstances presenting an affirmative reason for a new carrier there appears to be no inherent desirability of increasing the present number of carriers merely for the purpose of numerically enlarging the industry. 2 CAB 447, 480 (1941).

they generally refer to past operating experience that demonstrates ability, financial fitness and soundness (with emphasis on past financial history), and operating equipment and organization (once more based on past operations). In all cases, it is rather difficult for a new carrier to demonstrate it is "fit, willing and able," particularly since much of the interpretation of the terms turns on experience or past operation. It is much easier for existing carriers to "extend" their operations into a new territory and develop as demand grows than for new carriers to enter a market under regulatory statutes.

The obvious result of the use of certificates of public convenience and necessity, plus the grandfather clause, plus the requirement of being "fit, willing and able," plus regulatory policy, is that competition in the sense of new carriers is severely controlled. There is a definite preference for existing firms and it is almost impossible for new ones to enter the transportation market. Empirical investigation shows that in air, bus, and rail passenger transportation, the existing firms have continued since the time of regulation (grandfather carriers) and have expanded and changed as the market has expanded and changed. Very few new firms have begun under regulation.

Given these regulatory conditions, the matter of competition turns mostly on expanding the route pattern of passenger transportation carriers. Regulatory authorities can and do allow competition by certificating existing carriers on routes already served; indeed, the awarding of competitive routes is the major way in which most competition in passenger transportation comes about.[14] Route certification is a very powerful tool of control, especially in air transportation, and its use has been subject to considerable criticism.[15]

Additionally, as part of entry controls (as well as financial controls) of carriers, all mergers have to be approved. The concept was originally found in the Transportation Act of 1920, which dealt mainly with railroads, and which was based on the idea that the carrier might endanger itself financially by undue expansion via mergers and consolidations, thus impairing its ability to serve. The

---

[14]Samuel B. Richmond, *Regulation and Competition in Air Transportation* (New York: Columbia University Press, 1961), Chap. 5: "Methods for Creating and Controlling Competition," pp. 62-97, and Chap. 6: "The Policy of the Civil Aeronautics Board Toward Competition," pp. 98-100, and Fruhan, *The Fight for Competitive Advantage*, pp. 110-123.

[15]Richard Caves, "Performance, Structure, and the Goals of Civil Aeronautics Board Regulation," *The Crisis of the Regulatory Commission*, Paul W. MacAvoy, ed. (New York: W. W. Norton and Company, Inc., 1970), pp. 131-151 and Fruhan, *Ibid*.

idea was that regulation should promote economically strong carriers in order to assure good service. Control over mergers was incorporated in each act subsequent to the 1920 act as the newer modes of transportation were regulated.

In addition to the original rationale, it should be realized that if mergers were not controlled, the carrier could subvert the regulation of entry and routes by simply taking over existing firms. Merger controls and certificates of public convenience and necessity are mutually interdependent regulatory devices. However, the result of this logic is firmer control of entry and the pattern of competition, not simply regulation of new entrants.

Finally, there are many possible patterns of competition in passenger transportation. The public itself may choose to provide the service through a municipally owned carrier such as a city bus line. The publicly owned carrier may compete with a privately owned for-hire carrier. Additionally, private passenger transportation via the personal automobile probably will always exist and compete with both public and for-hire carriers. We will return to the important matter of financial support for publicly owned transportation and subsidy of for-hire transportation under social regulation. Suffice it to say for now that the control of entry into the passenger transportation market is not absolute and that various patterns of existing and potential competition exist.

Service Regulation

The final device of economic regulation is the control over the level of service of the carriers. This aspect of regulation, although less well known than price and entry control, is equally a part of and is interrelated with price and entry regulation as a "system" of economic regulation.

From a philosophical viewpoint, the goal of regulation in this area is to see that the public is offered good service. Economically, service regulation must accompany price and entry regulation because, when a monopoly or near monopoly is granted and prices are set, there may be a natural tendency on the part of the firm to maximize by decreasing the quality and level of service. Once a carrier is granted the "right" to operate exclusively, the natural stimulus of competition is removed. The whole point of service regulation is to substitute administrative action for the stimulus of the impersonal marketplace—with its financial rewards for good service.

Service regulation is a very old concept, and the natural tendency to have deteriorating service levels once entry is controlled has existed almost as long as regulation itself. Historically, this problem was solved by imposing a series of "rights and duties" on the carrier or regulated firm by the sovereign. Thus, in exchange for the "right" to operate exclusively, the regulated firm assumed four duties: the duty to serve, the duty to deliver, the duty to avoid discrimination, and the duty to charge only reasonable prices. Later, these "duties" became part of the "common law" or the doctrine of "common callings" and were uniformly recognized as part of the fabric of regulation.[16]

While the four "common law duties" (sometimes called "common carrier obligations") dealt mainly with freight carriers, at least three of them apply equally to passenger transportation. The "duty to serve" means that the regulated firm must serve all comers, that it may not limit its "public" except for due cause and unless physically limited in some way. Hence, an airline must sell tickets to travelers and may not refuse to serve a given group, nor may it otherwise pick and choose its customers. Likewise, once given the right to serve a point, a carrier may not abandon its service without permission.

The "duty to avoid discrimination" and the "duty to charge reasonable prices" have been formalized in rate control as noted previously. Discrimination here refers both to price discrimination and service discrimination (both preferential and prejudicial) between points and between classes of passengers. Reasonableness as used here refers to both the rate level and the rate structure, as previously noted, and in general means that a carrier may not exploit its monopoly privilege. In both these "duties," an administrative commission has been granted the task of interpreting the meaning of the terms, subject to court review, and establishing rules and regulations to see that those duties are fulfilled. The "duty to deliver" refers to freight and concerns delivery to the proper consignee with dispatch and in the same physical condition as originally tendered to the carrier.

In passenger transportation, the "duty to serve" is perhaps the most important of the four common carrier obligations. Once oper-

---

[16]Roy J. Sampson, and Martin T. Farris, *Domestic Transportation: Practice, Theory and Policy,* 3rd ed. (Boston: Houghton Mifflin Co., 1975), Chap. 7, "Legal Service Obligations," pp. 109-120.

ating authority to serve a point has been granted, the carrier must continue to serve and must carry all passengers. In the words of the law, the carrier must "hold himself out to serve all comers." Planes must fly, trains must operate, and buses must roll to fulfill this basic type of service regulation and retain the right to a franchise or a certificate.

It should be pointed out, however, that the "extent of service" is usually not closely regulated. By "extent of service," we mean simply: "How often?" Certainly a minimum of service exists—a train once a week, say, or a plane once a day—to fulfill this duty, but until recently there has been little concern beyond this minimum. In recent times, however, there has been concern with both the minimum and maximum extent of service.

Prior to Amtrak, the ICC and state regulatory commissions were involved in trying to ascertain what minimum level of rail passenger service was necessary in order to properly serve the public. Likewise, the CAB has been concerned over the continuation of air passenger service to small communities and the fact that the "duty to serve" may impose a substantial financial and operating burden on the carrier where points of small traffic generation are involved.[17] This becomes a difficult problem where the carrier, such as a regional or feeder airline, is subsidized by public revenues. One attempt to solve this problem was the so-called "use it or lose it" rule in the late 1950s, whereby a small city had to generate a minimum of deplaning or enplaning passengers per day or it would lose its service.[18] Additionally, there have been some attempts to connect earnings regulation to minimum service levels. On some occasions the CAB has indicated that it would allow a carrier a certain percentage return only if it served its territory a specified number of times per week or month.

[17]While abandonment of service is not possible, a substitution of another carrier to fulfill this obligation or the substitution of another type of service (bus for rail—regional airline for trunk airline) is an alternative. For an interesting discussion of substitute service in air transportation, see Virgil D. Cover, "The Rise of Third Level Air Carriers," *Transportation Journal* (Fall 1971), pp. 41-51.

[18]When the local-service airlines were granted permanent certificates of public necessity (in response to a Congressional amendment to the basic 1935 Act in 1955), the CAB decided that an intermediate point must show an average of at least five passengers a day emplaned over a test period in order to warrant authorization of permanent service. 28 CAB 680, 752 (1958). Enforcement of this policy in the 1960s led to deletion of service to a number of smaller cities.

Until recently, there has been little concern with the maximum levels of service. The assumption has been that the carriers would follow the profit motive and would not serve more often than was necessary in their own self-interest. In the late 1960s and early 1970s, however, some control of maximum levels of service has occurred.

The rationale for this was that the competitive nature of some markets, particularly in air transportation, forced the carrier to serve more frequently than necessary, and some markets had become "oversaturated." No single carrier could cut back the frequency of service without losing a substantial share of a given market and the earnings of all carriers were unduly depressed due to "too much competition." Hence, in the depressed earnings conditions of the airlines in the early 1970s, the CAB was forced to concern itself with petitions to decrease the number of flights and was under pressure to control the maximum level of service. As an experiment, the CAB allowed the three largest domestic air carriers (United, American, and TWA) to get together with a veiw to decreasing the number of flights coast to coast. The idea was to help the airlines financially since the intensity of competition had forced the carriers to offer duplicating flights, many of which were being flown with very low load factors. It was generally agreed that the experiment was a success and it was extended several times.

These experiments, plus considerable research by regulatory authorities as well as by the Department of Transportation, point up the fact that the level of service is but a part of the overall system of regulation. Indeed, it is difficult to consider earnings or rate control in isolation without considering service levels and entry control. This is particularly true of air transportation.[19]

Another control over maximum levels of service came in late 1973 with the energy crisis. As fuel shortages became severe due to Middle East hostilities as well as to the "shortfall" of supply over demand, the CAB allowed all the air carriers to meet and collectively adjust the number of flights. This action was part of the national effort to control the use of energy and bring demand down to meet available supply. Many schedules were canceled and the frequency of service was curtailed in all of passenger transportation including buses and trains. However, as noted in the previous chapter on pricing, it is

[19] George W. Douglas and James C. Miller, III, "Quality Competition, Industry Equilibrium, and Efficiency in the Price-Constrained Airline Market," *American Economic Review* (September 1974), pp. 657-669.

not unusual for carriers and private automobiles to operate with excess capacity—often with less than half the seats occupied. It was possible, therefore, to sometimes decrease the frequency of service to conserve fuel while still maintaining the level of service by consolidating two duplicating half-full flights into one full one. The same remarks apply to car pools for private automobiles and consolidated bus and train schedules.

Finally, there has been little concern with the "condition of service" until recently. By the term "condition of service" we mean the physical condition of equipment, the comfort of the passenger, and the general environment within which the service was rendered. Once more the assumption was made that the carrier would render some minimum standard of service in order to meet competition in the marketplace. If the condition of service was inferior, the passenger would simply shift to another carrier or another mode—that is, intermodal and intramodal competition and elasticity could be relied on to regulate the condition of service.

This position fails to recognize the interrelated nature of the regulatory system. Poor conditions of service can exist, especially where monopoly privilege is found and it is not possible for all passengers to shift to other modes. Likewise, the conditions of service can become a vehicle of discrimination against points or classes of customers as well as a competitive tool to assure a large share of the market.

To make rate and entry regulation effective, conditions of service, as well as extent of service, may have to be controlled. Recognition of this necessity to control service in a comprehensive manner (both minimum and maximum) has come slowly and reluctantly to regulatory boards and commissions. Prior to Amtrak, the ICC grappled reluctantly with the problem of poor passenger train service. The problem was not just seeing that the trains ran but the physical condition of the equipment, the quality of the meals, the "on-time" performance of service and so forth.[20] Likewise, as it considered the general level of air fares, the CAB has recently become concerned with seating configuration, meals served, free drinks, private clubs for preferred passengers, pitch of seats, leg room, and a whole host of matters relating to condition of service.[21] Both of these problem areas

----

[20] *Adequacy—Passenger Service—Southern Pacific Co. between California and Louisiana*, 335 ICC 415 (1969).

[21] *Domestic Passenger Fare Investigation, 1971.*

of recent concern are examples of the fact that once entry is controlled and price regulated, the third aspect of service must also be regulation.

Consistency

It is fairly obvious that the three devices of economic regulation, price, entry, and service regulation, are a whole "package," or a system of interrelated controls. It is sometimes difficult to regulate one without affecting another. A cut in rates may mean a cut in frequency of service or the quality of service, a raise in rates to meet a desired revenue level may cause discrimination and preference. Too many carriers in a given market can lead to economic chaos for all if wasteful service levels are not controlled or frequency of service becomes too great. All sorts of compromises and trade-offs are necessary and the whole system of economic regulation must be considered as a whole—not as individual regulatory devices.

Unfortunately, economic regulation has not always been consistent. Rates have been raised or lowered without concern over regulation of services; entry has been allowed with little recognition of its effects on earnings or on service; inconsistency in regulation has abounded. Much of this inconsistency arises from the failure to realize that economic regulation is a system of three interrelated and quite complicated devices.

Inconsistency in the application of economic regulation of for-hire passenger transportation is matched by inconsistency in the pattern of providing and controlling passenger transportation. As we shall discuss shortly, all modes are not regulated equally, and some modes, such as private passenger transportation, are not regulated at all (economically). Publicly owned transportation is controlled by different groups than those regulating for-hire passenger transportation even though they compete, which may lead to inconsistency. For instance, Amtrak and Greyhound compete on intercity travel and the level of rates of one will greatly affect the demand for the other. Yet the rates on Amtrak are set by a quasi-governmental board which has little or no concern with the effect on Greyhound, and the ICC in approving Greyhound rates is relatively unconcerned with the success or failure of Amtrak. Further, public transportation, such as rapid transit systems and city bus lines, may be subsidized by revenues collected in part from the users of for-hire transportation, and so forth. While consistency for its own sake is not sacred, it is possible to say that inconsistency seems to be a predominant factor in the economic regulation of passenger transportation.

Direct Regulation

Finally, it is well to note that the system of economic regulation is imposed directly on the for-hire carriers. Some board or commission, such as the CAB, ICC, or FMC, imposes these controls directly. In public transportation the action of a city council, public authority, or public board or commission, in effect imposes the same three devices of the economic regulatory system upon the passenger transportation system as well. While regulation and control of the for-hire carrier and the public transportation system may be clothed in a legal framework, its effect is directly economic. The carriers must live in this regulatory environment and system, for the public has come to expect it in pursuit of the two general goals of (1) protecting the public, and (2) promoting the best possible system of passenger transportation.

After discussing the regulation of the physical aspects of transportation and social regulation, we shall be concerned briefly with the various agencies imposing these controls.

REGULATION OF THE PHYSICAL ASPECT OF TRANSPORTATION

The second aspect or type of control in the regulatory system concerns the physical aspects of passenger transportation. In general, these are regulations imposed on the conditions of transportation, both by society as a whole and, in some instances, the industry itself.

The term "regulation" as used here may be somewhat different from "regulation" in the above section on economic regulation. All systems must have ground rules—"rules of the road," so to speak. Some structure of operating procedures is necessary for an ordered and efficient society. Many of these ground rules or rules of the road or operating procedures are called "regulations"—but irrespective of what they are called, they serve the same function of establishing order and relative operating efficiency in the daily life of society. Yet, as is the case with specific economic regulation, these rules of the road restrict and impinge upon the freedom of the individual whether he be operator-owner, a for-hire firm, or a publicly owned passenger transportation system. In this sense they are "regulations" just as surely as the actions of an administrative commission or board are "regulations."

Everyone lives with a whole series of restrictions upon his individual freedom and choice. Passenger transportation is no exception. Restrictions have always been present and probably always will be. It is well to remember that when man came down out of the trees he had to set up ground rules!

Objectives of Physical Regulation

Applying these general remarks to passenger transportation, it is possible to note that two rather specific interrelated objectives seem to be at the base of all this regulation of the physical aspects of transportation. These are safety on the one hand and reliability on the other.

Perhaps the most important objective of physical regulation is the safety of the user and the co-user of the highway, airway, street, railway, ocean shipping lane, or whatever. Society acts to protect its members from physical danger, of course, but in addition to safety it wants a reliable passenger system. Many rules are imposed with the idea that not only will the public be served in a safe manner but that it will be served when it demands service and with some assurance that a journey, once stated, will be completed. While the objective of reliability might be thought of as economic, and indeed is involved in two of the economic regulatory devices of control of entry and control of service, we are concerned here with physical reliability. The close connection between physical reliability and economic reliability only illustrates once more that rules are interconnected and interrelated—a system of regulation exists.

Finally, it should be noted that the objectives of safety and reliability fit nicely into the general goals of the regulatory system noted above: protection of the public, and promoting the best possible system of transportation.

Devices of Physical Regulation

Most physical regulation of transportation is found in three groups or devices of control: regulation of the conditions of equipment, regulation of the qualifications of operators, and regulation of operating procedures. While we do not claim to present a comprehensive list of all regulation in each group, each will be discussed in turn and the reader is invited to supply his own additional examples.

Regulation of Condition of Equipment.   Rules and regulations governing the physical condition of equipment are found in every phase and type of passenger transportation. In private transportation it is becoming common for states to require periodic safety checks of brakes, lights, steering mechanisms, windshields, and so forth. Generally this is carried on under state jurisdiction but federal action is involved, for the federal government requires that a portion of federal highway grants be withdrawn unless approved safety-inspection state programs are enacted.

Commercial highway vehicles, including buses, are checked. Standards were prescribed by the ICC for many years, but since 1966 this work has been handled by the Department of Transportation. State authorities check safety features of buses and prescribe weight, height, width, and length regulations with the goal of safety of the passenger and the co-user of the highway as at least part of the rationale. Protection of the highway itself from damage is generally also a consideration in these regulations. Publicly owned vehicles generally must meet state standards, but the condition of equipment in this instance is a matter of operating policy rather than conforming to rules established by an outside agency.

In air transportation much of the work of the Federal Aviation Administration, also part of the Department of Transportation, concerns the condition of equipment and the airworthiness of planes. Inspections are but a part of this task and levels of maintenance are specified as well. Parts must be replaced or reconditioned after a specified number of hours of operation and rigorous requirements to protect the safety of the user of air transportation are common. Navigational aids and devices are also controlled by the FAA and become part of the physical equipment necessary for passenger transportation. Even in international air transportation, rules and regulation relative to equipment are prescribed by the International Civil Aviation Organization (closely associated with the International Air Transport Association, better known as IATA).

In water transportation, the U.S. Coast Guard, now a part of the Department of Transportation, inspects the condition of equipment and is concerned with operating safety. In rail transportation the Federal Railroad Administration, also a part of the Department of Transportation, sets standards for roadbed, alignment, gauge and surface structure, condition of the rails, and other basic requirements. These are only some of the many regulations concerning the condition of equipment established by the many agencies involved with the regulation of the physical aspects of transportation.

Regulation of Qualification of Operators.   Rules and regulations governing the qualifications of personnel, and particularly operating personnel, are common in transportation. In the private passenger transportation sector, the requirement that everyone have a current driver's license is a familiar example. Driving tests are normally given to assure knowledge of safety laws, and regulation is almost uniformly found in all jurisdictions. In most states operator qualification requirements are more rigorous where commercial vehicles are involved.

In for-hire passenger transportation, operator qualifications may be regulated by several boards or groups at several levels. Not only is the highway operator expected to qualify for a commercial operator's license at the state level but federal rules relative to hours of rest and hours of continuous service are also involved for highway vehicles. In commercial air transportation, pilot training is supervised, operating personnel must submit to periodic physical examination, and conditions of operation, such as hours of service and rest, are rigorously specified. In water transportation, ships' pilots are licensed and must meet regulatory qualifications.

In public transportation, most drivers must meet state standards if they operate buses on the public streets. Qualifications and training of operating personnel in street-railway and transit systems are more a matter of local operating policy.

Some inconsistency may be involved in having different qualifications for private owners as compared to for-hire operators as compared to public employees but, as noted above, transportation is filled with inconsistency. In general, however, operators' qualifications are highest in the for-hire intercity area of passenger transportation and lowest in the private passenger transportation area.

Regulation of Operating Procedures.   There are a whole host of rules and regulations concerning operating procedures, some quite obvious (like limits on speed), and others quite indirect and less obvious (for example, driving on the right in some countries and on the left in others). It would be impossible to list all the "rules of the road" in transportation but the alert reader knows that highway vehicle speeds are regulated, that traffic signals restrict uninhibited traffic flow, that planes must fly at specified altitudes, that ships pass one another in a specified fashion, that cars traveling in the same direction use a given side of the highway, that the physical distance between planes and railroad trains is regulated, that buses must stop before crossing a railroad track, and that planes approach an airport in a prescribed fashion irrespective of where the airport is located. The point is that there are a series of "systems" of operating procedures for each means of passenger transportation prescribed by many authorities and levels of government and principally designed to accomplish the objectives of safety and reliability for passenger transportation. It might be added in closing this subject that the regulation of operating procedures tends to be similar regardless of ownership (with a few exceptions) whereas regulation over the qualification of operators and condition of equipment tends to be stricter for for-hire transportation firms than the publicly owned or the private passenger transportation sectors.

REGULATION BY SOCIAL POLICY

The third and final aspect of the regulatory system is regulation by social policy. It is a common practice, of course, to refer to economic regulation (rates, entry, and service) as "social policy," since an agency of government typically imposes these controls. Likewise, it is a common practice to refer to the regulation of the physical aspects of transportation as "social policy" since society imposes ground rules to protect itself with the idea of safety and reliability in mind. But even beyond these aspects there remain the broader social aspects of public support and repayment, the ownership patterns and structure of competition permitted, and the relatively new environmental restraints. This portion of the overall regulatory system we call regulation by social policy.

Finally, it should be noted that this area of the regulatory system more than any other leads to "problems" in passenger transportation. In that sense our discussion here is only introductory to a more detailed consideration in Part Two: Problems of Passenger Transportation.

Public Support and Repayment

Society has always imposed its general economic philosophy on individuals in the form of rules and regulations that set a framework within which economic activity takes place. Examples of this are the statutes prohibiting fraud and misrepresentation, the money and credit system, the weights and measures system, and the legal system protecting ownership. In the United States the system of antitrust and the reliance on the economic philosophy of competition is a further illustration. These all tend to be negative aspects of social policy in the sense that each forces economic activity into a desired framework.

Positive aspects of social policy also exist, of course. By the use of public resources (monetary and physical), or by the taxing power or by public economic power (such as tariffs and import quotas, for example), various economic activity can be aided, promoted, and directed into various desired areas. Social policy is not all negative and the positive aspects are of particular interest in the study of transportation.

Historically, transportation has been aided and promoted in the United States. Almost without exception each mode of transportation has benefited from either direct or indirect aid by the whole of society as it developed. The railroads had their land grants; motor transportation benefited from programs to develop highways; air transportation has been aided technologically by public research and development, been directly subsidized, and continues to have the airway provided and operated for its benefit; water carriers have been subsidized; public transit receives federal developmental grants; and the private automobile uses public streets at least partly provided by property taxes. It is beyond the scope of this book to analyze all means, goals, and methods of public aid, and the interested reader should consult a basic transportation text for such a discussion.[22] However, it is well to realize that passenger transportation has been greatly aided by these methods of social policy.

There is also the broader question of promoting transportation as an economic function as compared to other economic functions. Public resources are never infinite. Priorities must be established and choices made. It is a very real problem whether it is better in the interests of the social good to promote transportation and not some other function, say water resource development, the public school system, slum clearance, or agricultural production. It is inappropriate to enter this interesting debate here and we shall merely observe that transportation is indeed aided and promoted by society, and concern ourselves with some of the ramifications of that fact of life.

Also a part of social policy is the provision for repayment of public aids. While some support has been in the form of outright grants, more often than not the firm or the user of the means of transportation has made some repayment through the tax system or by way of services of some nature. The problems arise not from the existence of public support but rather from the uneven application of the public support, the various methods or lack of methods of repayment, and the competitive ramifications of aiding one mode of transportation over another at a given period of time.

Examples of aid and support at different time periods, the various repayment devices, and the social policy ramifications are numerous. Railroads received tremendously large grants of land from all levels of government during the mid-nineteenth century. These acts promoted rapid development of a rail system in the United States and vastly improved passenger transportation and communication. In return the railroads were forced to haul federal government cargo and passengers at greatly reduced rates for almost 100 years. Some studies have shown that several times the value of the land given by the federal government was recouped in reduced charges.[23]

Later, in the early twentieth century, our social policy sponsored

---

[22] Sampson and Farris, *Domestic Transportation*, Chap. 27: "Public Aids and Promotions of Transportation," pp. 437-452.

[23] Over 130 million acres were granted. Depending on the value assigned to the land, this meant somewhere between $130 and $440 million in subsidy. Reliable estimates place the savings in the Federal government from special land grant rates (generally 50 percent of regular rates from the time of the grants in the 1850-1870 period up to 1948) in excess of $580 million. Locklin, *Economics of Transportation*, pp. 133-138.

the building of highways. The provision of an improved highway greatly aided and promoted motor transportation, including buses and private passenger cars. While some early funds came from general revenue sources, in recent times most new highway construction has depended upon "user charges" in the form of federal and state gasoline taxes to provide for highway improvements. Here a different "repayment" device was utilized.[24]

Also early in the twentieth century, social policy sponsored air transportation. The federal government has regularly developed military aircraft for war purposes that have had passenger transportation ramifications; sponsored the experiment of air mail, which was an important early revenue source that contributed considerably to the development of air passenger transportation; established and operated the airways for private and commercial aviation without a toll or charge; paid public service revenues to airlines[25] (recently restricted to regional airlines only), and made grants for airport improvement by cities. Municipalities have provided and operated airports, sometimes renting facilities at less than the cost of operating them, often not recovering the initial cost of airport facilities in rents, and often recovering only a portion of operating airports in landing fees. Until recently, no user tax was charged for providing these services to the air passenger industry, and in the Airport and Airway Improvement Act of 1970, it is well to note that the 8 percent passenger fare surcharge is to be used solely for improvement, not to recover the substantial operating cost of the airway.

Maritime subsidies are a study in themselves but it is well known that shipowners are paid both a construction subsidy and an operating subsidy if the maritime fleet can be used to carry military personnel and cargo. Even the private automobile, which generally provides a considerable portion of highway revenue in gas tax, is partially subsidized since a portion of the street system is provided by property taxes and not user taxes. Finally, in the mid-twentieth century, social policy turned belatedly to the problem of urban transportation. Federal grants for experimentation in rapid transit started in the 1960s.

---

[24]The argument here is generally not over the fact that "user charges" pay for the building and improving of the highway but rather whether a given class of vehicle (say large trucks and buses) pays its proper "share" of user charges compared to the added or incremental cost of building the highway to accommodate it.

[25]Ronald Dean Scott and Martin T. Farris, "Airline Subsidies in the United States," *Transportation Journal* (Summer 1974), pp. 25-33.

Capital grants for equipment improvements, federal grants for planning, and local operating subsidies from the general revenue with matching provisions by local governments were authorized in 1974. The Highway Act of 1973 permits a portion of highway-user taxes to be applied to urban-transit capital acquisitions and illustrates the use of social policy to shift repayment from one group to another. The point is that transportation has been aided and promoted over time with various means, and several different methods of repayment or no repayment at all have existed. Also, some passenger transportation operations have been aided, promoted, and subsidized while in competition with other operators not (at that point in time) equally aided, promoted, or subsidized. This "unevenness" of public aid has caused a considerable number of economic problems and shall concern us in a later chapter.

Ownership Patterns and Structure of Competition

Obviously, various repayment devices, plus subsidy of one mode at one time in exclusion of a competitive mode, will cause a problem. Social policy has, in effect, structured competition in passenger transportation. It makes considerable difference if one mode has an operating subsidy and hence needs to charge a somewhat lower rate to survive in a world of competitive choice by passengers (air or maritime passenger transportation versus rail or bus transportation; urban rapid transit versus for-hire city buses). So, too, repayment of an indirect subsidy via user charges that are carrier operating costs is quite different from repayment of capital invested, at interest, where the way is privately provided (the rail versus the bus; rail versus private automobile). Other examples and combinations are also possible, but the point is that social policy directly or indirectly affects the structure of competition.

Finally, ownership patterns are also a reflection of social policy. By and large our system of passenger transportation has been based on the pattern of private ownership of the means of transportation with public ownership of the way. Hence, the automobile is privately owned, the highway is publicly provided; the airline is a private profit-seeking firm, the airway is publicly owned and operated; and so forth. Ownership patterns are "mixed" with both private and public ownership existing together. Rail transportation provides the major exception to this pattern. Traditionally, the means of carriage *and* the way were both privately owned. The pattern of private means and public way has just been reversed under Amtrak. The public operates the passenger trains through Amtrak but over privately owned railways.

Now, these ownership patterns and their exceptions are, in a very real sense, social policy. As a nation we have deliberately chosen to maintain private ownership of the for-hire means of passenger transportation (with the exception of Amtrak) and public ownership of the transportation way. Many nations have chosen to have public ownership of both means and ways. We will return to these ownership patterns and their effect on the transportation structure and carrier competition in the following chapters.

Environmental Restraints

A final type of regulation by social policy is found in the recent concern over the quality of life and the effect of human action on the environment. Perhaps somewhat belatedly, society has moved to impose environmental restraints on passenger transportation. Standards for permissible emissions of hydrocarbons, lead, nitrogen compounds, carbon monoxides and dioxides are being developed; noise pollution standards are of some concern; water pollutants emitted from passenger ships and the ever present problem of petroleum spills are being controlled. Another environmental concern is with congestion, and some progress is being made in dealing with airway, highway, and street congestion. In each case, what is involved is society operating through public policy with a concern for the environment.

It should be noted that these restraints should be imposed irrespective of ownership. The privately owned automobile should be controlled just as strictly as the for-hire vehicle. Likewise, the publicly owned passenger operation ought to assume the role of "demonstration and example" for environmental controls. Unfortunately, this is not always the case and the private automobile remains one of the major sources of pollution while the opportunity to implement social policy by "clean" operation of publicly owned vehicles is not always seized. Once more the problem may turn, in the case of private automobiles, on the multiplicity of ownership and the natural hesitancy of the individual to forgo his freedom to act as he wishes.

This is the reason, of course, why social control in the form of imposition of standards at the manufacturing level holds out the chance of some positive action and is being pursued. As to publicly owned operations and the lack of "environmental examples," one can only point once more to the fact that different public agencies are involved and note that no one ever suggested that governments are consistent, even where the same levels of government are involved.

These environmental restraints are destined in the future to become more important, not less. This type of social action is, of course, the basis of a whole series of problems. We feel so strongly about this whole area that an entire chapter in the "problems" part of this book will be devoted to the subject. But the point for now is that environmental restraints are but a third example of regulation by social policy.

In summary, regulation by social policy, a phrase with many meanings, is concerned principally with methods of public aid and promotion, and the accompanying structure of repayment systems, the patterns of ownership imposed by society and the resultant structure of competition developed or allowed, and, finally, the host of new environmental restraints that are still developing but that are destined to become more important as a future type of social regulation.

AGENCIES OF CONTROL

The whole regulatory system, made up of economic regulation, regulation of the physical aspects of transportation, and regulation by social policy, is imposed and administered by a host of agencies, boards, commissions, and groups. We designate these as the "agencies of control." While we do not intend to analyze each group in depth, some elementary discussion of the major agencies of control is necessary to understand the conflicting and interrelated aspects of the regulatory system.

It is possible to classify these agencies of control into two groups: agencies of primary control, and agencies of ancillary control. This classification is based mainly on the function of the agency and does not imply that the action taken by the agency is not direct or important. Rather, we suggest that some agencies have a primary function of controlling transportation, whereas other agencies have the control of transportation as one of many functions or, in some cases, have a primary function in an area other than transportation, and transportation control is but a secondary function. Finally, it should be noted that our discussion does not include every single agency that affects transportation. Such an approach would be quite beyond the scope of this book. Many other agencies exert influence on passenger transportation.

Agencies of Primary Control

There are 15 agencies primarily concerned with administering economic regulation and the control of the physical aspects of passenger transportation or directly providing passenger transportation (six of which are part of the Department of Transportation). Each will be briefly noted.

1. **Interstate Commerce Commission.** The oldest of the federal agencies directly concerned with passenger transportation is the ICC. Established in 1887, this agency has led the way in the development of the economic regulation of transportation. Its role is now basically to control rates and earnings, issue certificates of public convenience and necessity, control entry, and control the service aspects of bus and rail passenger transportation carriers in interstate commerce. Many of the regulations of the physical aspects of transportation developed initially in the ICC were transferred to the Department of Transportation in 1966. The ICC is an independent regulatory commission with its 11 commissioners appointed by the President with consent of the Senate for staggered seven-year terms with no more than six commissioners from one political party. The President designates the chairman of the commission.

The ICC is organized into three divisions: Operating Rights; Rates, Tariffs and Valuation; and Finance and Service. Besides control of rates and fares, and certificates of public convenience and necessity, the ICC controls mergers and acquisitions, prescribes accounts, controls the issuance of securities, and has numerous controls over freight transportation.

2. **Civil Aeronautics Board.** The second major independent regulatory agency is the CAB. Established in 1938 to undertake the conflicting tasks of promoting air transportation and regulating the economic aspect of the air transportation industry, the CAB is con-

cerned mainly with economic control. The board has five members, no more than three from one political party, appointed by the President with consent of the Senate, for staggered terms of six years each. The President designates the chairman and vice chairman of the board.

The board grants authorizations to carriers to engage in interstate and foreign air transportation. Domestic carriers must secure certificates of public convenience and necessity, while foreign carriers are issued permits to engage in air transportation between the United States and foreign countries. The CAB has jurisdiction over tariffs, rates, and fares, and authorizes and pays subsidies to certain air carriers for service to communities where the traffic does not pay the cost of service. Additionally, the CAB passes on mergers, agreements, acquisitions of control, and interlocking relationships between carriers. It also has jurisdiction over unfair competitive practices of air carriers and ticket agents. Finally, the CAB regulates air carrier accounting and requires each carrier to file regular financial and operating reports.

3. Federal Maritime Commission.   The third independent federal regulatory agency is the FMC. Though it was established in 1920, its jurisdiction and function were revised and clarified in 1961. The commission is composed of five members, no more than three from one political party, appointed by the President with the consent of the Senate, for staggered terms of five years each. The President designates the chairman.

While the FMC is primarily concerned with maritime freight transportation, many ocean freighters carry passengers and a few passenger lines still come under FMC control and regulation. Basically, the FMC approves or disapproves agreements filed by common carriers and conference agreements, regulates shipping practices, controls tariffs or charges of carriers, issues or denies certificates of financial responsibility, and administers the passenger indemnity laws. The FMC was also given control in 1970 of issuing certificates of financial responsibility where oil spills were involved.

4. National Transportation Safety Board.   The fourth independent federal agency regulating passenger transportation is the NTSB. This board was created in 1966 simultaneously with the Department of Transportation although it is independent of the latter. The board is composed of five members, no more than three from one political party, appointed by the President with the consent of the

Senate, for staggered five-year terms. The President designates the chairman and vice chairman.

The purpose of the board is to investigate, determine probable cause, and issue reports on all civil-aviation and surface-transportation accidents, make recommendations for the prevention of accidents and promotion of safety in transportation, and conduct safety studies, examine safety standards, and determine compliance with safety standards.

5. **Federal Aviation Administration.** The FAA, formerly called the Federal Aviation Agency, was an independent federal regulatory commission from 1958 until it became one of the major operating agencies of the Department of Transportation in 1967. As such, it is now a part of the executive branch of the federal government.

The FAA is charged with regulating air commerce to promote its safety and development; achieving the efficient use of the navigable air space of the United States; promoting, encouraging, and developing civil aviation; developing and operating a common system of air-traffic control and air navigation; and promoting the development of a national system of airports. To accomplish this mission, the FAA physically operates a network of airport traffic-control towers, air-route and traffic-control centers, and flight service stations. It also issues and enforces rules, regulations, and minimum standards for safety and manufacture and for operation and maintenance of aircraft. It is also responsible for rating and certification (including medical) of airmen, and certification of airports. Further, the FAA installs and maintains air navigation facilities and operates visual and electronic aids to air navigation. It registers aircraft, including foreign aircraft, and participates in the International Civil Aviation Organization. The FAA research and development program involved in developing and testing improved aircraft, engines, propellers, and appliances, plus new systems of air navigation and traffic control, is quite large and well known. Finally, the FAA administers a comprehensive airport planning and development program; it includes substantial grants of funds to assist other public agencies in airport development and improvement.

6. **Federal Highway Administration.** This agency is also a part of the Department of Transportation and has three broad functions that directly affect passenger transportation: the administration of the federal aid program for highway planning and con-

struction, highway safety, and motor carrier safety. The major work concerns the administration of the highway trust fund and the federal-aid aspects of highway construction via various revenue-matching plans. The best known highway program in the last few years has been the National System of Interstate and Defense Highways, commonly called the Interstate System, which has been a special program of improving an upgrading a small portion (42,500 miles, or about 1 percent of the 4-million-mile total in the United States) of intensively used streets and highways. Construction and safety standards involved in the Interstate as well as the federal, primary, secondary, and urban highway-aid systems come under the Federal Highway Administration. Standards are established as well as funds administered and highways coordinated. This program also includes beautification of the highways. Much of the work of this agency was under the Bureau of Public Roads in the Department of Commerce prior to 1966.

The final aspect of FHA work concerns the safety program for commercial motor carriers engaged in interstate commerce. Safety investigation and inspection, driver qualifications, hours of service on the road, bus and truck accident investigation, and vehicle inspection are the main elements of this program, which was formerly in the Bureau of Carrier Safety under the ICC.

7. Federal Railroad Administration.   This agency of the Department of Transportation consolidated the administration of the Bureau of Railroad Safety and Services (formerly part of the ICC), the Office of High Speed Ground Transportation (formerly in the Department of Commerce), and the administration of the Alaska Railroad (formerly in the Department of Interior). The work of this agency affects passenger transportation in its concern with rules and regulations designed to promote railroad safety, the demonstration projects of the Office of High Speed Ground Transportation in the Northeast Corridor of the U.S. (the turbo-train and Metroliner projects), and in the Passenger operations of the Alaska Railroad (service between Anchorage and Whittier, and Anchorage and Fairbanks).

8. Urban Mass Transportation Administration.   This agency was transferred from the Department of Housing and Urban Development to the Department of Transportation in 1968. It has three purposes: (1) assisting in the development of improved mass transportation facilities, equipment, techniques, and methods; (2) encouraging the planning and establishment of mass transportation systems; and (3) assisting state and local governments in the financing of mass transportation systems. These purposes are pursued by a program of agency research and development and grants to outside agencies for research and development (both to public and university agencies, and private research groups); grants or loans to assist communities to improve capital equipment and facilities; grants for planning and design of mass transportation systems; grants for managerial training; and unrestricted grants that may be used for operating subsidies. Since 1974 UMTA has also been involved with matching grants for operating subsidies.

9. National Highway Safety Administration.   The fifth agency of the Department of Transportation involved in primary control of passenger transportation is the National Highway Safety Administration. Various programs are involved, the best known of which is probably the Federal Motor Vehicle Safety Standards program of establishing and administering prescribed safety features in the private automobile (seat belts, shoulder harness, air bags, vehicle design, and so forth). The agency also carries on important research and development into vehicle design and the "crashworthiness" of vehicles. Further, it provides matching federal funds for state and local motor-vehicle and driver-safety programs. A portion of the work of this agency was part of the Department of Commerce prior to 1966, but the main thrust of this safety mission came out of the Highway Safety Act of 1970.

10. United States Coast Guard.   The sixth and final agency of the Department of Transportation involved in transportation regulation is the U.S. Coast Guard. Formerly part of the Department of Treasury, the Coast Guard is also a branch of the Armed Forces. The Coast Guard maintains vessels and stations to pursue its program of search and rescue; provides enforcement of federal laws on the high seas and navigable waters of the United States (including boat inspection); maintains ocean stations (four in the North Atlantic and two in the Pacific) to provide meteorological information, search and rescue services, and oceanographic data and navigation information to ships and aircraft; and is responsible for merchant marine safety (including licensing personnel), inspection of vessels for safety of personnel and passengers, and the aids to navigation program (lightships, buoys, electronic aids, and so forth). Other Coast Guard programs, such as boating safety, port security, icebreaking services, Great Lakes pilotage staff, and military preparedness, are less related to passenger transportation.

11. Amtrak.   With the creation of the National Railroad Passenger Corporation in late 1970, a drastic change in intercity rail passenger transportation took place. Called Amtrak, this quasi-public corporation undertook the operation of intercity rail passenger service in conjunction with cooperating railroads. Rail carriers invested equipment and some funds, the federal government invested funds and made loan guarantees, and an agency to continue rail passenger service was established. The rail carriers who chose to join Amtrak (all but three railroads so chose) were relieved of the responsibility of providing interstate rail passenger transportation service; those that did not join were forced to continue service until 1975. Much of the existing passenger service personnel and equipment were transferred to Amtrak, which operates trains over privately owned railway of the rail carriers under a lease arrangement.

Rail passenger service routes were severely restricted under Amtrak, the Secretary of Transportation being given authority to designate which of a limited number of routes in a basic system of essential passenger transportation would be used (initially only 16 routes between 14 major cities—later the routes were expanded somewhat). However, service was to be upgraded, new equipment acquired, and new programs to promote rail transportation undertaken. The National Railroad Passenger Corporation is governed by a 15-man board of directors, 8 of whom are appointed by the President with the consent of the Senate, 3 of whom are elected by the common stockholders (common stock can be owned only by the cooperating railroads) and 4 of whom are elected by preferred stockholders (preferred stock is to represent the public and cannot be owned by railroads). Amtrak is not a governmental agency but it is a quasi-governmental corporation subject to the District of Columbia Business Corporation Act.

Amtrak began operations May 1, 1971, and has been actively pursuing its goals of upgrading the quality of railroad passenger service on a limited number of essential routes. For all practical purposes, the Amtrak program contains all rail passenger transportation service in the United States, except commuter service and a few routes not under Amtrak. It is too early to judge whether or not the experiment is a success.

12. IATA and ICAO.   The activities of the International Air Transport Association (a trade association) and the International Civil Aviation Organization (a United Nations agency) provide "regulation" in the broadest sense of the term. With over 100 airlines from over 80 nations as members, the self-regulatory work of these international agencies greatly affects international passenger transportation.

IATA, organized in 1945, was a successor to the International Air Traffic Association, organized in The Hague in 1919. It is a nongovernmental organization and private trade association chartered under a special act of the Canadian Parliament. Membership is open to all airlines of the world, and the vast majority of them, whether governmentally or privately owned, belong to the organization. Membership by a nation in the International Civil Aviation Organization (ICAO) automatically qualifies an airline for membership in IATA. The distinction between the two organizations, aside from one being part of the United Nations and the other a private association, is that IATA is concerned with the commercial and economic aspects of international air transportation, while ICAO with the technical aspects. ICAO establishes standard and recommended practices for international airlines whereas IATA deals with accounting and offers a clearinghouse service whereby interline accounts may be settled, as well as problems of air law and liability, problems of traffic exchange (forms, procedures, handling agreements), problems of dealing with passenger and cargo agents, problems of reservations, and the problem of rates and fares. IATA is probably best known for its activities in this last-named function.

The policy decisions of IATA are arrived at through annual general meetings at which the members exchange information, draw up agreements, and coordinate their activities. Biannual traffic conferences, where rate and fare agreements are negotiated, ratified, and approved, are of major economic importance. As a voluntary trade association, IATA itself cannot regulate rates, although it does maintain a "compliance office," which attempts to ensure that members respect the obligations they have voluntarily assumed. Changes in fares are subject to vote by any member and considerable discussion, negotiation, and hard bargaining goes on prior to a change of international air fares. It is not unusual for a traffic conference to be in session for several months.

13. **State Commissions.** At the other end of the spectrum of passenger transportation are the regulatory commissions and boards of the various states. Almost every state has one or more agencies charged with the economic (and sometimes the physical) regulation of transportation. Jurisdiction over firms will vary by state, of course,

but in all cases the authority of these boards is limited to intrastate transportation. Intrastate rail, bus, and airline fares are regulated, certificates or permits for intrastate operation are often issued, and occasionally the carriers' service is regulated. Sometimes these agencies also have control of taxi services and a portion of urban passenger transportation service.

14. Local Agencies.   Various local agencies are involved, generally at the municipal level but sometimes as an association of municipalities. These may be aimed at economic regulation (such as where a city council controls entry of taxicabs or bus lines, or establishes rates) or they may be operative (where a city-owned service is provided). Also, various authorities or agencies (titles vary) may operate transportation systems for several local governments. A good example of this is the Port of New York Authority, which operates equipment, airports, and port facilities in the Greater New York area. It is impossible to list all the various authorities or agencies involved, and they will vary with the location and the situation involved. The point is, however, that local authorities often exert considerable regulation over passenger transportation.

15. Ship Conferences and Industry Groups.   Self-regulation of firms, somewhat like that practiced by IATA, exists in all aspects of passenger transportation. In maritime transportation, ship conferences have existed for years and affected fares as well as procedures in passenger transportation. Maritime ship conference agreements must be approved by the FMC. Voluntary associations of firms and operators exist in all areas of passenger transportation and their activity often involves self-regulation of fares, procedures, entry, and so forth.

In concluding this section on agencies of primary control, it should be pointed out that some agencies are more concerned with economic regulation (ICC, CAB, or state commissions, for example), some with regulation of the physical aspects of transportation (FAA, Federal Railroad Administration, National Highway Safety Administration, Coast Guard), some with regulation by social policy (Federal Highway Administration, Urban Mass Transportation Administration), and some with actually operating transportation facilities (Amtrak, local governments, authorities). It should also be pointed out that a firm or an individual will often be subject to the regulatory action of more than one of these agencies—often a substantial number of them, as a matter of fact—and that the problem of consistency remains as ever a difficult but annoying one.

Agencies of Ancillary Control

Many agencies are involved in the control of transportation, of course. Some have a primary function that is other than regulation of transportation, others affect transportation only indirectly. We have arbitrarily designated these as "agencies of ancillary control" and note only three broad groups of the many agencies involved herein.

1. **State and Local Law Enforcement.**   Regulation of the physical aspects of transportation may often rest partly with state and local peace officers. This is particularly true relative to private passenger transportation and for-hire passenger transportation. Traffic control, speed limit enforcement, and operator qualifications are familiar aspects of this type of regulation. These agencies, such as state highway patrols, sheriffs' departments, and local police, have functions other than transportation regulation and often have a primary function much more comprehensive than traffic control. Accordingly, they are a good example of agencies of ancillary control.

2. **Municipal, County, and State Governments.**   A portion of the function of government is to regulate transportation through rules of operation. Increasingly, however, these agencies also control passenger transportation through providing governmentally owned transportation in competition with private passenger transportation and for-hire passenger transportation. Sometimes decisions at these governmental levels are of prime importance to passenger transportation, and public transportation services may often be the only alternative available to some passengers. Control also comes from capital decisions of these agencies, not just in upgrading or subsidizing public transportation operations but in allocating funds to street and road improvements or construction, airport construction and improvement, harbor and port development, and the like. The primary function of these governmental agencies is not primarily to regulate transportation, but their rule-setting actions, their operating decisions, and their capital decisions do a great deal to control transportation.

3. **Federal Agencies.**   A whole group of federal agencies with primary functions in matters other than transportation regulate and affect transportation. Some familiar examples are the operation and rules of the Customs and Immigration Service, research grants and programs of the Department of Housing and Urban Development, the policies and operations of the United States Postal Service, the operating procedures of the various branches of the Armed Forces.

Many of these actions regulate passenger transportation in an indirect manner.

SUMMARY ON TRANSPORTATION REGULATORY SYSTEMS

The regulatory system in passenger transportation has many interrelated parts and facets. The three main aspects of the system are economic regulation (rate regulation, entry regulation, and service regulation), regulation of the physical aspects of transportation (regulation of the condition of equipment, regulation of qualifications of operators, and regulation of operating procedures), and regulation by social policy (public support and repayment, ownership patterns and the structure of competition, environmental restraints). These aspects of the regulatory system are imposed and administered by a multitude of governmental and private agencies, some of which are primarily concerned with transportation control (we have noted 15 such groups), and some of which are primarily concerned with other than transportation control. In view of the complexity of the regulatory system, it is not surprising that regulations are often inconsistent and overlapping, and that a person or firm is subject to many regulations by many agencies at many levels. This is part of what we mean by a regulatory "system." Even so, the regulatory system does seem to function, by and large, in its two general goals of protecting the public and promoting the best possible system of passenger transportation. Given the complexity of the regulatory system, it is not surprising that many problems arise. We shall concern ourselves in the second part of this book with the problems of passenger transportation.

ADDITIONAL READINGS

CAVES, RICHARD, "Performance, Structure, and the Goals of Civil Aeronautics Board Regulation," *The Crisis of the Regulatory Commission*, Paul W. MacAvoy, ed. (New York: W. W. Norton and Company, Inc., 1970), pp. 131-151.

DAVIS, GRANT M., *The Department of Transportation* (Lexington, Massachusetts: Heath Lexington Books, 1970).
    Chap. 5:   "Operating Agencies of the Department of Transportation and the National Transportation Safety Board," pp. 106-150.

DOUGLAS, GEORGE W. and JAMES C. MILLER, III, "Quality Competition, Industry Equilibrium, and Efficiency in the Price-Constrained Airline Market," *American Economic Review* (September 1974), pp. 657-669.

FARRIS, MARTIN T. and ROY J. SAMPSON, *Public Utilities: Regulation, Management and Ownership* (Boston: Houghton Mifflin Co., 1973).

Chap. 3:   "The Legal Basis for Regulation," pp. 35-46.

Chap. 5:   "Regulatory Methods and Principles," pp. 60-79.

Chap. 6:   "Rate Regulation: Valuation," pp. 79-92.

Chap. 8:   "Rate Regulation: Percentage Return," pp. 118-135.

FRUHAN, WILLIAM E., JR., *The Fight for Competitive Advantage: A Study of the United States Domestic Trunk Air Carriers* (Boston: Division of Research, Graduate School of Business Administration, Harvard University, 1972). ·

JORDAN, WILLIAM A., *Airline Regulation in America: Effects and Imperfections* (Baltimore: The Johns Hopkins Press, 1970).

Chap. 2:   "Entry and Exit," pp. 14-33.

Chap. 3:   "Rivalry Through Service Quality," pp. 34-56.

Chap. 4:   "CAB Fare Authorizations," pp. 57-72.

LOCKLIN, D. PHILIP, *Economics of Transportation,* 7th ed.(Homewood, Illinois: Richard D. Irwin, Inc., 1971).

Chap. 9:   "Beginning of Railroad Regulation," pp. 211-220.

Chap. 10:   "Federal Legislation 1887-1920," pp. 220-239.

Chap. 13:   "The Agencies of Control," pp. 282-310.

Chap. 25:   "Railroad Service and Service Regulation," pp. 607-621.

Chap. 34:   "Development of Air Transport Regulation," pp. 797-810.

Chap. 35:   "Problems and Policies in Air Transport Regulation," pp. 811-843.

NORTON, HUGH S., *Modern Transportation Economics,* 2nd ed.(Columbus, Ohio: Charles E. Merrill Publishing Co., 1971).

Chap. 11:   "Development of Regulation 1887-1920," pp. 221-233.

Chap. 15:   "Regulation of Air Carriers," pp. 278-290.

PHILLIPS, CHARLES F., JR., *Economics of Regulation,* rev. ed. (Homewood, Illinois: Richard D. Irwin, Inc., 1969).

Chap. 12:   "Service and Safety," pp. 400-439.

Chap. 14:   "Public Policy and the Transportation Industries," pp. 483-536.

RICHMOND, SAMUEL B., *Regulation and Competition in Air Transportation* (New York: Columbia University Press, 1961).

Chap. 2:   "Regulation of Domestic Airlines," pp. 10-20.

Chap. 5:   "Methods for Creating and Controlling Competition," pp. 62-97.

Chap. 6:   "The Policy of the Civil Aeronautics Board Toward Competition," pp. 98-120.

SAMPSON, ROY J. and MARTIN T. FARRIS, *Domestic Transportation: Practice, Theory and Policy,* 3rd ed. (Boston: Houghton Mifflin Co., 1975).

Chap. 3:   "Environmental and Sociological Aspects of Transportation," pp. 40-48.

Chap. 7:   "Legal Service Obligations," pp. 109-121.

Chap. 20:   "The Regulation of Transportation Monopoly," pp. 315-335.

Chap. 22:   "The Regulation of Transportation Competition: Evolution," pp. 352-366.

Chap. 23:   "National Transportation Planning: A New Era," pp. 368-383.

Chap. 24:   "Regulatory Institutions," pp. 384-400.

Chap. 28:   "Passenger Transportation Policy Problems," pp. 455-472.

TAFF, CHARLES A., *Commercial Motor Transportation,* 4th ed. (Homewood, Illinois: Richard D. Irwin, Inc., 1969).

Chap. 19:   "Intercity Passenger Operations," pp. 429-455.

Chap. 20:   "Urban Mass Transit," pp. 456-477.

PART TWO

Problems
Of
Passenger
Transportation

Now that the general framework of the four systems of passenger transportation has been analyzed, we can turn to the more specific problems of passenger transportation. Once more, it will be impossible to analyze in depth or even to enumerate all the problems of passenger transportation. Accordingly, we once more fall back on our approach of attempting to present a broad framework within which specific problems can be viewed.

To our way of thinking, the four interacting and interrelated systems (physical, economic, pricing, and regulatory) of passenger transportation bring forth four broad problem areas: marketing, urban transportation, social benefit vs. social cost, and passenger transportation policy. A chapter will be devoted to each of these four problem areas.

5

*THE
MARKETING
OF
PASSENGER
TRANSPORTATION
SERVICES*

Almost everyone has had some contact with passenger transportation marketing. In most cases, this experience has taken the form of an advertisement for a particular carrier seen on television, read about in a magazine, or heard on the radio. Therefore, most people do know something about marketing. However, there is much involved in this process that is not immediately evident. Marketing activities constitute an important function in the overall operation of passenger transportation carriers.

Passenger transportation marketing may be defined as a total integrated system of activities organized to achieve an effective relationship between the needs of present and potential passengers and the service offerings of carriers. The interface between carriers and markets is achieved through a judicious mix of service, promotional, and distribution strategies as well as the utilization of the pricing alternatives available under conditions of regulation. The marketing function is important to public agencies providing passenger transportation services and to individual firms operating in the private sector.

A diagram of the marketing process as it is discussed in this chapter is presented in Fig. 8. This model, a "picture" of the complex whole defined above, is organized in a manner that relates various operational subsystems to the functioning of the marketing system as a whole. It is intended to be a point of departure for our analysis of the role of marketing in passenger transportation and as a source for referral as the chapter is read.

In recent years marketing has become increasingly relevant to transportation planners for a number of reasons. First, marketing is the revenue-producing function of any firm or agency. There is no operating income until services are sold to passengers, and marketing encompasses all sales activities.

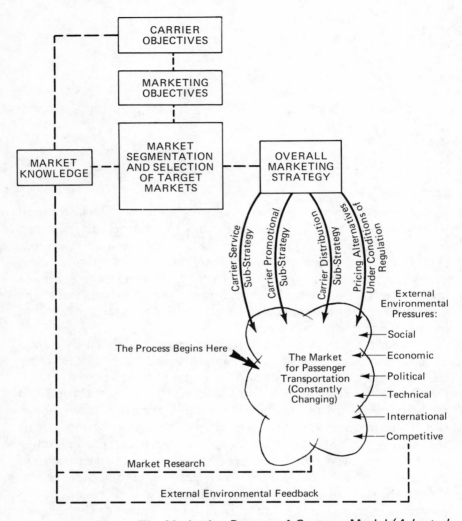

Figure 8.   The Marketing Process: A Systems Model *(Adapted from George D. Downing,* Basic Marketing: A Strategic Systems Approach *(Columbus, Ohio: Charles E. Merrill Publishing Company, 1971), p. 61.)*

Second, there has been a significant squeeze on profits and operating budgets during the 1970s. Labor, capital, and fuel costs have tended to increase more rapidly than carrier revenues. Under these conditions, increases in productivity are sought through more efficient utilization of carrier capacity. Increasing the ratio of paying passengers to available seats is an important marketing problem area.

Third, the separation of the producers and consumers of passenger transportation services continues to increase. Accurate information concerning the wants and needs of passengers and potential passengers are more important at the same time such data become more difficult to obtain. Marketing research activities can provide information useful in enhancing the communication between carriers and their markets.

Fourth, the long lead time required to obtain the approval of regulatory agencies for changes in routes, rates, or conditions of service and the difficulty in obtaining changes in previous agency action, emphasize the importance of accurate market forecasting and analysis.

Fifth, because of increasing risk factors and the higher costs involved in the development of new routes or in the expansion of capacity, it is essential that demand for these services be sufficient to produce adequate return on investment.

Finally, recent events relating to passenger transportation underlie the concept of dynamic market conditions. The demand for these services has gone through significant cycles and patterns of change. The marketing function provides a link between those producing transportation services and their markets, through which adaptation to change may be accomplished.

THE ROLE OF MARKETING IN PASSENGER TRANSPORTATION

Passenger transportation services may be understood to be a "bundle" of satisfactions. Some of these satisfactions are tangible: frequency and reliability; efficiency of ground service; quality of the vehicles of transportation and of the terminal facilities; courtesy and efficiency of carrier personnel; comfort and convenience of travel; and the speed, safety, and price of the service offerings. Other passenger satisfactions, however, are intangible and may be thought of as psychological satisfactions. Here we are referring to factors such as carrier image, how comfortable a traveler feels with a certain mode

of transport or specific carrier, and many other subjective considerations. It is important to recognize that both tangible and intangible
satisfactions are involved in the process of passenger decision making.
For example, a person may choose his automobile over public transportation because he feels more secure in the familiar surroundings of
his car. This intangible feeling of security may outweigh a myriad of
economic advantages of public transportation. Or, a certain air
carrier may be selected because it is more "friendly" than its competition. It might even be suggested that first-class travel offers as
many psychological satisfactions as it does tangible ones.

The marketing function, both of entire modes of transportation
and of individual carriers, is responsible for the planning, communication, and delivery of both tangible and psychological satisfactions. In
service industries, without a "product" to focus upon, the marketing
of satisfactions is important indeed.

THE INFLUENCE OF MARKETING ON SUPPLY AND DEMAND

Marketing activities influence both the supply and demand sides
of the transportation industry. If we take air transportation as an example, we see that the supply of passenger transportation has been
affected by changes in the composition of fleets of aircraft operated
by various carriers. Table 14 reveals a trend toward wide-bodied,
high-capacity aircraft (Boeing 747, Lockheed L1011, and McDonnell-
Douglas DC-10). As these models have become operational, they have
become a focal point of the marketing activities of individual carriers
(that is, promotional campaigns stressing "More wide-body seats to
New York than any other airline"). It might also be argued that the
supply of transportation exerts a significant influence on the demand
in all modes. For example, scheduling and frequency of service are
characteristics of supply with important demand implications for
buses, trains, urban transit, and so forth.

Although the supply of passenger transportation services is influenced by the marketing function, the major thrust traditionally
has been toward the demand for these services. In Chap. 3, eight
specific demand characteristics were discussed in detail. It will be recalled that these are (1) instantaneous demand, (2) extreme variability
of demand, (3) multiplicity of demand, (4) intermodal competition,
(5) intramodal competition, (6) intraclass substitutability, (7) dollar

TABLE 14

Aircraft in Service: U.S. Scheduled Airlines, 1963 — 1973

MANUFACTURER	MODEL	1973	1972	1968	1963
Boeing	B707 (Jet)	315	337	380	133
	B720 (Jet)	44	56	134	104
	B727 (Jet)	710	662	516	—
	B737 (Jet)	134	134	66	—
	B747 (Jet)	109	106	—	—
Convair	240	—	1	3	49
	340/440	6	7	46	153
	580/600 (Turbo)	129	135	148	—
	880 (Jet)	37	41	41	46
	990 (Jet)	—	—	9	19
Lockheed	Constellation	—	—	—	40
	Super C'stell	—	—	—	111
	Electra (Turbo)	19	19	86	117
	L-382B (Turbo)	1	3	9	—
	L1011 (Jet)	48	17	—	—
McDonnell-Douglas	DC-3	—	2	14	197
	DC-4	—	—	—	14
	DC-6	3	3	7	217
	DC-7	—	—	15	164
	DC-8 (Jet)	207	227	217	104
	DC-9 (Jet)	335	329	260	—
	DC-10 (Jet)	86	59	—	—
Other		177	257	349	144

Source: *Air Transport 1974* (Annual Report of the U.S. Scheduled Airline Industry. Washington, D.C.: Air Transportation Association of America, 1974), p. 17.

competition and income elasticity, and (8) conditions of service and nonprice competition.

These eight characteristics, all but unique to passenger transportation, give rise to a number of problems, the solution to each of which requires major inputs of marketing planning and activity. The first of the eight demand characteristics has to do with the problem of excess capacity in nonpeak traffic periods brought about largely as a result of the instantaneous and variable demand for passenger transportation services. A major concern of those providing service must be to create marketing programs designed to even out some of the peaks and valleys of demand so that better utilization of equipment and personnel may be achieved.

Another marketing problem is related to the multiplicity of demand. The market for passenger transportation is, in reality, composed of several distinct submarkets or market segments. For example, business travelers and those who travel for pleasure belong in separate categories—for there is a different motivation for travel, a different response to price changes, a difference in frequency of trips. The problem of catering to distinct and heterogeneous market segments has implications for scheduling, promotional decision making, and many other areas relating to the nature and scope of the service offering. Much will be said about market segmentation later in the chapter.

A third problem area is that of competition between modes of transportation. While intermodal competition exists between for-hire carriers, by and large it has been reduced to private versus public transportation. Or, more simply, competition between private automobiles and "the field." Energy-imposed restrictions on the operation of the family car may result in prominent new market opportunities for all modes of public transportation.

Fourth, the intense intramodal competition that characterizes air travel has brought about high levels of marketing activities. The airlines have been oriented toward a marketing approach to the solution of intramodal competitive problems. Involved have been the use of scheduling and frequency as marketing tools, extensive advertising programs, special services such as passenger-service representatives or champagne flights, innovative seating configurations, passenger lounges, in-flight movies and television, and even novel "packaging" through decoration of the interior or exterior of aircraft. Clearly, this demand characteristic (intramodal competition) has been interpreted as a marketing problem and the carriers have utilized a number of techniques to protect or expand their market share.

Fifth is the unique demand characteristic of intraclass competition and elasticity. Seldom in other industries do firms find themselves in direct competition with themselves to the extent of passenger carriers. The already segmented market for transportation services may be further divided by class of service. The task of matching the various classes of service offered (that is, first, tourist, economy, night coach, military, or whatever) to appropriate market segments is a distinct and sophisticated marketing task in that each class of service is unique in terms of potential profit contributions, volume requirements, and labor inputs.

A sixth demand characteristic of passenger transportation is dollar competition and income elasticity. Involved here is the competition between all goods and all services for the consumer's discretionary dollar. Pleasure travel competes with many luxury goods, including new automobiles, jewelry, and furs, and certain nonluxury expenditures, such as home improvements, education, and retirement investment. Because pleasure travel is especially subject to the forces of dollar competition and because travel of all types is affected by income elasticity, carrier management must endeavor to maintain their share of the consumer's discretionary dollar. Clearly, this is a most profound marketing task.

Finally, because of the homogeneity of fares charged by competing scheduled intramodal carriers, conditions of service and nonprice competition are stressed and constitute another important demand characteristic of passenger transportation. Here we find one of the most evident "arenas" for marketing battles among competing carriers. In the airline industry, for example, it has been established that the price, speed, type of aircraft, and airport facilities offered by various carriers serving the same city pair markets are frequently identical. The carriers, therefore, are reduced to differentiating their service offerings by other means. These other means generally include competition involving conditions of service (food service, friendly personnel, in-flight entertainment) and in other dimensions of their operation not related to price. The nature and scope of these services have become a marketing problem of consequence for the entire air-travel industry.

In addition to these broad categories of marketing problems that grow out of passenger-transportation-demand characteristics, there are virtually hundreds of specific marketing problems that encompass important aspects of the day-to-day and week-to-week operations of passenger carriers. The success of a carrier may well turn on the ability of its management to find effective and innovative solutions to these problems.

THE MARKETING PROCESS: A FRAMEWORK OF ANALYSIS

The remainder of this chapter will entail the presentation of a framework of analysis (paralleling the diagram presented in Fig. 8) which is offered as an approach to the understanding of the marketing process and to offer suggestions that may be helpful in the solution of marketing problems in passenger transportation. Air transportation examples will be extensively used but the same framework is applicable to other modes of passenger transportation.

External Environmental Pressures and Market Change

The marketing process begins and ends with an analysis of the market. All markets are composed of people, people with money and a willingness to spend it. Markets are dynamic; they are constantly going through patterns and cycles of change. Although we will return to the management of change in the concluding chapter of this book, it is necessary here to state a premise—that the key to the management of change is to be found in successful adaptation to changing market conditions. To adapt successfully, transportation planners must be aware of the factors that cause and influence change. We suggest that pressure from changing external environmental conditions can influence the market and cause variability.

In our framework of analysis, the external environment is defined as those social, economic, political, technical, international, and competitive forces that are linked, directly or indirectly, to various markets for passenger transportation services. It is suggested that there is a time lapse between the occurrence of change in one or more of the dynamic external environmental areas and the resulting impact on transportation markets. The external environment, therefore, is a potential lead indicator for planners that may be useful in their attempts to anticipate, understand, and manage change. The specific linkages between the external and market environments will be explored in the concluding chapter of this book.

Market Knowledge

Given dynamic conditions in both market and external environments, it is essential that accurate and up-to-date information be available to decision makers on a regular basis. Here we are referring to market research information and external environmental feedback, which, in sum, constitute that which carrier management knows and understands about the markets for their service offerings.[1]

The entire marketing process rests on market knowledge. This is true because both short- and long-term objectives are based on the assumptions held by carrier management in regard to present and future market opportunities and challenges. If accumulations of information accurately reflect market conditions, the likelihood of effective planning is enhanced. Faulty assumptions, however, invite miscalculations and ineffective planning.

Recognition of the importance of accurate, up-to-date, and relevant market knowledge has prompted and stimulated the introduction of computers to automate and systematize approaches to the management of information. Such intelligence systems can generate large quantities of diverse, interrelated, and relevant data with a wide range of practical passenger-transportation applications.[2]

In short, we would emphasize that market knowledge is the foundation upon which rests the entire structure of the marketing process. The success of all subsequent actions is affected by the manner in which data flows are collected, organized, and analyzed.

Carrier Objectives

Objectives are statements of intended goals. Written, attainable objectives that clearly define both the task to be accomplished and the time limits for accomplishment are the basis for the planning and control of any organization, public or private. The overall objectives of a passenger-transportation carrier provide guidelines for the coordinated activities of the entire organization. For a carrier to operate in a systems context (that is, by emphasizing the coordination and integration of its various functional efforts), it must, as a prerequisite, set specific overall objectives. The objectives will become the points of reference from which each functional area may take

---

[1] For a complete discussion of the information-gathering process, see Harper W. Boyd, Jr. and Ralph Westfall, *Marketing Research: Text and Cases* (Homewood, Illinois: Richard D. Irwin, Inc., 1972).

[2] For an interesting discussion of such applications see Harold D. Watkins, "Computer Filling Crucial Passenger Role for Airlines," *Aviation Week and Space Technology*, vol. 99, no. 17 (October 22, 1973), pp. 44-55.

direction. They will also be standards against which to measure performance.

Although the importance of clear overall objectives is generally acknowledged by carrier management, frequently the objectives that have been written are too general or too vague to be utilized as guidelines for action. A usable objective is specific in both purpose and time. For example, at the beginning of his term of office, President John F. Kennedy stated that the United States was committed to landing a man on the moon by 1969. Here was an attainable objective, specific in both purpose and time. If he had said, "It is our intent to support the concept of lunar exploration," it would have been an interesting position but hardly an objective upon which planning could be based and responsibility assigned. But once 1969 had been established as a target date, it was possible to work backward, setting sub-objectives around which work could be organized, schedules established, and performance compared. Carrier objectives for traffic, market share, expansion, and return on investment should be established with similar specificity.

A guideline for setting objectives that might be useful to transportation planners may be found in the writings of Peter Drucker.[3] Drucker offers five questions designed to assist the planner in thinking about his operation in a way that lends itself to the setting and evaluation of overall carrier objectives. The five questions: (1) What is our business? (2) Who is the customer? (3) What is value to the customer? (4) What *will* our business be? (5) What *should* our business be?

The question "What is our business?" sounds simple—deceptively so. However, the inability of management to properly define the real nature of a carrier's business can lead directly to failure. A good example is to be found in an examination of railroad passenger service. Many railroad executives made the mistake of defining their business as running trains rather than providing transportation services. As a result, both passenger and freight business was taken away from the railroads by competing modes of transport.[4] In the same context, the business of computer manufacturers can best be perceived as providing management information rather than as building computer

[3] Peter F. Drucker, *The Practice of Management* (New York: Harper and Row, 1954), pp. 49-61.

[4] For a more developed discussion see Theodore Levitt, "Marketing Myopia," *Harvard Business Review*, XXXVIII (July-August, 1960), pp. 45-56.

hardware. Or, the business of the giant petroleum companies has accurately been described as the distribution of energy rather than the selling of oil products. In short, the nature of any business is determined by the market and not by management. Because markets are dynamic, it is important that the question "What is our business?" be thought through and answered as part of the objective-setting process.

"Who is the customer?" Involved here is not only the need for a precise definition of the economic, demographic, or geographic characteristics of passengers currently being served, but also a consideration of the nature of high-priority potential market segments. Once again, the dynamic nature of markets challenges carrier management in seeking answers to this question.

"How does the customer buy?" is a question related to an understanding of "Who is the customer?" To the passenger transportation planner, the problem of effective distribution has long been of interest. Generally, passengers have been ticketed by the carrier at the terminal of departure. However, independent travel agents, retail extensions of travel wholesalers, carrier-owned ticket outlets, unlimited mileage passes, and the integration of passenger transportation with other travel services into tour packages have emphasized the innovative contemporary approach to the distribution of passenger transportation services. Many of these are direct outgrowths of answers to the question "How does the customer buy?"

Also related to "Who is the customer?" is the question "How can the customer be reached?" Involved here are analyses of various advertising and promotional media and the match of media and target market segments. It is clear that the communication process between carrier and potential passenger be one based on an orientation toward the passenger. The content, delivery, and basic appeal of any advertising campaign must fit into the experience of the passenger (rather than those of the individuals planning the campaign). In other words, being understood is the responsibility of the communicator and not the responsibility of the audience. More will be said about promotional substrategies later in this chapter.

The third question posed by Drucker is "What is value to the customer?" It is crucial that passenger transportation planners understand what various market segments consider value. Value may be defined in terms of frequency, speed, safety, convenience, price, luxury, ground service, terminal facilities and location, status and prestige, departure and arrival times, and a number of other factors.

The main point, however, is that each market segment may have a different perception of value. Value, then, must be perceived as a subjective factor keyed to the desires of specific passenger groups.

The fourth of Drucker's five questions is "What will our business be?" This question may be answered by relating past and present operations to future plans. Involved would be a synthesis of past trends tempered by specific future plans. The focus of the planner is directed toward a forecast of the intermediate future of the carrier. Where will we be in five years if we continue our present course of action? Where will we be in ten years?

The final question in this analytical series is "What should our business be?" This is the "crunch" question. The first task involved in answering it is an analysis of change in the external environmental areas and in the market environment. The second step in the process is a comparison of future external environmental conditions and resulting market requirements and the answers generated from the previous question ("What will our business be?"). If there is a substantial difference between the direction in which a carrier is headed and where it should be going, a careful reappraisal of previous planning definitely is in order. In any case, answers to the question "What should our business be?" are material considerations for those who are given responsibility for setting carrier objectives. Answers to this question often lead to revisions in the definition of the nature of a carrier's business and another round in a continuous process of self-evaluation and appraisal.

Marketing Objectives

Once specific objectives for overall carrier operations have been established, it is possible to proceed to the setting of marketing objectives. The prime requisite of marketing objectives is that they be consistent with both overall carrier objectives and with market requirements.

There are certain general guidelines that may be useful to those involved in the marketing of transportation services as they consider the articulation of objectives. These are: (1) The marketing activities of every carrier should be oriented toward meeting the needs of passengers instead of the conveniences of carrier management. (2) Marketing activities should be planned and should take place in a systems context. (3) Efficiency (or profitability) of operation should be a prime carrier guideline.

By passenger orientation we mean that marketing activities should reflect the requirements of the market rather than the philosophies (or prejudices) of carrier management. This implies an external rather than an internal focus of executive attention. Transportation planners must begin with an analysis of the market and then work backward toward assessment of carrier requirements to meet market needs. This is the exact opposite of beginning with an internal analysis of carrier capabilities and then making a decision on marketing activities based substantially on carrier convenience. While the latter approach may have considerable short-run appeal, its potential for success over a longer period is a most risky proposition. Passenger orientation should be the basic tenet supporting marketing objectives. Sensitivity to markets and changing market conditions is a prime requisite for passenger orientation.

By operation in a systems context, we are suggesting that there is a need for the integration of marketing activities with those of all the other functional areas of the carrier (operations, finance, and so on). It is unfortunate that internal competition rather than cooperation is often the modus operandi for carrier personnel in every mode of passenger transportation. For example, marketing people may be at odds with those in finance. Or, marketing people from one geographic area or division may overzealously compete with their counterparts in other areas or divisions. In each of these situations, an unwritten goal might be to look good at the expense of others. While this approach could advance one's position within his functional area or division, it does little to further the position of the carrier in its competitive struggle with other carriers. If each functional area operated in a systems context, with overall carrier objectives as guidelines for the integration of division efforts toward common goals, the competitive position of the carrier could significantly improve.

By citing efficiency (or profitability) of operation as a prime carrier guideline, we are suggesting that efficiency of operation (or profitability) be emphasized over simple expansion. Americans tend to worship at the altar of growth. The success of an enterprise is often measured in terms of quantity rather than in terms of the quality of operation. More significantly, the rewards for executive excellence are frequently tied to volume rather than to efficiency or profit-ability. The best marketing executive, then, is thought to be the one responsible for the highest volume of sales. The best salesman is the one who sells the most. Seldom does contribution to carrier profits enter as a criterion for rating performance—and perhaps understand-ably, since many firms simply cannot determine the profit contribu-tion of the various phases of their operations. It is encouraging, how-ever, to note that direct costing systems have found favor with many contemporary businessmen. These systems create "profit centers" that can yield profitability and efficiency data on specific phases of an operation.

A third consideration, therefore, for those developing marketing objectives is related to carrier profitability and efficiency. Growth is an important, but not an exclusive, consideration. Many carriers have expanded their operations into new markets only to subsequently realize that the expansion resulted in a drain rather than a contribu-tion to carrier resources. Further, because of regulations covering market entry and exit, it is often either difficult or impossible to withdraw from markets once a commitment has been made.

Once the marketing activities of a carrier have been reviewed and its objectives have been articulated, more specific aspects of marketing strategy may be considered.

Market Segmentation and the Selection of Target Markets

Market segmentation is a process through which prospective passengers (the market) are categorized into a number of subgroups or segments. The assumption underlying this process is that the market as a whole lacks homogeneity. This is to say that the responses of individuals to various marketing efforts will differ and that certain groups of individuals within this broad market will represent greater economic potential to carriers than will other groups. The objective of market segmentation is the division of markets into categories that have certain geographic, economic, demographic, or life-style simi-larities.[5] It is expected that with these similarities will go a certain

---

[5] For an overview of the market segmentation literature, see James F. Engel, Henry F. Fiorillo, and Murray A. Cayley, eds., *Market Segmentation: Concepts and Applications* (New York: Holt, Rinehart and Winston, Inc., 1972). For a new dimension in market re-search technology, see Joseph T. Plummer, "The Concept and Application of Life Style Segmentation," *The Journal of Marketing*, vol. 38 (January, 1974), pp. 33-37.

homogeneity in transportation wants and needs.

A simplified example of how a market might be segmented is illustrated in Table 15. Suppose that a market research study was undertaken by a carrier in a given city to determine the broad demographic and economic characteristics of its passengers and its potential passengers. Perhaps this study would conclude that the group currently traveling the most was traveling for business, male, between 35 and 50 years of age, with some education at the college level, employed as salesmen, earning $21,000 to $30,000 per year, and residing in the northeast section of the city and in suburban communities "B" or "D." Here would be a profile of the dominant market segment within the whole of the passenger market. Other market segments, once isolated, could be evaluated to determine whether they generate enough traffic to be included in the market plan.

TABLE 15

Market Segmentation Example

NATURE OF TRAVEL	SEX	AGE	EDUCATION IN YEARS	OCCUPATION	INCOME	RESIDENCE
Business		Under 18	0 − 8	Student	Under $5,000	Section of City:
			9 − 12	Blue Collar		NE
	M	18−25			$5,000- $10,000	SW SE
			13 − 15	Clerical		S
		26−35				Central
					$11,000- $20,000	Etc.
			16 and	Sales		
		36−50	Over			
Pleasure				Technical	$21,000- $30,000	Suburban Commun- ity:
		51−65				
				Managerial		"A"
	F	Over 65			$31,000- $50,000	"B" "C"
				Professional		"D" "E"
					Over $50,000	Etc.
						Rural

This process of segmentation directs attention from broad general market considerations toward more specific high-potential segments. Transportation planners, as well as other businessmen, must recognize that they cannot efficiently offer enough services to cover every possible passenger or customer. Instead, they must direct scarce resources into the market segments that will yield the highest return. These high-return segments may be termed "target markets." The recognition and selection of target markets can be accomplished only after a process of market segmentation has been completed.

There are several major advantages of market segmentation and target-market selection for transportation planners. First, the designing of passenger transportation services to fulfill the needs of high-potential customers will be made easier. Second, this approach will be useful in allocating promotional dollars to market segments where they will have the greatest return. Third, market segmentation can be of value in creating advertising appeals appropriate to certain demographic or economic groups. Thus, the diluting effect of trying to develop advertising appeals for entire markets will be minimized. Fourth, the use of market segmentation in advertising planning will result in better media choices and more enlightened allocation of the advertising budget among available media. Fifth, the timing of marketing efforts can be made more effective if the travel needs of high priority segments are considered individually. Finally, focusing on a limited number of market segments rather than on a market as a whole will enhance the prospects of discovering the first signs of major trends that may indicate changing market conditions, and therefore allow added time for adaptation.

Once target markets have been selected, marketing strategy may be planned. It is clear that effective strategy will be tailored to these high-potential market segments. In short, market segmentation and the selection of target markets may be thought of as a point of balance between the general and specific phases of marketing planning.

Overall Marketing Strategy

Overall planning of marketing strategy must be completed before specific services, promotional, or distribution substrategies are contemplated. If these substrategies are to be goal-oriented, an overall plan of action to achieve these goals must first be developed.

The planning of overall market strategy is largely a task of determining the carrier's current marketing needs, given market conditions. This calls for assessing three factors: the carrier's current economic position, the nature of its competition, and the characteristics of its passengers. An example from air transportation will illustrate the application of these factors.

Carrier's Current Economic Position.   Assessments of a carrier's current economic position could include five-year data on: (1) total operating revenues, (2) revenue passenger miles flown, (3) available seat miles, (4) load factors, (5) revenue ton miles, (6) available ton miles, (7) revenue ton-mile load factors, (8) yields, (9) public service revenues, (10) return on investment. Since some of these terms are not self-explanatory, Table 16 will help the reader to understand the significance of each.

TABLE 16

Definitions of Relevant Air Transportation Terms

Revenue Passenger-Mile.   One fare-paying passenger transported one mile.

Available Seat Miles.   The total number of seats available for the transportation of revenue passengers multiplied by the number of miles which those seats are moved.

Revenue Passenger Load Factor.   The percentage of seating capacity actually sold and utilized. Computed by dividing revenue passenger-miles by available seat miles.

Revenue Ton-Mile.   One ton of revenue traffic transported one statute mile. Revenue ton-miles are computed by multiplying tons of revenue traffic (passengers, freight, mail, etc.) by the miles this traffic is moved.

Available Ton-Miles.   The total number of tons available for the transportation of passengers, freight, and mail multiplied by the number of miles this capacity is moved.

Revenue Ton-Mile Load Factor.   The percentage of total capacity available for passengers, freight, and mail which is actually sold and utilized. Computed by dividing total revenue ton miles actually moved, by total available ton-miles.

Yield.   The average amount of revenue received per revenue passenger-mile. Computed by dividing total passenger revenue by the total number of revenue passenger-miles.

Public Service Revenues (Subsidies).   Payments that provide for transportation (especially air transportation) to communities in the United States where traffic levels are such that service could not otherwise be supported.

Source: Adapted from *Air Transport 1973* (Annual Report of the U.S. Scheduled Airline Industry). Washington, D.C.: Air Transportation Association of America, 1973, p. 42.

Next, some assessment of the share of the market controlled by the carrier and competitive carriers should be made. Four possible measures of market share in airlines are presented in Table 17: total operating revenues, passenger revenues, revenue passenger-miles flown, and available seat miles. All of these data are for 1973.

The soundness, strength, and probable future of a carrier's economic position could be evaluated through analysis of five-year trends in these and other relevant categories (especially those measures of the economic health and well-being of a carrier generated by the accounting function).

TABLE 17

Total Operating Revenues, Passenger Revenues, Revenue Passenger-
Miles, and Available Seat Miles for Top Ten U.S. Air Carriers, 1973

Total Operating Revenues

1. United	$1,904,963,000
2. American	1,475,359,000
3. Trans World	1,452,905,000
4. Pan American	1,424,639,000
5. Eastern	1,259,807,000
6. Delta	1,122,971,000
7. Northwest	584,748,000
8. Braniff	428,099,000
9. Western	414,717,000
10. National	413,849,000

TOTAL INDUSTRY $12,418,771,000

Passenger Revenues

1. United	$1,654,540,000
2. American	1,296,318,000
3. Trans World	1,154,069,000
4. Eastern	1,130,279,000
5. Pan American	1,049,914,000
6. Delta	1,021,122,000
7. Northwest	474,060,000
8. National	382,959,000
9. Western	379,824,000
10. Braniff	370,954,000

TOTAL INDUSTRY $10,275,689,000

Revenue Passenger-Miles Flown

1. United	27,029,304,000
2. American	20,654,338,000
3. Trans World	20,440,696,000
4. Pan American	19,518,694,000
5. Eastern	16,875,804,000
6. Delta	15,022,048,000
7. Northwest	8,007,850,000
8. Western	6,357,481,000
9. National	5,900,240,000
10. Continental	5,661,379,000

TOTAL INDUSTRY 161,957,307,000

Available Seat Miles

1. United	49,383,884,000
2. American	39,005,759,000
3. Trans World	38,611,925,000
4. Pan American	36,234,006,000
5. Eastern	30,532,145,000
6. Delta	29,311,469,000
7. Northwest	19,593,377,000
8. National	11,886,451,000
9. Continental	11,692,700,000
10. Western	11,043,425,000

TOTAL INDUSTRY 310,597,107,000

Source: Air Transport 1974 (Annual Report of the U.S. Schedules Airline Industry. Washington, D.C.: Air Transportation Association of America, 1974), pp. 5, 7, 20, and 25.

This is the first step in establishing the needs and parameters inherent in the planning to overall marketing strategy.

Nature of Competition.   Data similar to those considered above would also be helpful in assessing the nature of carrier competition and the activities of competitors.   However, it is pointed out that analyses of competition should be made for each city pair served. In other words, each city pair is to be considered a separate market for the service offerings of a given carrier.

The following information, classified by city pairs, is important in analyses of competition: (1) the number of competitors; (2) the share of the market held by each competitor; (3) changes in frequency of service offered by competitors; (4) changes in the schedules of competitors, that is, in the times of day when service is offered during each day of the week; (5) variations in the market-share percentage held by the carrier over a five-year period; (6) a qualitative assessment of the marketing activities of competing carriers to identify the substance and impact of these activities on revenues and market shares.

Until accurate evaluations of the nature of competition are completed, it is not possible to maximize the effectiveness of the overall thrust of one's own marketing structure.

Assessments of the Characteristics of Passengers.   Assessments of the characteristics of the users of a carrier's service offerings should begin with market segmentation and the selection of target markets. Extending beyond this dissection could be: (1) estimates of the numbers of potential passengers in high-priority market segments for each major city pair and geographic region; (2) some demographic characteristics of target markets in each city pair, that is, occupation, age, income, education, sex, and so forth; (3) where the potential passengers tend to reside, that is, sections of the city or suburban communities; (4) how passengers are ticketed; (5) breakdowns of when various passengers tend to travel—time of day, day of week, time of month, and season of year; (6) what passenger segments are actually buying—time, convenience, price, service, luxury, entertainment, or whatever; (7) differences, if any, between the use of transportation services and the actual buyers of these services (Do secretaries or corporate travel offices arrange for tickets? If so, what factors influence *their* choice of carriers?); (8) passenger satisfaction or dissatisfaction; (9) indications of changes in the travel patterns of key market segments, for example, shifts from private to public transportation or shifts from one vacation area to another; (10) other passenger characteristics isolated by individual carriers.

Once candid assessments of current economic position, nature of competition, and passenger characteristics have been made by a carrier, its marketing needs are likely to emerge. From a close review of these needs comes an awareness of overall marketing strategy requirements.

After the general thrust of marketing strategy has been decided upon, it is possible to establish service substrategies, promotional substrategies, distribution substrategies, and pricing alternatives.

Carrier Service Substrategies

We have previously referred to the offerings of passenger carriers as "bundles" of passenger satisfactions having both tangible and intangible dimensions. The service substrategies of carriers, therefore, may be thought of as that mix of its offerings which is designed to maximize the satisfactions of present or potential customers. There are a number of alternative service substrategies available to carrier management.

Scheduling.   Scheduling is a potentially important carrier service substrategy. When used as a marketing tool, the schedule of a carrier correlates carrier capacity to passenger needs. The result is an optimization of the service offering. For example, we know that each city pair market has two basic classifications of travelers: business and pleasure. Both business and pleasure travelers have different peak-demand periods according to the day of the week or the hour of the day. Table 18 reveals that in many city pair markets there are four apportionments of days within a normal week: Monday through Thursday, Friday, Saturday, and Sunday.

The demand for business travel tends to peak Monday mornings and Friday afternoons and is heavy during the morning and early evening hours Mondays through Thursdays. The demand for pleasure travel tends to peak on Friday evenings or on Sunday afternoons and early evenings. Saturday normally is the lightest travel day of the week.

The use of a carrier's schedule as a marketing tool implies a recognition of these demand characteristics and the allocation of individual offerings of service to meet the needs of both classifications of travelers.

TABLE 18

Scheduling as a Service Substrategy: Peak Demand Periods

DAY OF WEEK	BUSINESS DEMAND	PLEASURE DEMAND
Monday through Thursday	Heavy early morning and early evening. Very heavy Monday morning.	Generally light.
Friday	Very heavy Friday afternoon and early evening.	Very heavy Friday early evening.
Saturday	Light mornings. Very light afternoons and evenings.	Moderate early mornings. Light afternoons. Very light evenings.
Sunday	Very light mornings. Moderate evenings.	Moderate mornings. Very heavy afternoons and evenings.

Expansion of Contraction of the Service Offering. Related to the use of scheduling as a service substrategy are the expansion and contraction of service offerings. Here we are referring to actions such as increasing the capacity of the carrier in certain markets (that is, shifting from Boeing 737s to 727s, increasing the frequency of service, or other activities which have the effect of expanding the quantity of service offered. As the demand for passenger service increases and as the adult population grows, the expanding of capacity is a natural reaction.

Expansion, however, necessarily requires heavy capital expenditures in equipment, which may require long production cycles and obligate a carrier financially for extended periods. Therefore, carrier management must plan carefully before making capacity-expansion decisions. Management will be forced to live with overly optimistic expansions of capacity for a long time.

Contracting the service offering is the opposite of expansion. Because both entry and exit from markets are controlled in regulated transportation industries, neither expansion nor contraction of service offerings is easily accomplished.

Contraction is often a difficult decision for carrier management to make and for regulatory agencies to approve. We have already suggested that American businessmen tend to worship at the altar of growth. Contraction, then, is a strategy often likened to defeat. Further, certain routes or markets are protected for political or social reasons. As a result, attempts by carriers to contract service in these areas may be interpreted as antisocial acts on the part of carrier management. Finally, there is the problem of tradition. After serving particular city-pair markets for long periods of time, carriers may be perceived as "residents" of the communities by regulatory agencies. As a result, they may not be permitted to contract operations if demand diminishes.

Even in the face of these difficulties, it is recommended that carrier management continually review its service offerings for both expansion and contraction possibilities. Both of these strategies are of merit in achieving profitable and efficient levels of operation.

Alteration.   Another service substrategy is to alter the service mix in response to market change. This strategy has frequently been used by passenger carriers. Air carriers currently are altering their service mix by upgrading the quality of their coach-class service and by converting the interiors of conventional jet airliners to create an illusion of spaciousness with a wide-body look. A Southeastern railroad has added automobile carrying cars to passenger trains so vacationers may take their cars with them at a nominal cost. Bus service is being altered with the inclusion of cabin attendants, lavatories, and food service. Urban passenger carriers are attempting to upgrade the quality, dependability, and security of mass transit service. Many cities are turning to "express" type bus service during peak hours. In each of these cases, the carriers are utilizing the strategy of service-mix alterations to achieve better harmony with the changing wants and needs of their customers.

New Uses for Existing Service Offerings.   Finding new uses for present service offerings is also a service mix substrategy. Here the question of adding freight capacity to already existing passenger operations may be relevant (as would the addition of passenger service to existing freight operations). The Greyhound Corporation effectively introduced a small package service on its scheduled intercity buses. Airlines have converted aircraft from daylight carriers of people to haulers of freight at night and back again within a 12-hour period. A new version of the Boeing 747 is being designed as a simultaneous passenger and freight carrier. Certainly urban highway systems are most efficiently used when truck transport is limited to nonpeak hours. Perhaps future urban rapid-transit systems will include freight-carrying capacity to help offset operating costs.

In all of these cases, finding new uses for existing operations has resulted in a more complete utilization of facilities and hence, a greater return on capital and labor investments.

Service Differentiation.   Another service substrategy alternative may be termed service differentiation. This maneuver has previously been discussed. It will be recalled that differentiating service offerings involves providing unique aspects of service—dimensions of service not offered in the same form by competing carriers. Clearly, each mode of transport is differentiated by inherent modal characteristics. For example, the downtown-to-downtown convenience of intercity rail travel or the capacity of a steamship to double as a hotel while in port are important reasons why passengers choose rail or steamship service.

Intramodal service differentiation has also been a prominent competitive strategy. The airlines have been especially creative here. Champagne service, roomier seating configurations in coach, substantial leg room for all passengers, lounges, unique decorations of the interior or exterior of aircraft, special food service, and improved terminal facilities are a few examples of the efforts of carriers to differentiate their service offerings from those of their competitors.

Differentiated service makes the task of marketing the offerings of a specific passenger carrier considerably less difficult in highly competitive markets. This is true because it provides the marketers with certain tangible differences to promote in an industry that is marked by standardization of services and prices required by governmental regulatory agencies. Sometimes these service differentiations provide the theme for an entire marketing program. For example, Braniff has stressed "packaging" of their services through decoration of aircraft exteriors. They have decorated their entire fleet with unique colors, culminating in a multicolored design of a DC-8 by famed sculptor Alexander Calder. This original work of art bears the signature of Calder, but has no other distinguishing lettering, not even the Braniff name.

Carriers must carefully evaluate the relevance and impact of dollars spent on the differentiation of service within the context of the wants and needs of target-market segments. First-class leg space in coach may be an important differentiating factor to business travelers, whereas the color or exterior decor of aircraft may not.

In summary, it should be pointed out that service-mix sub-strategies may be of greater consequence to those providing passenger transportation services than to other businessmen. This is the case because price competition, which is such an important consumer consideration in most other industries, is not a major factor in domestic intramodal carrier competition. In the absence of price differentials, service-mix substrategies become perhaps the most basic single element in the total marketing mix.

Carrier Promotional Substrategy

The mix of promotional activities available to carrier management consists of advertising, personal selling, public relations, and sales promotion. Advertising is indirect communication with markets through the mass media or the mail. Personal selling involves interpersonal communication with representatives of target-market segments. Public relations includes those activities designed to communicate with a broad range of "publics" in a manner designed to enhance public approval of carrier conduct. Sales promotion efforts support and supplement advertising, personal selling, and public relations; many include point-of-purchase displays, trade-show participation, and promotional gifts or novelties.

The promotional substrategy is crucial for every carrier. Here is the only communications link between carrier and passenger, between the producers of passenger transportation and the consumers of these services. This link may take on even more substantial proportions in the decades ahead as the distances between carrier management and diverse markets increase and as an already highly competitive market becomes even more so.

Promotion generally accounts for the largest share of a carrier's marketing budget. Dollars spent here should be expected to yield a return just as are dollars invested in other aspects of carrier operations. Although the difficulty in evaluating the returns from specific promotional campaigns is well known, it is essential that these campaigns be carefully planned and made an integral part of the entire operation of a carrier. The costs are too high to do otherwise.

A prerequisite to evaluating promotional efforts is to have clear promotional objectives that define the task to be accomplished, the time allotted for accomplishing the task, and the target markets to be reached. It is also important that the promotional theme adopted be consistent with overall carrier objectives and the total marketing effort. Unless clear objectives have been established as criteria for evaluation, it will not be possible to measure the effectiveness of any promotional effort.

Advertising is the most visible element of the promotional mix. Most carriers employ the services of advertising agencies as an adjunct to their marketing programs. It is important that the agency be included in marketing planning sessions and encouraged to be innovative and creative in developing advertising campaigns. The agency should be made aware of the carrier's marketing objectives so that all advertising proposals can be oriented toward these objectives.

In evaluating the efforts of an advertising agency or in selecting a new agency, the following criteria may be helpful to carrier management: (1) experience with the transportation industry, (2) market research capability and expertise, (3) knowledge of external environmental conditions and pressures in relevant market areas, (4) expertise in media selection and evaluation, (5) ability to develop strong advertising programs coordinated with the total marketing program, (6) willingness to assign its best people to the account, and (7) the ability to create an innovative advertising strategy and the desire to excel in promoting a carrier's service offering.

Finally, it is essential that carrier management personally make periodic qualitative evaluations of their advertising programs. They must ask themselves if this is really what they want to say to their customers or to potential travelers. They must also make sure that the message is appropriate for selected target-market segments. In any communication effort, the burden lies with the communicator to make sure that his message is relevant, clear, and persuasive.

Personal selling is the other major ingredient in a carrier's promotional mix. Here is a face-to-face, person-to-person confrontation with representatives of target-market segments that extends the impact of carrier advertising and adds the dimensions of interaction and response.

Most carriers have sales staffs that are used in conjunction with major accounts. However, it is important that other carrier personnel be made aware of their responsibilities as company salesmen. This is a notable consideration in that for most passengers, operational and ground personnel *are* the carrier. These employees are, in fact, the only company representatives with whom they generally have personal contact. Therefore, even the best of marketing plans could be rendered ineffective if ticket agents, baggage handlers, stewards and stewardesses, bus drivers, conductors, and others do not assume the role of company salesmen in their everyday contact with the traveling public. It is recommended that the total job performance of these public-contact employees be appraised in terms of their ability to function as company representatives as well as in terms of their ability to carry out their regular duties.

Carrier public relations are directed toward the achievement of public acceptance and understanding of carrier policies and actions. These activities are taking on greater importance as certain dimensions of carrier operations become more subject to public scrutiny and criticism. Candor and truthfulness are the most important qualities for effective public relations.

Sales promotion is the remaining element of the promotional mix. Point-of-purchase displays in travel agencies, various company trinkets, calendars, flight bags, and diverse activities are included in this classification. Sales promotion is used to support the other elements in the marketing mix.

Carrier Distribution Substrategy

Scheduling is the carrier's system of distributing its inventory, and seats are inventory. Sophisticated scheduling (that is, scheduling based on knowledge of the needs of major target markets in each city pair served) is the technique used to achieve optimization of carrier inventories. As mentioned earlier in this chapter, a schedule that features the same arrival and departure times seven days a week may be a convenience for the carrier but it is not utilizing the potential of the schedule as a marketing tool. Peak-demand periods for major passenger groups tend to vary according to season of the year, time of month, day of week, and hour of day. Creative utilization of its schedule enables a carrier to increase load factors, enhance its competitive position, and maximize the distribution of its inventory of seats.

We have previously briefly mentioned that travelers gain access to transportation services primarily through individual carriers and independent travel agencies. However, a new concept of distribution strategy is emerging. This approach is the travel systems concept.

Travel industry institutions are creating a marketing systems complex with both national and international dimensions. This systems approach reflects the mutual interests of airlines, steamship carriers, travel agents, Amtrak, bus lines, hotels, restaurants, rental car agencies, and various park, recreational, and cultural centers. In other words, the common interest of those providing travel services is recognized, and cooperation between the institutions is stressed. The objectives are growth of the entire travel market and an increase in operational efficiency and marketing effectiveness.[6]

The travel systems approach has taken several forms. First, independent travel companies have emerged to organize all the necessary components of travel into individualized marketable packages. There are three categories of travel companies. Wholesalers who arrange the specifics of a tour are one such group. They provide services associated with travel (hotels, sightseeing, automobile rental, entertainment, restaurants) as well as transportation by air, rail, bus, or steamship. A second group comprises retail travel agencies serving as independent distributors for wholesalers in cooperation with individual airlines and carriers in other modes of transportation. Retail travel agents deal directly with potential customers and are, in effect, salesmen of the travel package. The third group consists of wholesalers-retailers who package their own tours or who buy packages from other wholesalers for distribution through their own retail outlets or through independent travel agents.

Second, the marketing of tourism on a national or regional basis is emerging to supplement the efforts of individual carriers or others providing services to travelers. For example, the State of Hawaii has created a Hawaii Visitors Bureau to promote the islands as a tourism center. Various national governments and a number of cities have taken similar initiatives.

Third, there has been an integration of the service offerings of firms in the private sector. For example, representatives of certain airlines and hotel chains have tied together their services through price-guarantee programs or other packages designed for the vacation traveler. Also, seasonal programs, such as ski packages, have been organized and promoted cooperatively by transportation carriers and firms providing supporting services.

[6] See Edward M. Barnet, "Travel Industry Institutions Meld into Marketing Systems Complex Among Pacific Area Nations," *Passenger Transportation,* Stanley C. Hollander, ed. (East Lansing, Michigan: Michigan State University Business Studies, 1968), pp. 498-505.

Finally, there has been a kind of vertical integration taking place in the economic structure of the travel industry as airlines have acquired control of hotel chains, restaurants, and car-rental agencies. All of these activities reflect the movement toward the integration of travel-service distribution within a marketing systems context.

Implementation of the travel systems concept has interesting potential implications for the entire industry. Involved would be the mass distribution of travel services that could be coupled with the mass "production" already brought about by technological advances within the industry. This movement could bring some of the mass marketing efficiencies evident in modern supermarkets, department stores, drug chains, and discount houses. Since travel ranks behind only manufacturing among the world's income-producing industries, the potential economic impact could be profound.

Pricing Alternatives Under Conditions of Regulation

A previous chapter was devoted exclusively to an examination of the economics of pricing in passenger transportation. Therefore, it will be sufficient here to focus on pricing alternatives under conditions of regulation.

Prices for passenger transportation services are controlled by the governmental regulatory agencies assigned jurisdiction over each mode of transport. The approach to rate making has tended to be exclusively a reflection of operating costs. In other words, rates are calculated on the basis of the average costs of carriers serving particular markets plus a reasonable return on investment. This cost-plus approach does not encourage efficiency in carrier operations and, in fact, tends to reward inefficient carriers. Further, it does not take into consideration the various price elasticities inherent in the travel market.

For example, the price theory embraced by the Civil Aeronautics Board is structured to protect the economic viability of the entire industry. The industry is regulated as a utility with prices based on the average costs of all the CAB-certified air carriers. Specific fare levels are calculated by estimating expenses and investments required for operations conducted at a standard load factor of 52.5 percent.

This approach does not acknowledge the fact that carrier revenue is a function of both prices *and* utilized capacity (load factor). An aircraft operating at the standard 52.5 percent load factor is only about half filled with passengers. Since underutilization of capacity constitutes a major drain on potential carrier revenues and since unused capacity cannot be stored (revenue lost due to vacant seats is lost forever), it is reasonable to suggest that price be considered against a backdrop of load-factor maximization rather than as merely a reflection of carrier operating costs.

Pricing Alternatives: the California experience.   Air transportation in California is regulated by both the CAB and the California Public Utilities Commission (PUC). The name given to this arrangement is duo-jurisdiction. The PUC regulates and sets all air fares for *intra*state service and grants service certificates to the air carriers operating only within California (Pacific Southwest Airlines, Air California, and several others). The CAB sets all *inter*state fares and grants service certificates to the interstate carriers, which may include routes within California.[7]

The fares for air travel within California are among the lowest in the world on a per-mile basis. This fare structure grows out of a market philosophy to pricing embraced by the PUC that is the opposite of the cost-plus approach of the CAB. The market approach to pricing, commonly used in other industries, begins with price estimates based on market conditions. The experience in California was that for each 1 percent fares were reduced below CAB levels there was a 1.3 percent increase in traffic. As the PUC approved market-determined prices submitted by California intrastate carriers, the load factors of these carriers steadly increased above the 52.5 CAB standard. In 1973, for example, Air California had a systemwide load factor of 66.7 percent.

What happened in California was that the elasticities in the market for air service were utilized to increase the efficiency of carriers through better utilization of capacity. At the same time, of course, California travelers reaped the benefits of low air fares.

---

[7] For an in-depth study of the California situation as well as its implications nationally, see: William A. Jordan, *Airline Regulation in America: Effects and Imperfections* (Baltimore: The Johns Hopkins Press, 1970).

The California experience as a pricing alternative under conditions of regulation is worthy of consideration by the CAB and other regulators of interstate passenger transportation. Taking into consideration the two general goals of regulation discussed in Chap. 4 (the protection of the public and the promotion of the best possible system of passenger transportation), the California approach to pricing seems to be a most prudent alternative to present rate-making policies.

Evaluating the Marketing Effort

The effectiveness of implemented marketing strategy should continually be appraised. Not only should marketing activities be examined for appropriateness in the face of changing market conditions, but it also must be recognized that the marketing efforts of major carriers exert pressure on the market that can, in themselves, produce variations in demand.

The objectives that formed the foundation for marketing planning must be utilized as standards against which performance is measured. It is stressed that unless objectives have been established that are precise as to both purpose and time, it will not be possible to evaluate marketing efforts in a meaningful way.

A periodic marketing audit is suggested as a relevant tool of evaluation. In addition to measuring performance against objectives, the operating effectiveness of each marketing subsystem can be appraised. The model of the marketing process presented earlier in this chapter should facilitate the assessment of the impact of the total strategic effort, the accuracy of market knowledge, the appropriateness of selected target markets, and the integration of overall marketing strategy with corporate objectives.

Finally, the overall quality of carrier service offerings should continually be assessed. An indicator of service quality is to be found in examinations of the CAB data on written passenger complaints, which are compiled and published on a regular basis. Figure 9 (pp. 181-82) illustrates the trend of such complaints over the past several years for 11 of the largest CAB carriers. The total number of passenger complaints, as well as the relative measure of passenger dissatisfaction

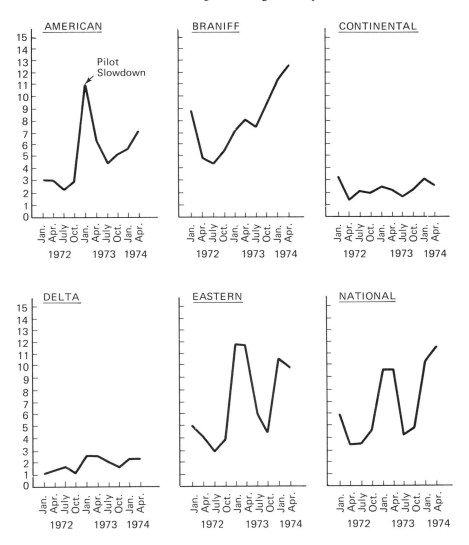

Figure 9.   Passenger Complaints Per 100,000 Emplanements
(Copyright Aviation Week and Space Technology,
*May 27, 1974, pp. 30-31. Graphs represent Civil
Aeronautics Board figures based on air transporta-
tion passenger complaints. Data converted to
three-month moving average.)*

Figure 9 *(cont)*

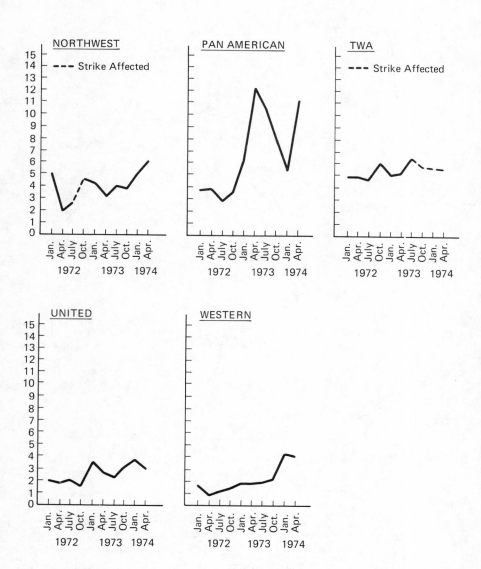

(that is, compared to competing carriers), should be of substantial interest to carrier management when evaluating overall performance.

SUMMARY ON MARKETING

The marketing of passenger transportation services has been shown to be a system of integrated activities oriented toward selected target-market segments. It has been suggested that the marketing of passenger transportation services may be approached through a series of steps: (1) the accumulation of market knowledge, (2) the setting of carrier objectives, (3) the development of related marketing objectives, (4) the selection of target market segments, (5) the planning and implementation of market strategies and substrategies tailored to these target market segments, and (6) the evaluation of the marketing effort.

The importance of marketing to those providing passenger transportation services is undeniable. Increasingly, it may be said that the successful operation of a carrier may be defined in terms of its success as a marketer of its service offerings.

ADDITIONAL READINGS

BARNET, EDWARD M., "Travel Industry Institutions Meld into Marketing Systems Complex Among Pacific Area Nations," *Passenger Transportation,* ed. Stanley C. Hollander (East Lansing, Michigan: Michigan State University Business Studies, 1968), pp. 498-505.

BARTON, ROGER, ed., *Handbook of Advertising Management* (New York: McGraw-Hill Book Company, 1970).

BOYD, HARPER W. and RALPH WESTFALL, *Marketing Research: Text and Cases* (Homewood, Illinois: Richard D. Irwin, 1972).

BRITT, STEVART HENDERSON and HARPER W. BOYD, JR., eds., *Marketing Management and Administrative Action* (New York: McGraw-Hill Book Company, 1973).

CASHER, J. D., *Marketing and the Computer* (Morristown, N.J.: General Learning Corporation, 1971).

DOTY, LAWRENCE, "Automating the Airline System," *Aviation Week and Space Technology*, XCIX, no. 17 (1973), pp. 40-55.

DOWNING, GEORGE D., *Basic Marketing: A Strategic Systems Approach* (Columbus, Ohio: Charles E. Merrill Publishing Company, 1971).

DRUCKER, PETER, *The Practice of Management* (New York: Harper and Row, 1954).

ENGEL, JAMES F., HENRY F. FIORILLO, and MURRAY A. CAYLEY, *eds. Market Segmentation: Concepts and Applications* (New York: Holt, Rinehart, and Winston, Inc., 1972).

FREY, ALBERT WESLEY, ed., *Marketing Handbook* (New York: The Ronald Press Company, 1965).

GIBSON, LAWRENCE D., CHARLES S. MAYER, CHRISTOPHER E. NUGENT, and THOMAS E. VALLMANN, "An Evolutionary Approach to Marketing Information Systems," *Journal of Marketing*, XXXVII, no. 2 (1973), pp. 2-6.

HOOPER, TERRY J. and EVERETT JOHNSTON, "Marketing High Speed Ground Transportation," *High Speed Ground Transportation Journal*, vol. 8, no. 3 (Fall 1974) pp. 275-282.

HOLLOWAY, ROBERT J. and ROBERT S. HANCOCK, *Marketing in a Changing Environment* (New York: John Wiley and Sons, Inc., 1973).

JORDAN, WILLIAM A., *Airline Regulation in America: Effects and Imperfections,* (Baltimore, Maryland: The Johns Hopkins Press, 1970).

KELLEY, EUGENE J., *Marketing: Strategy and Functions* (Englewood Cliffs, N.J.: Prentice-Hall, Inc., 1965).

KOTTLER, PHILIP, *Marketing Management: Analysis, Planning and* Control (Englewood Cliffs, N.J.: Prentice-Hall, Inc., 1972).

PLUMMER, JOSEPH T., "The Concept and Application of Life Style Segmentation," *Journal of Marketing*, XXXVIII, no. 1 (1974), pp. 33-37.

QUERA, LEON, *Advertising Campaigns: Formulation and Tactics* (Columbus, Ohio: Grid, Inc., 1973).

SEVEN, CHARLES H., *Marketing Productivity Analysis* (New York: McGraw-Hill Book Company, 1965).

STASCH, STANLEY F., *Systems Planning and Control* (Glenview, Illinois: Scott Foresman and Company, 1972).

UHL, KENNETH P. and BERTRAM SCHONER, *Marketing Research: Information Systems and Decision Making* (New York: John Wiley and Sons, Inc., 1969).

6

URBAN TRANSPORTATION

There has always been a direct and intimate link between the availability of transportation facilities and man's ability to create an effective urban environment. Throughout history, natural conditions, such as navigable waterways, have generally provided the basis for the establishment and growth of cities. In fact, until steam power was harnessed and applied to land transportation, most major cities of the world adjoined a body of water.

The availability of transportation facilities has contributed to urban development by stimulating trade between various urban areas, thus making available both employment and low-priced goods. In addition, the population attracted to the cities tended to create additional demand in the domestic sector, which led to the growth of residentiary business, which provided varieties of locally produced goods and services. These residentiary businesses, in turn, created further demand and employment opportunities along with the need for better transportation. In short, industrialization bred urbanization, and the availability of transportation facilities was a prerequisite for industrial growth.

In the United States, urbanization has been a relatively recent phenomenon. Until the twentieth century, the majority of Americans lived in rural communities, and the orientation of the country tended to be more agricultural than industrial. However, it is clear that a transition to an urban society has largely been completed in the contemporary United States. And with urbanization has come a paralleling complex array of transportation problems, the most conspicuous of which are related to the movement of people. Many of these problems will be outlined in this chapter and some proposed solutions explored.

THE GROWTH OF THE UNITED STATES AS AN URBAN SOCIETY

Early Development

At the beginning of the nineteenth century, the United States rested peacefully in a pastoral environment characterized by single-family agriculture, small businesses, and a commercial rather than an industrial national economic focus. As the eighteenth century came to a close, the proportion of the population living in cities (communities of over 2,500) was about 5 percent. The largest of these cities were New York (49,401), Philadelphia (28,522), and Boston (18,320). The population of the United States was 3,929,214.

The population steadily increased during the next three decades, growing to 5,308,483 in 1800, to 7,239,881 in 1810, and to 9,638,453 in 1820. By 1820 almost 20 percent of all Americans were urban dwellers. During the 40 years between 1820 and 1860, the population boomed, increasing by 226 percent (to 31,443,321). More significantly, the proportion of the population classified as urban increased almost eightfold. Just under one-half of all Americans were residing in the cities.

Urbanization in the Twentieth Century

By 1920, those living in urban areas had achieved majority status. By 1970, the percentage had increased to over 67 percent and U.S. Census Bureau projections indicate that by the year 2000 more than 70 percent of the nation's population will live in urban areas.

Growth of Individual Cities. The growth of individual American cities is illustrated in Fig. 10. Here the population growth of the 15 largest cities is measured as a percentage of the 1970 population attained by 1850, 1900, and 1950. We can see, for example, that

---

[1] Unless otherwise indicated, the source of all data presented in this section was the United States Bureau of the Census.

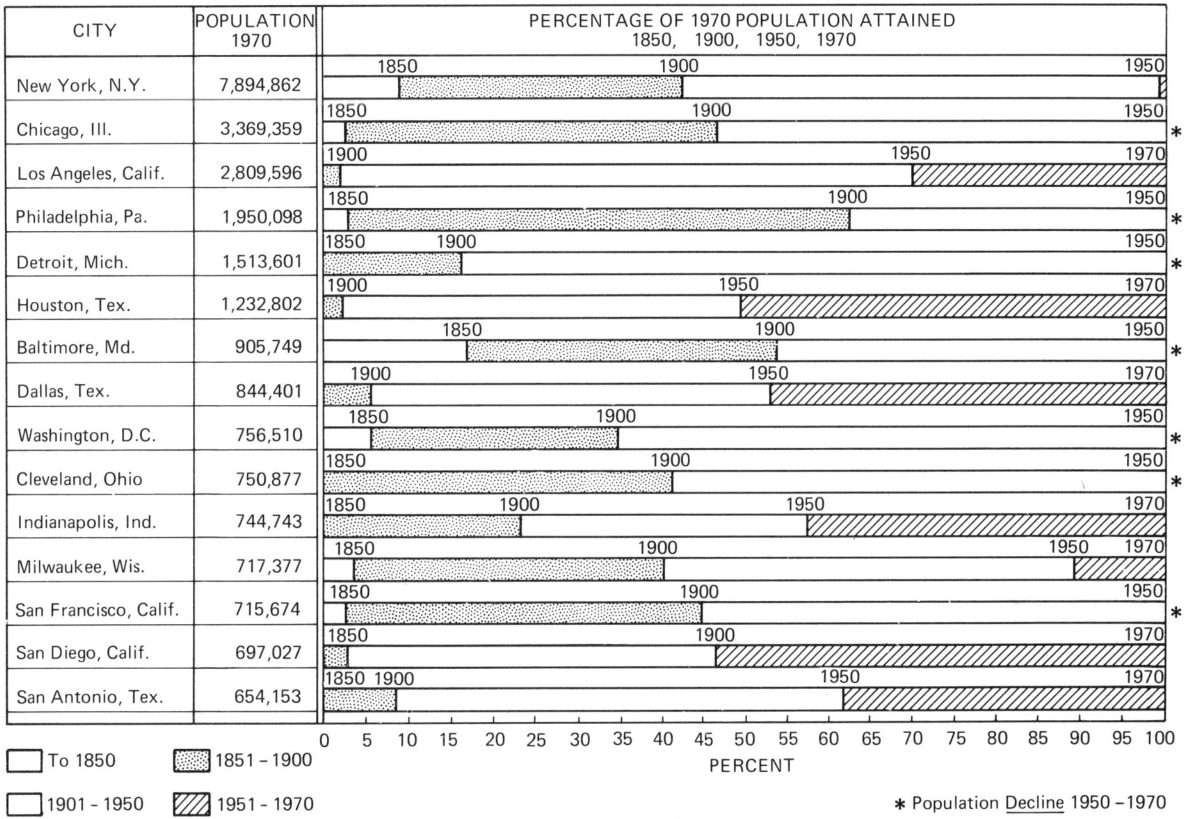

Figure 10. Population Growth By Percentage in 15 United States Cities. (Source: *Bureau of the Census.*)

New York City attained about 9 percent of its 1970 population by 1850, 42 percent by 1900, and over 99 percent by 1950. Los Angeles, on the other hand, located a continent away from eastern population centers, attained less than 1 percent of its 1970 population by 1850, only 3.6 percent by 1900, and 70 percent by 1950.

Decline of the Central City.   Interestingly, examination of Fig. 11 reveals that seven of America's 15 largest cities (Chicago, Philadelphia, Detroit, Baltimore, Washington, D.C., Cleveland, and San Francisco) had reached their population peaks by 1950 and lost inhabitants between 1950 and 1970.

This phenomenon becomes more apparent when evaluating the decade between 1960 and 1970. During this period, half of our 30 largest cities experienced a population loss. Table 19 lists these 15 cities, showing their 1960 and 1970 populations and the net loss of population in inhabitants and percentages during the decade.

The largest number of inhabitants were lost by Chicago (–181,045), Detroit (–156,513), St. Louis (–127,790), and Cleveland (–125,171). The cities losing the greatest percentage of their 1960

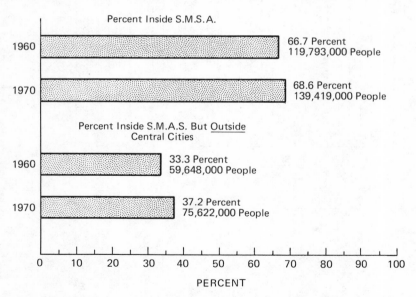

Figure 11.   Distribution of United States Population By Standard Metropolitan Statistical Areas (SMSA), 1960 - 1970. (Source: *Bureau of the Census.*)

TABLE 19

Major United States Cities Experiencing Net Population Loss, 1960 – 1970

CITY	1960	1970	NET LOSS	PCT. LOSS
Chicago	3,550,404	3,369,359	–181,045	– 5.1%
Philadelphia	2,002,512	1,950,098	– 52,414	– 2.7%
Detroit	1,670,114	1,513,601	–156,513	– 9.4%
Baltimore	939,024	905,759	– 33,455	– 3.5%
Washington, D.C.	763,959	756,510	– 74,460	– 1.0%
Cleveland	876,050	750,879	–125,171	–14.3%
Milwaukee	741,324	717,372	– 23,952	– 3.2%
San Francisco	740,316	715,674	– 24,672	– 3.3%
Boston	697,197	641,071	– 56,126	– 8.0%
St. Louis	750,026	622,236	–127,790	–17.0%
New Orleans	627,525	593,471	– 34,054	– 5.4%
Seattle	557,087	530,831	– 26,256	– 4.7%
Pittsburgh	604,332	520,117	– 84,215	–13.9%
Buffalo	532,759	462,768	– 69,991	–13.1%
Cincinnati	502,550	452,524	– 50,026	–10.0%

Source: Bureau of the Census

populations were St. Louis (–17.0 percent), Cleveland (–14.3 percent), Pittsburgh (–13.9 percent), and Buffalo (–13.1 percent).

Growth of Metropolitan Areas.   The growth of suburbia and the geographic dispersion of urban populations into sprawling metropolitan areas accounted for much of the population loss experienced by the central cities. Since World War II, more than two-thirds of the new single-family homes constructed in the United States have been located in suburban communities. During this period, more than 5,000 new shopping centers were built in the suburbs, and employment opportunities outside the central cities significantly increased. Reflecting these important demographic trends, population density in urban areas has been diffused from 6,580 people per square mile in 1920 to 4,230 in 1960.

Suburban communities, along with the central city they surround, have been grouped by the Bureau of the Budget into classifications termed "Standard Metropolitan Statistical Areas" (SMSAs). A metropolitan area is defined as a county or group of counties that contains at least one city of at least 50,000 population. Counties adjacent to the county in which the central city is located might be

TABLE 20

Ranking of Top Twenty Standard Metropolitan Statistical Areas, 1970 — 1973

SMSA	RANK	1970 POPULATION	RANK	1973 POPULATION
New York, N.Y.-N.J.	1	11,571,899	1	9,973,557
Los Angeles-Long Beach	2	7,032,075	2	7,032,075
Chicago	3	6,978,947	3	6,978,947
Philadelphia, Pa.-N.J.	4	4,817,914	4	4,817,914
Detroit	5	4,199,931	5	4,431,390
San Francisco-Oakland	6	3,109,519	6	3,109,519
Washington, D.C.-Md.-Va.	7	2,861,123	7	2,909,801
Boston	8	2,753,700	8	2,899,101
Nassau-Suffolk, N.Y.	New SMSA, post - 1970		9	2,553,030
St. Louis, Mo.-Ill.	10	2,363,017	10	2,414,163
Pittsburgh	9	2,401,245	11	2,401,245
Dallas-Ft. Worth	16	1,555,950	12	2,377,979
Baltimore	11	2,070,670	13	2,070,670
Cleveland	12	2,064,194	14	2,064,194
Newark	14	1,856,556	15	2,054,928
Houston	13	1,985,031	16	1,999,316
Minneapolis-St. Paul	15	1,813,647	17	1,965,159
Atlanta	20	1,390,164	18	1,597,816
Seattle-Everett	17	1,421,869	19	1,421,869
Anaheim, Santa Ana, Garden Grove, Calif.	18	1,420,386	20	1,420,386

Source: Bureau of the Census, 1973

included within the metropolitan area depending on specific requirements of population density and economic dependence on the central
city. There currently are 267 SMSAs, an increase of 55 since 1960.

Almost 69 percent of the population of the United States now
lives in standard metropolitan statistical areas, up from 66.7 percent
in 1960. Of these, 37.2 percent now live *outside* the central city compared to 33.3 percent in 1960. These figures are illustrated in Fig. 11.

The relative size of the largest SMSAs is presented in Table 20,
which is a ranking of the top 20 based on their total populations in
1970 and 1973.

The makeup of the top 20 SMSAs has remained basically the
same between 1970 and 1973 although some variances in the rank-
ings did occur. The eight leading areas maintained their positions, but

the ninth rank was occupied by the Nassau-Suffolk, N.Y., SMSA, which was created out of the eastern Long Island counties formerly in the New York classification.

California leads all states, with 92.7 percent of its population in SMSAs. New York is second with 86.5 percent. In other words, over 9 out of 10 Californians live in the state's metropolitan areas and only 1 out of 10 may be categorized as rural. In 28 states more than 50 percent of the population reside in SMSAs. Of the total population of the United States, approximately 69 percent live in metropolitan areas. Table 21 is a ranking of the states according to the concentration of their populations in metropolitan areas.

TABLE 21

Concentration of Population in Standard Metropolitan Statistical Areas by State, 1970

STATE	PCT. IN SMSA	STATE	PCT. IN SMSA
California	92.7%	Minnesota	56.9%
New York	86.5%	Louisiana	54.8%
Massachusetts	84.7%	Alabama	52.3%
Rhode Island	84.7%	Oklahoma	50.1%
Maryland	84.3%	Georgia	49.7%
Connecticut	82.6%	Tennessee	48.9%
Hawaii	81.9%	Nebraska	42.8%
Nevada	80.7%	Kansas	42.3%
Illinois	80.1%	Kentucky	40.0%
Pennsylvania	79.4%	South Carolina	39.3%
Ohio	77.7%	North Carolina	37.3%
Utah	77.6%	Iowa	35.6%
New Jersey	76.9%	West Virginia	31.3%
Michigan	76.7%	New Mexico	31.1%
Arizona	74.5%	Arkansas	30.9%
Texas	73.5%	New Hampshire	27.3%
Colorado	71.7%	Montana	24.4%
Delaware	70.4%	Maine	21.6%
Florida	68.6%	Mississippi	17.7%
Washington	66.0%	Idaho	15.8%
Missouri	64.1%	South Dakota	14.3%
Indiana	61.9%	North Dakota	11.9%
Oregon	61.2%	Alaska	0.0%
Virginia	61.2%	Wyoming	0.0%
Wisconsin	57.6%	Vermont	0.0%

United States: 68.6 Percent

Source: Bureau of the Census

Summary on Urbanization in America

There have been three phases in the evolution of the United States into an urban society. At first, cities were largely islands of commercial activity located in a country dominated by agriculture. Then urban centers emerged as industrial nuclei, characterized by their relatively compact size and population density. Finally, there has been a decentralization of population from the central cities into large metropolitan complexes.

The central cities have tended to decline both in population and in terms of their commercial importance. Improved transportation and communication have had a significant impact on this change in the structure of urban areas by reducing the economic advantages of centralization. As a result, additional parcels of land have become acceptable for commercial and industrial activities. This tendency toward greater homogeneity in the usefulness of urban land has made it economically advantageous to increase nonresidential utilization of the outer rings of urban areas.

Paralleling the dispersal of industrial and commercial activities away from the central business districts (CBDs) has been a decentralization of employment opportunities. This development has tended to stimulate a prior trend of movement away from the central cities for residential reasons. This evolution in the structure and substance of American cities has brought increased pressure and changing requirements for passenger transportation within urban areas.

THE TRANSPORTATION OF PEOPLE IN AN URBAN ENVIRONMENT

Historical Overview

Until steam power was applied to transportation, people were moved either by animals or by their own energy. Because mobility was so distinctly limited, cities radiated outward little more than two or three miles from their political or economic cores and tended to cover geographic areas of not more than 20 square miles. Virtually all employment took place in the center of the city and concentric circles of residential neighborhoods surrounded this core.

With the mechanization of transportation, as well as of manufacture, the stage was set for the rapid development of urban areas. Industrial, commercial, and residential enterprise grew along the ribbons of steel railroad tracks that converged on the economic hubs of cities.

As the nineteenth century drew to a close, electricity became available as a municipal power source that made available alternative means of transportation within the cities. In 1884, the first commercially operated electric urban railway was established in Cleveland. Similar systems were adopted by other communities. The Chicago version utilized tracks elevated above the normal traffic of urban streets. Elsewhere, tunnels were dug so that electric railways could be operated underground. New York City expanded such a subway system into the backbone of an effective urban transportation network.

Around the turn of the century, the trolley appeared. Powered by electricity received through sliding contacts on overhead wires, it rapidly achieved popularity throughout the world. Soon networks of track and overhead wires became commonplace, crisscrossing neighborhoods as they radiated outward from metropolitan focal points.

All of these forms of mechanized transport enhanced urban mobility and contributed to substantial increases in residential flexibility. Townsmen could reside as far as five miles from the city core, and some very early indications of transportation's contribution to urban sprawl subtly began to take form.

The Automobile

For those who have been caught in a rush-hour traffic jam, the statement that the automobile has become the most widely used form of urban transportation will come as no surprise. As we noted in Chap. 2 (Fig. 4), there were 101,237,000 passenger cars registered and 118,414,000 drivers licensed in the United States for the year 1973. Eighty-three percent of all U.S. households own at least one car and over 28 percent own two or more. Of these, 11 percent own at least one "new car" (current or previous model year) and 10 percent own an imported car.

The average American automobile is driven about 11,500 miles a year, a national total of over one trillion miles. Eight of ten commuters choose their automobiles over all alternative forms of urban transportation, and within standard metropolitan statistical areas a remarkable 90 percent of all travel is by car.[2]

Many factors have contributed to the popularity of the motorcar in the United States and throughout the world. It is a personal vehicle, the ultimate in convenience. It stands waiting to come to life at the whim of its owner, a powerful tool for overcoming the problems of time and space. Also, great status has been connected with automobile ownership. A car is a symbol of power, wealth, and speed. In addition, the family car reflects dimensions of privacy, comfort, and security that parallel one's home and that cannot be duplicated by other modes of transportation. Finally, the automobile has brought individual mobility and a sense of freedom to large segments of the American population.[3]

Highway Development

Public acceptance of the importance of motor vehicle transportation has been reflected in the demand for new streets and roads. Federal and state cooperation in meeting this need through programs of highway construction was assured by passage of the Federal-Aid Road Acts of 1916 and 1934. New Deal programs of the 1930s and the Federal Highway Act of 1944 provided the means for continued construction of both country highways and urban streets.

But it was the Federal-Aid Highway Act of 1956 that created the interstate highway system, the largest public-works program in American history, and one of the major contributions in modern times to the diffusion of central cities and the growth of large metropolitan areas throughout the United States. As these limited-access roadways were completed, city dwellers realized that it was possible to commute greater distances by auto between job and home within

---

[2] Data from *Automobile Facts and Figures* (New York: Motor Vehicle Manufacturers Association, 1970, 1971, 1972, 1973).

[3] For a discussion of the symbolic meaning of automobile ownership see Ernest Dichter, *Handbook of Consumer Motivations: The Psychology of the World of Objects* (New York: McGraw-Hill Book Company, 1964), pp. 262-285.

given time constraints. Population diffusion, started earlier by rail commutation, was given a new dimension.

The United States currently has over 3,758,000 miles of streets and highways, of which almost 3 million miles are surfaced. Table 22 presents the total road and street mileage for each state. Texas has 248,340 miles of highways and streets, California has 165,990, and Kansas ranks third with 134,182. Texas also leads with 49,476 miles of urban streets. California is second with 45,997, Illinois third at 27,753. Both rural and urban mileage are important because inter-

TABLE 22

Street and Road Mileage by State, 1971

STATE	URBAN	RURAL	TOTAL	STATE	URBAN	RURAL	TOTAL
Ala.	11,462	67,574	79,036	Neb.	6,681	92,084	98,765
Alaska	862	6,955	7,817	Nev.	1,919	47,783	49,702
Ariz.	6,166	40,919	47,085	N.H.	4,816	10,110	14,926
Ark.	9,231	69,449	78,680	N.J.	17,512	14,725	32,237
Calif.	45,997	119,193	165,990	N.M.	4,836	63,535	68,371
Colo.	7,581	74,289	81,870	N.Y.	40,618	65,872	106,490
Conn.	13,168	5,363	18,531	N.C.	13,885	72,593	86,478
Del.	766	4,338	5,104	N.D.	3,130	103,400	106,530
Fla.	22,275	71,035	93,310	Ohio	23,563	85,677	109,240
Ga.	15,028	85,186	100,214	Okla.	14,246	93,626	107,872
Hawaii	998	2,593	3,591	Ore.	6,348	91,105	97,453
Ill.	27,753	102,434	130,187	Pa.	24,171	91,487	115,658
Ind.	15,507	75,401	90,908	R.I.	4,444	1,017	5,461
Iowa	13,663	99,168	112,831	S.C.	6,838	52,791	59,629
Kan.	11,088	123,094	134,182	S.D.	2,973	81,105	84,078
Ky.	5,852	63,271	69,123	Tenn.	11,926	68,364	80,290
La.	10,993	42,347	53,340	Texas	49,476	198,864	248,340
Maine	2,449	18,957	21,424	Utah	4,412	36,569	40,981
Md.	4,146	22,376	26,522	Vt.	1,004	13,508	14,512
Mass.	21,858	7,497	29,355	Va.	8,636	52,872	61,508
Mich.	20,115	94,959	115,064	Wash.	9,965	70,254	80,219
Minn.	17,201	110,543	127,744	W. Va.	3,612	32,329	35,941
Miss.	6,599	60,167	66,766	Wis.	14,222	89,130	103,352
Mo.	15,386	100,158	115,544	Wyo.	1,287	39,253	40,540
Mon.	2,333	75,587	77,920	D. of C.	—0—	1,087	1,087

United States: Urban 593,047; Rural 3,165,895; Total 3,758,942

Source: Department of Transportation, Federal Highway Administration

city travel combines with urban travel to aggravate urban transportation problems.

Limitations of the Automobile

While it is true that the private automobile is the most flexible and convenient means of travel, it has become apparent that our love affair with the automobile has produced some rather burdensome offspring. The health of urban residents is threatened by pollution of the atmosphere. The esthetics of cities throughout the world are being blurred by automobile exhaust fumes. Scarce urban land has been consumed by roads and parking facilities. It has been estimated, for example, that about 85 percent of the downtown area of Los Angeles is directly or indirectly devoted to automobiles.[4]

Energy shortages and increases in the price of crude oil charged by the oil-producing nations have caused serious economic problems in the United States and throughout the industrialized world. This crisis in energy may be traced to increased motor vehicle usage, the depletion of many of the older oil fields within the United States, constraints placed on the drilling of new wells in environmentally sensitive areas, a general lack of conservation of scarce fuels, increases in the populations of consuming countries, and many other factors.

As domestic fuel supplies dwindled, American oil producers were forced to increase their dependence on foreign suppliers. At the same time, the motor vehicle revolution that had swept the U.S. several decades earlier was repeated in Western Europe and Japan, resulting in increased competition for limited supplies of fuel. The higher prices that generally accompany conditions of rapidly increasing demand soon followed. In short, a long period of abundant low-cost energy has come to a rather abrupt halt.

As a result of the increases in the prices of oil and other raw materials, the economic cost of automobile ownership has risen. The Department of Transportation estimates that a 1974 standard-size automobile will cost its owner $15,893 over a 10-year, 100,000

---

[4]Charles Luna, *The UTU Handbook of Transportation in America* (New York: Popular Library, 1971), p. 24.

mile lifetime. Gasoline for the 10-year period will total $3,521. The cost of operation per mile has increased to 15.8 cents.[5]

Another major economic cost is the construction and maintenance of highways. As we noted in Chap. 2, between 1920 and 1974 more than $312 billion was spent by state and local governments and more than $88 billion by the federal government to develop the road and highway system of the United States. The cost of constructing the national system of interstate highways (to be completed in 1977) has been placed at about $77 billion. The Bureau of Public Roads estimates that the cost of maintaining roads and highways exceeds $18.5 billion a year. In other words, it costs approximately $6,000 to own and operate each mile of street, road, or highway in the United States each year.[6]

The dollar outlays necessary to obtain right of way for urban highway construction are enormous. For example, eight miles of Chicago's Eisenhower Expressway cost over $50 million.

In addition to these economic considerations, there are social costs growing out of our dependence on the automobile for transporting people in urban areas. These costs are difficult to measure. How can the decline in job performance of individuals subjected to a daily commuting battle on the freeways be quantified? What is the impact on primarily lower income or minority-group neighborhoods when they are sealed off or isolated by the routing of urban highway systems? How many Americans are unemployed or underemployed because they are unable to afford a car and public transportation is unavailable? How is it possible to measure the toll being taken on the health and well-being of urban dwellers subjected to a polluted atmosphere? And, finally, what are the social and political implications for an industrial nation unable to meet its energy needs?

Motor vehicle accidents account for almost half of all accidental deaths in the United States. The National Center for Health Statistics reports that 2,150,000 people were injured in highway mishaps during 1972. Of these, 170,000 suffered permanent impairments and

[5] U.S. Department of Transportation, Federal Highway Administration, *Cost of Operating an Automobile* (Washington, D.C.: Office of Highway Planning, Highway Statistics Division, April 1974), p. 9.

[6] J.R. Meyer, J. F. Kain, M. Wohl, *The Urban Transportation Problem* (Cambridge: Harvard University Press, 1965), p. 67.

56,600 were killed. Over $6 billion in wages were lost as a result of motor vehicle accidents, and medical expenses of $1.4 billion were incurred.

It seems clear that if we weigh the disadvantages of heavy reliance on the current generation of private vehicles in urban areas and the continued growth of the highway and freeway systems against the advantages and conveniences of the automobile, we are compelled to conclude that alternative solutions to the problems of moving people in our cities must now seriously be considered. What is sought is not an elimination of the private car in urban environments, for many benefits of the automobile are necessary and desirable, but rather a more balanced system that would include several alternative modes of transportation.

THE MASS TRANSIT ALTERNATIVE

Conditions attributable to contemporary urbanization (that is, congestion, pollution, resource depletion, and the decline of the central city) have stimulated a resurgence of public interest in mass transportation. However, the present deteriorated condition of many mass transit systems, the substantial cost and lead-time periods involved in constructing new components, the extended areas enveloped by urban sprawl, and public preference for private transportation have compounded the already complex problem of developing more efficient means of moving people within metropolitan regions.

The Decline of Mass Transit Ridership

The general state of the public transportation systems currently in operation within the United States is marginal at best. In most communities, mass transportation has been assigned to a low priority position since World War II. During the war, ridership had peaked as a result of governmental restrictions on the operation of private vehicles. In the postwar years, there has been a steady deterioration of facilities and ridership despite rapid population increases in metropolitan areas brought about by high birth rates and migration from rural regions. Figure 12 illustrates the decline in mass transit

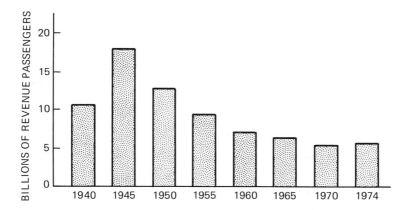

Figure 12.   Mass Transit Ridership, 1940-1974. (Source: *American Public Transit Association, '74-'75 Transit Fact Book, p. 14.*)

ridership—from 18,981 billion revenue passengers in 1945 to 5,341 billion revenue passengers in 1973. By and large, mass transportation in American cities has become outmoded, unpleasant, and erratic—when service is available at all.

Among the many factors contributing to this decline, four are especially noteworthy: (1) There has been a substantial increase in the cost of operating the systems. Labor costs alone, about two-thirds of total operating costs, increased 25 percent between 1970 and 1972. (2) Short-run productivity increases to offset increased costs have been difficult to produce because of right-of-way limitations and the "peak load" problem. The latter is the tendency for mass transportation to be utilized extensively during the weekday morning and evening rush hours. During other hours of the day or on weekends, the systems have excess capacity. This, of course, leads to inefficient use of both labor and capital. (3) Revenue losses, the result of a decline in passengers carried, have created major operating deficits. Fare increases, reductions in the number of neighborhoods served, contracted service frequency, and other similar measures have done little more than to assure new cycles of passenger losses. (4) Finally, there has been a general lack of regional transportation planning. Instead, independent solutions to transportation problems have been proposed by individual communities. The result has been a lack of coordination or integration of policy within metropolitan areas.

Mass Transportation and the Quality of Urban Life

Even after taking the operational problems of mass transportation into consideration, it is clear that these systems offer a myriad of potential solutions to problems associated with urban life. Thoroughfare congestion could be reduced since many mass-transit systems utilize their own rights of way and therefore do not compete with automobiles for street and highway space. Even buses, which do use urban thoroughfares, have much more capacity than the three automobiles they represent in space occupied.

In addition, mass transportation can conserve scarce fuel supplies and, at the same time, contribute to the reduction of air pollution. Some mass-transit vehicles are powered by electricity and are pollution-free while others use clean-burning natural gas. But whatever fuel they use, all have the effect of reducing use of the private automobile, the primary source of urban air pollution and a dominant consumer of fossil fuel.

It is also important to note that mass-transportation fares are usually considerably cheaper than the cost of operating a private vehicle over the same distance. Many urban residents are unaware of the high cost of operating their automobiles. In addition to fuel, oil, and tires, automobile owners must include maintenance, depreciation, insurance, parking, license fees, and repairs in their calculations. Conservative Department of Transportation estimates of the expense of operating a motor car are 15.8 cents a mile for a standard-size automobile, 12.8 cents for a compact, and 11.1 cents for a subcompact. So, a family that drives a typical 11,500 miles a year can expect to spend from $1,276 to $1,817 for automobile transportation.

There are also psychological and sociological rationales for increased emphasis on public transportation. The psychological well-being of many commuters could be improved in direct proportion to a reduction in the frustrations of rush-hour driving and parking experiences. The availability of public transportation facilities could mean increased occupational and recreational opportunities for those who are unable to afford private transportation or who are too old or too young to operate a motor vehicle, or physically incapable of doing so.

Further, the presence of mass-transportation systems could alter land-use decisions by shifting priorities from road and parking construction to the development of parks, playgrounds, or greenbelts.

These amenities could reverse the present tendency of American families to spend proportionately larger percentages of their budget on transportation as they move away from the central city in quest of low-density suburban living arrangements.

Finally, it is encouraging to note that the decline in mass-transit ridership seemed to have "bottomed out" in 1972, for there was a small increase in revenue passengers in 1973 and in 1974.[7]

Financing Mass Transportation

If improved mass-transportation systems are to become available, substantial improvements in public support will be required. This support must take the form of both financial commitment and public willingness to make use of such systems.

The precedent for public financial assistance in the development of transportation systems has been well established. Right of way has been provided for both the railroads and, indirectly, truck lines. The airways and waterways are maintained at public expense for, respectively, the airlines and inland water carriers. Only the construction of the pipeline systems did not involve substantial governmental subsidies.

Programs of public support of mass transportation can take several forms. A city may, for example, exempt a private carrier from municipal taxes, franchise payments, or other related charges. Here the objective would be to lower the operating costs of the urban carrier through an indirect subsidy. The importance and impact of this type of support is largely a function of the tax structure of individual communities.

A second possibility is that a direct subsidy could be paid from the city treasury to the carrier. This is a traditional form of assistance to those providing essential services, and has been used at one time or another by federal, state, and local governments. Because there are no offsetting costs related to funds obtained in this manner, carrier revenues are enhanced in a significant way. In most instances, public ownership of mass-transit systems has become a necessity. With few

---

[7] Revenue passengers in transit stood at 5.61 billion in 1974 as compared to 5.27 billion in 1972, the first year that ridership had increased since 1945. American Public Transit Association, '74-'75 *Transit Fact Book*, p. 14.

exceptions, municipal ownership has been the only way to rescue urban transportation systems from financial collapse and to upgrade the operation in a manner consistent with the immediate transportation needs of the community.

Once owned, the city may apply for federal matching grants under the 1974 Urban Mass Transit Act (80 percent federal, 20 percent local for capital improvements; 50-50 for operating subsidies). Even though the funding of public transportation remains the responsibility of municipal governments under federal legislation, substantial amounts of assistance are available, including $11.8 billion in federal funds between 1974 and 1980.

In addition, it may be possible to divert revenues from federal and state gasoline taxes to help fund public transportation. The Federal Highway Act of 1973 allows considerable state and local flexibility in the use of highway trust funds for the first time. Once the magnitude of highway construction maintained in recent years is lessened, much of the revenue that would thereby be available could logically be allocated to mass transit.

Further, a municipal bond issue could be floated. In the past, voters have been reluctant to finance mass transportation through public indebtedness; however, general concern about the availability of energy and the quality of our physical environment could reverse this posture. Then, too, matching funds are available from the federal government in recent times, thereby making municipal bond issues for "matching funds" more appealing.

Marketing Urban Transportation

Even if adequate public financial support for mass transit becomes available, it still will be necessary for urban residents to regularly patronize the system. The response of urban dwellers to public transportation facilities, however, has been less than enthusiastic. To promote public transportation, it will be necessary to make a number of improvements in facilities and bring about certain changes in the operational environment. Among the most apparent of these would be: (1) The system must be dependable, clean, and reasonably esthetically pleasing. This is extremely important since virtually every study of transit fare and service charges indicates that demand elasticities are significantly greater for service improvements. That is, ridership is more sensitive to improvements in levels of service than to changes in fare.[8] (2) Passengers must be guaranteed safety, being protected both from collisions and equipment malfunctions and from violence and robbery. (3) The prices charged for service must be kept reasonably low. (4) Auxiliary services, such as parking at points of origin, must be made available. (5) Sophisticated marketing programs must be developed to support the mass-transit system. (6) Bold governmental measures, perhaps including high taxes on downtown parking or the creation of vehicle-free pedestrian malls in central business districts, could encourage the use of public transportation.

THE BICYCLE ALTERNATIVE

For relatively short distances, perhaps up to five miles, the bicycle offers an interesting alternative for urban commuting and for general travel. In some geographic locations where the weather is relatively mild, bicycles are a year-round alternative to the automobile. Further, an urban area with a relatively flat terrain makes this alternative even more appealing to certain groups of travelers.

The twin developments of the ecology movement and the energy crisis of the early 1970s have called attention to the bicycle as more than just a means of recreation and have led some to proclaim that a "bike boom" exists. In fact, sales of bicycles have always been large and have equalled or exceeded sales of new automobiles in recent years, as shown in Table 23. Indeed, the use of the bicycle predates the automobile, and its recent popularity is reminiscent of several bike booms of the past.[9]

It is generally conceded that a bicycle is an alternative commuter transportation choice only within a five-mile radius of the place of employment. Yet given the structure of many American cities, this could be a viable choice for a considerable portion of the workforce. One analyst claims that 37 percent of the present population already uses bicycles. Still, the U.S. is far from "saturation" and far from approaching the 76 percent of the Netherlands population that uses

[8]"Making Mass Transit Work," *Business Week* (February 16, 1974), p. 76.

[9]Robert A. Smith, *A Social History of the Bicycle* (New York: American Heritage Press, 1972).

TABLE 23

Sales of Bicycles and New Automobiles in the United States, 1968–1972
(IN MILLIONS)

	BICYCLES	NEW AUTOMOBILES
1968	7.5	8.8
1969	7.1	8.2
1970	6.9	6.5
1971	8.9	8.6
1972	13.7	11.0

Source: Robert C. Podolske, "Investing in Urban Bicycle Facilities," Bicycles, U.S.A.(Washington: Department of Transportation, 1973) p. 43.

bicycles.[10] While this may be so, it is also true that the major demand for bicycle transportation will be higher (a) for those persons who use the bicycle for recreation as well as travel to work or school, (b) for those who feel exercise is important, and (c) for those persons not owning an automobile.[11]

But even within these limitations, considerable savings in pollution, energy, and money are made possible by the use of the bicycle. One study shows that a 90 percent savings in BTUs of energy is possible by switching from automobile to bike and that if only 10 percent of all automobile urban travel under five miles (in good weather and during the day) were to shift to bikes, 180 trillion BTUs would have been saved in 1971.[12] Translated into dollars, the savings in using a bicycle under certain conditions can amount to $675 per bicycling person per year.[13]

Part of the problem of using the bicycle as an alternative turns on the lack of bikepaths and the traditional lack of interest on the

[10]Robert C. Podolske, "Investing in Urban Bicycle Facilities," Bicycles, U.S.A. (Washington: U.S. Department of Transportation), p. 43.

[11]See Michael Everett, "Commuter Demand for Bicycle Transportation in the United States," Traffic Quarterly, XXVIII, no. 4 (Oct. 1974), pp. 585-601.

[12]Eric Hirst, "Bicycles, Cars and Energy," Ibid., p. 583; also see Richard A. Rice and Jeffrey L. Thompson, "The Search for the Ideal Urban Vehicle," Bicycles, U.S.A. (Washington: U.S. Department of Transportation, 1973), pp. 7-17.

[13]Everett, Traffic Quarterly, p. 589.

part of public authorities. Unlike the automobile, the bicycle does not produce its own revenue and bikepaths are not inexpensive.[14] However, the public policy problems of bikepaths seem to be changing rapidly and with the new flexibility in the use of the Highway Trust Fund allowed by the Federal Highway Act of 1973, it is logical to expect accelerated interest and development of bikepaths.

Finally, some very interesting intermodal transportation combinations utilizing the bicycle are possible. With a relatively simple and small investment in trailers or in storage racks, combinations of transit-bike, bus-bike, and auto-bike are possible.[15] This merely emphasizes the need for broad thinking and innovative planning.in passenger transportation.

THE NEED FOR REGIONAL PLANNING

Urban transportation is a regional problem. Inevitably, the transformation needs of metropolitan residents are intercommunity or intercounty and sometimes even interstate. Therefore, regional frameworks for public transportation planning reflecting the integration of representatives of all levels of government and all modes of transportation are requisites for the maximization of effectiveness and the optimization of returns on dollars invested. The need for regional planning is particularly acute in mass transit and at present, there are few centralized and coordinated bodies with authority over the planning, administering, and financing of public transportation. Instead, there are haphazard programs and shreds-and-patches management, which are unlikely to have the capability of coping with the difficult urban transportation problems that will be present for the remainder of this century unless there are considerable changes in approach and policy. Recognition of the need for regional planning

---

[14] Podolske estimates per-mile costs at $500 for a bike route marked and signed on an existing roadway, $3,050 for a protected bikepath of a lane on existing roadway protected by a physical barrier, and over $10,000 for a bike-track or bikeway completely separated from the existing roadway. Podolske, *Bicycles, USA*, p. 47.

[15] See Wesley Luar, "Bicycles in Mixed-Mode Travel" *Bicycles, USA* (U.S. Department of Transportation, 1973), pp. 82-88, and David M. Eggleston, "Toward a Dual-Mode Bicycle Transportation System," Ibid., pp. 88-99.

was contained in the 1974 Urban Mass Transit Act, and federal matching funds will be available only where a regional plan exists.

URBAN TRANSPORTATION OUTLOOK

Technological breakthroughs cannot be counted on to revolutionize the means through which people are moved within urban areas. Although advances in technology will occur, progress in urban transportation is more likely to be the result of innovative applications of presently available transportation technology. In other words, by the turn of the century it is likely that improved versions of present day automobiles, buses, trolleys, railroads, subways, and bicycles will remain the basic modes of urban transportation.

Perspectives on urban transportation should be organized according to time constraints. There should be a short-range period during which no new transportation systems can be constructed and no alterations in industrial and residential patterns can take place within urban geographic structures. There should be an intermediate time frame where investments in new transportation facilities can take place. There should be the long-run approach, where construction of new transportation facilities and technological advances may be coupled with certain changes in the location of the community's residential, commercial, economic, and political centers.

Short-Range Outlook

In the short run, the primary objective of urban transportation planning should relate to obtaining maximum impact and efficiency from existing facilities. In most cases, this means more effectively utilizing a mix of public and private modes of transport.

In communities where public transportation networks are presently operating, the problems tend to be concerned with upgrading the quality of service and of effectively marketing the offerings. The major objective would be to modify the behavior of automobile-oriented commuters through educational programs and other pro-mass-transit incentives. Increased fuel costs and potential fuel shortages have increased the probability that these programs can achieve measurable success.

In urban areas where public transportation facilities do not exist, or where they are inadequate to meet community needs, the problems are obviously more complex. The primary objective here would be to make automobile travel more efficient and to introduce bus and bike alternatives to supplement private transport wherever possible.

It has been suggested that the automobile will remain the dominant form of urban transportation throughout this century. If so, increased automobile efficiency should be an immediate focal point. The most direct method is to simply increase the number of passengers in each available vehicle. Random observations of rush-hour traffic reveal that the majority of automobile trips have an average occupancy of 1.1 persons. In other words, each vehicle is operating at only 20 to 25 percent of its passenger-carrying capacity, an intolerable situation given the high cost of energy, the congestion of highways, and present levels of air pollution. Applying computer technology on a regional basis to the task of matching those who potentially could form car pools is a solution to this problem that could be rapidly implemented.

In addition to this course of action, proposals have been made to reduce automobile traffic by staggering work hours or by shifting to a four-day workweek. Staggering work hours could reduce rush-hour congestion and ease the peak-load problem by diffusing the demand for public transportation.[16] Four-day workweeks, where feasible, would tend to reduce traffic and conserve energy.

Only buses and bicycles can be pressed into public transportation service rapidly enough to provide an alternative to the automobile in the short run. Buses are currently the backbone of many urban transportation systems and are likely to be such for the remainder of the century. A key to improving public transportation service, therefore, is to be found in more innovative bus utilization. Examples of innovative proposals include the establishment of exclusive bus lanes along major freeways and city streets and a number of park-and-ride proposals. Here drive-in theaters, church parking lots, athletic-facility parking, and other parking areas outside the central business district could be utilized as point-of-origin parking where buses could begin and end their express runs to various points throughout the metropolitan areas. The advantages of this concept include immediate availability of essential parking facilities and a better utilization of scarce

---

[16]Mathew J. Betz, "Traffic and Staggered Working Hours," *Traffic Quarterly*, XIX, no. 2 (1965), pp. 188-203.

urban land since drive-in theaters, church parking lots, and athletics-connected parking facilities generally are vacant during normal working hours.

Bus service should continually be evaluated to assure that passenger needs are being met. Clear and informative signs are a prime requisite along with secure, well-lit shelters at major points of departure. Human factors, including the esthetics of design, should be recognized as an important determinant of passenger satisfaction.

In addition, other ideas, such as equipping buses with traffic-signal-control devices to avoid unnecessary intersection delay, providing racks for bicycles, and even making beverages available, are being tried in various cities. All of these innovative programs are designed to increase demand by better meeting the needs of present and potential passengers.

Intermediate Outlook

During the intermediate time frame, it would be possible to construct and put into operation new urban transportation facilities. Several alternatives are available.

The BART System. In September, 1972, after more than 15 years of planning and construction, the first train of the Bay Area Rapid Transit System (BART) began service between Oakland and Fremont, California. Throughout the now completed system, passengers enjoy a smooth and quiet ride at speeds up to 80 miles per hour in carpeted and air-conditioned comfort. The trains travel over a right-of-way apart from city streets, which includes a series of tunnels constructed along the bottom of San Francisco Bay.

While BART continues to struggle with technical, financial, and operational problems, it is the first totally new urban transportation system built in the United States since Philadelphia completed its Market Street Subway in 1907. The system is operating on a seven-day-a-week, 15-hour-a-day schedule and, according to the Bay Area Rapid Transit District, the number of riders has already reached 97 percent of the original goal. In Fig. 13, the various technical and geographical dimensions of the BART system are presented.

Demand-response Transit Systems. An innovative integration of computer technology and minibuses has produced demand-response, or "doorstep transit," systems, which are now being tested in small to medium-size communities throughout the United States. The

Costs of System.	$1.6 bil.
Miles of Route	71 Bart
	4 SF Muni
Stations	34
Track Gage	5 ft. 6 in.
Cars on Order and Delivered.	450
A Cars (control/cab).	176
B Cars (mid train).	274
A Car Length	75 ft.
B Car Length	70 ft.
A Car Weight	59,000 lbs.
B Car Weight	56,000 lbs.
Car Width and Height	10 ft. 6 in.
Seating Capacity, Each Car	72 Persons
Maximum Speed	80 MPH
System Voltage	1000v, dc
Motors, Four 150 HP/Car.	500v, dc
Ticketing	Magnetically Stored Fare

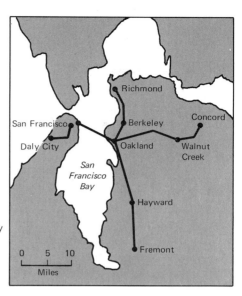

Figure 13.   Dimensions of the BART System. (Source: *Bay Area Rapid Transit District.)*

basic concept, sometimes called "Dial-a-Ride" or "Dial-a-Bus," combines the convenience of a taxi with the efficiency of a bus. A vehicle computer system keeps track of the location of all buses, noting their speed and the number of available seats. A centralized telephone network accepts calls from potential passengers. The location of individuals desiring service is fed into the computer, which plots these locations, selects the nearest vehicle, and dispatches it to the front door of the caller or to a convenient bus stop.

Demand-response systems have tended to be well-received and popular. By reducing the need for a second family car, they have been especially effective in low-population-density suburban areas where regular bus service is not economically feasible.

It is interesting to note that as a result of energy-related market changes, several manufacturers of recreational vehicles and motor homes have shifted to the production of a smaller generation of buses ideally suited to demand-response transit systems.

Public-Use "Private" Transport.   The concept of public-use automobiles has been introduced in Amsterdam and Tokyo. Here the idea of use without ownership has been extended to fleets of small, electrically powered, two-seat vehicles, which are available for short trips within central business areas. The vehicles are available in a series of designated parking areas and are activated with a membership card. When the driver reaches his destination, he simply returns the vehicle to the nearest parking area, where it becomes available for use by others.

Personalized Rapid Transit.   Automated mass transit systems called personalized rapid transit (PRT) and "people movers" have recently received much public attention. The typical PRT vehicles are smaller than the people-mover vehicles. Such systems operate like a huge horizontal elevator, utilizing their own rights-of-way and functioning with compact 12- to 20-passenger vehicles to provide either scheduled or on-demand service.

A passenger walks onto a platform and presses a button, much as he would do to summon an elevator. The message is transmitted to the nearest vehicle by the controlling computer through transmission lines built into the guideway. When the designated car reaches the assigned point, it automatically pulls off the main guideway, and stops to allow the passenger to board. As with an elevator, a button is depressed to establish a destination stop in the computer's memory bank. The vehicle is directed to stop at this predetermined point to allow disembarkation. Several major airports have established people-mover systems and the PRT experiment at Morgantown, West Virginia, is well known.

Denver is the first metropolitan area to have a voter-approved PRT system in the process of development. Specific testing of system hardware is being conducted by the U.S. Department of Transportation at Broomfield, Colorado.

The Automobile.   The motor car is not expected to change dramatically over the next few decades. It will be smaller, safer, more economical to operate, and it may even be powered by alternatives to conventional engines. Whatever its form, however, the automobile will remain the most widely used form of transportation in metropolitan areas.

The quest for an economical and pollution-free automobile engine has produced some interesting potential power sources. The stratified charge engine has a conventional up-and-down piston stroke but, in addition, it features a small extra combustion chamber and a double-barreled carburetor that feeds a rich mixture of fuel into the small chamber. The rich fuel burns and ignites a lean mixture, which is then fed into the larger combustion chamber. The initial rich fuel burn is not expelled as exhaust to the outside, however, and excess fuel remains in the chamber for the next burn. The result is an engine that is economical and that operates within acceptable emission levels.

Electricity has been used to power automobiles. Widespread use will not be practical until vastly improved storage batteries are developed to provide more power between charges and to generate greater surges of power for emergency situations.

The gas turbine engine is another power source that has been investigated. This is a kind of jet-propelled engine that creates thrust by expelling hot gases through a set of turbine blades, which turn a shaft. There are two problems associated with engines of this type: They are very expensive because they are built of hard metal alloys, and they consume a great deal more fuel than internal-combustion engines.

Steam engines seem to show somewhat more promise. They use a system that heats water to form the steam that turns a turbine. The steam then returns to water and is recycled through the system. While this process is a bit cumbersome for automobiles, it may become a low-polluting power source for a new generation of buses and trucks.

Long-Range Outlook

The long-range mass-transit outlook must be viewed against the dynamic backdrop of the total urban environment. In the short and intermediate ranges, the structure of cities and metropolitan areas tends to be regarded as given. That is, these variables are accepted as the parameters of an environment to which urban transportation facilities must be adapted. In the long run, however, significant alterations in the residential, commercial, industrial, economic, and political dimensions are to be expected. These must be considered along with strictly transportation-oriented issues.

A laboratory designed to aid in the conceptualization of such a broad range of variations in the urban environment and in the solution of long-range urban problems may become available in Orlando, Florida, as part of the "Experimental Prototype Community of Tomorrow" (EPCOT) under development by Walt Disney Productions.

Seven specific objectives have been identified by the Disney organization for the EPCOT project: (1) To encourage industry and the professions to introduce, test, and demonstrate new ideas, materials, and systems. (2) To showcase and prove the usefulness of promising concepts, technology, and specific prototype products. (3) To provide an ongoing "meeting place" where creative people from science, industry, and the arts may gather to discuss and develop specific solutions to urban problems. (4) To advance the excellence of environmental planning. (5) To bring together, in a living, working, creative environment, people of varied interests, talents, and backgrounds who will live together for days or weeks or months in a community and climate where experimentation is accepted and fundamental. (6) To create an artful and efficient environment, a community fashioned in human terms and on a human scale that begins with the belief that the people who live and work and play in the city are the heart of it. (7) To provide, for the first time, a practical basis for investigating and proving not only the popularity but also the economic feasibility of new ideas, materials, and systems.

Whether developed by a private corporation or by national or international governmental agencies, such an innovative milieu has potential for orderly long-range planning of transportation responses to changes in urban environments.

The Need for Modal Integration

An urban transportation outlook is incomplete without some reference to the need for integrating the various intracity, intercity, interstate, and international modes of transportation that serve a metropolitan area.

A number of European cities have effectively connected their multimodal transportation networks into single transportation systems. A most memorable one is in Frankfurt, Germany, where a modern international airport is linked with the German railroad network and with the hub of that city's extensive urban transportation facilities.

In the United States, coordinating air, rail, bus, auto, subway, bicycle, and other modes of urban transit into regional metropolitan transportation systems is an important objective for transportation planners that has positive short-range, intermediate, and long-range implications.

SUMMARY ON URBAN TRANSPORTATION

In this chapter we have discussed the nature of transportation in urban environmental settings. We have briefly surveyed the development of the United States from a rural to an urban society and noted the decline in the importance of central cities and the growth of metropolitan areas.

Relationships between changes in urban structures and maturing urban transportation networks were identified. The emergency of the automobile as the dominant form of urban transportation was traced and some of the positive and negative implications of this reliance were isolated.

An argument favoring mass-transit alternatives for urban areas was presented. Certain public transportation problems were discussed and several proposals for mass-transit improvements were evaluated.

Finally, an outlook for urban transportation in the short, intermediate, and long time frames was offered. The importance of modal integration and effective long-term planning was acknowledged.

ADDITIONAL READINGS

ANDERSON, J. EDWARD, "PRT," *Environment*, XVI, no. 3 (1974), pp. 6-11.

Automobile Facts and Figures (Detroit: Motor Vehicle Manufacturers Association of the United States, Annual).

BAILEY, S. STUART and HARRY T. DIMITRION, "The Commuter and Park and Ride," *Traffic Quarterly*, XXVI, no. 3 (1973), pp. 561-573.

BERRY, DONALD S., PAUL W. SHULDINER, GEORGE W. BLOMME, and JOHN HUGH JONES, *The Technology of Urban Transportation* (Evanston, Illinois: Northwestern University Press, 1963).

Bicycles, U.S.A. Symposium jointly sponsored by U.S. Dept. of Transportation and U.S. Dept. of Interior (Cambridge: U.S. Dept. of Transportation Systems Center, 1973).

BUEL, RONALD A. *Dead End: The Automobile in Mass Transportation* (Englewood Cliffs, N.J.: Prentice-Hall, Inc., 1972).

CATANESE, ANTHONY J., ed., *New Perspectives in Urban Transportation Research* (Lexington, Massachusetts: Lexington Books, 1972).

DICHTER, ERNEST, *Handbook of Consumer Motivations* (New York: McGraw-Hill Book Company, 1964).

EVERETT, MICHAEL, "Commuter Demand for Bicycle Transportation in the United States," *Traffic Quarterly*, XXVIII, no. 4 (Oct. 1974), pp. 585-601.

FITCH, LYLE C. and ASSOCIATES, *Urban Transportation and Public Policy* (San Francisco: Chandler Publishing Co., 1964).

HIRST, ERIC, "Bicycles, Cars and Energy," *Traffic Quarterly*, XXVIII, no. 4, (Oct. 1974), pp. 373-384.

KILBRIDGE, MAURICE D., *Urban Analysis* (Boston: Division of Research, Graduate School of Business Administration, Harvard University, 1970).

LUNA, CHARLES, *The UTU Handbook of Transportation in America* (New York: The Popular Library, 1971).

MEYER, J. R., J. F. KAIN, and M. WOHL, *The Urban Transportation Problem* (Cambridge: Harvard University Press, 1965).

MEYERS, EDWARD T., "BART Battles Complex Problems," *Modern Railroads,* XXIX, no. 4 (1974), pp. 68-73.

PAGE, ALFRED N. and WARREN R. SIEGFRIED, eds., *Urban Analysis* (Glenview, Illinois: Scott, Foresman and Company, 1970).

PIGNATARO, LOUIS J., *Traffic Engineering* (Englewood Cliffs, N.J.: Prentice-Hall, Inc., 1973).

ROOS, DANIEL, "Doorstep Transit," *Environment*, XVI, no. 5 (1974), pp. 19-28.

RAE, JOHN B., "The Mythology of Urban Transportation," *Traffic Quarterly*, XXVI, no. 1 (1972), pp. 85-98.

SEGELHORST, ELBERT W., "Transit Validation for City Centers," *Journal of Transportation Economics and Policy*, vol. 1 (1971), pp. 1-12.

SCHNIDER, LEWIS M., *Marketing Urban Mass Transit* (Boston: Division of Research, Graduate School of Business Administration, Harvard University, 1965).

SLOANE, EUGENE A., *The Complete Book of Bicycling* (New York: Trident Press, 1970).

SMERK, GEORGE MARTIN, "Evaluation of Federal Effort in Mass Transportation," *Traffic Quarterly*, XXVI, no. 4 (Oct. 1971), pp. 501-516.

SMITH, ROBERT A., *A Social History of the Bicycle* (New York: American Heritage Press, 1972).

SOAST, ALLEN, "Opening the Transportation Bottleneck," *Engineering News Record,* CXCII, no. 18 (1974), pp. 219-231.

Transit Fact Book (Washington, D.C., American Public Transit Association, Annual).

ZWERLING, STEPHEN, *Mass Transit and the Politics of Technology: A Study of BART and the San Francisco Bay Area* (New York: Praeger Special Studies, Praeger Publishers, Inc., 1974).

7

PASSENGER TRANSPORTATION:
The Social Benefits
and The Social Costs

Traditionally, major business decisions have been based almost exclusively on comparisons of the relative economic benefits to be gained vis-a-vis the economic costs that must be incurred. Consequently, the social impact of various alternative courses of action have tended to be given little consideration. Social benefits were viewed as a kind of incidental residual gain while social costs generally were ignored.

SOCIAL COSTS AND SOCIAL BENEFITS OVERVIEW

Social costs include a broad range of direct and indirect *losses* incurred by third persons or to the public generally as a result of private economic activity. Examples of social losses are air, water, or noise pollution, damage to human health, debasement of property value, esthetic deterioration.

Social benefits may be defined as those direct and indirect *gains* realized by third persons or by the general public as a result of private economic activity. The economist sometimes calls these "externalities." The transportation network within the United States permits the rapid and relatively inexpensive movement of people and goods within and between geographic regions. These advantages are shared by all members of society in enhanced individual mobility and in lower prices for goods.

A Matter of Balance

Generally included in economic activities are social costs and social benefits as well as economic costs and economic benefits. A positive balance between these sets of costs and benefits is an objec-

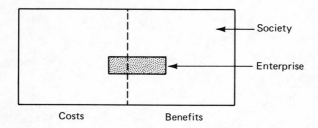

Figure 14.   Positive Cost and Benefit Balance: Society and Enterprise.

tive that is desirable for both enterprise and for the larger society. A conceptualization of this relationship is presented in Fig. 14. In this example, both society and enterprise receive a positive return of benefits for costs incurred.

It should be clear that it is also possible for private benefits to exceed private costs (that is, a firm operates at an economic profit) at the same time the costs to society of enterprise outweigh its benefits (that is, a firm causes a deterioration in drinking-water purity by dumping raw wastes into municipal water supplies). This situation is illustrated in Fig. 15. When imbalances of this nature occur over extended periods, social action to bring about a more equitable balance between private enterprise and society has historically taken place.

In the United States, relationships between the private and social effects of enterprise have become a major political and economic issue. Contemporary decision makers increasingly feel the pressure of organized consumer groups, environmentalists, community representatives, and the public at large to more fully account for and justify institutional action within a social context. This pressure has

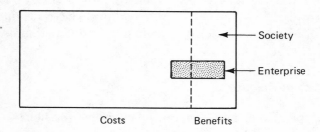

Figure 15.   Private Gain Social Loss.

taken the form of a new demand for business and businessmen to make concern for society central to the conduct of business itself.[1]

Social Costs and Economic Theory

Both classical and neoclassical economic theory tended to treat social costs as minor and exceptional disturbances.[2] Since private entrepreneurs were not easily held accountable for the harmful consequences of economic activity sustained by the community at large, social losses were considered external costs outside the realm of corporate accountability.

Accordingly, part of the cost of production was shifted to society. In other words, the responsibility of business generally was limited to the cost of land, labor, and capital, which were acknowledged as necessary inputs into the production process. Beyond these parameters of responsibility were the by-products of industrialization: pollution, poor land utilization, wasted natural resources, and unsafe, unhealthy, or exploitive working conditions. Many of these excluded factors, especially the atmosphere, water, and the waste-disposal capacity of land or water, were simply treated as "free goods" by entrepreneurs. As a result, society was compelled to assume part of the cost of enterprise.

In effect, therefore, the profitability of enterprise was computed without complete knowledge of the total costs involved. What was termed "profit" or "economic expansion" may merely have been the result of an unrecorded debit entry in some "invisible social ledger."[3]

The Railroads: an example of unrecorded social costs. Substantial social as well as economic subsidies were paid to railroad entrepreneurs to encourage rapid expansion of rights-of-way. Unlimited access to timber held by the government, gifts of land, and massive harvests of animal resources marked the initial phases of railroad de-

[1] Peter Drucker, ed., *Preparing Tomorrow's Business Leaders Today* (Englewood Cliffs, N.J.: Prentice-Hall, Inc., 1969), p. 77.

[2] An exception to the general classical and neoclassical treatment of social costs was the work of A. C. Pigou, in which he attempted to integrate social costs into the conceptual system of neoclassical equilibrium economics. See Arthur E. Pigou, *The Economics of Welfare* (London: Macmillan and Company, 1924).

[3] Hazel Henderson, "Toward Managing Social Conflict," *Harvard Business Review*, XLIX, no. 3 (1971), p.83.

velopment. Subsequently, open-immigration policies flooded the labor market and often forced workers to accept unsatisfactory conditions and low wages. At the same time, financial speculation and corporate manipulation by the railroads contributed to economic instability that affected every sector of society.

The total cost of constructing the railroad network of the United States should, therefore, be revised to include these substantial, but unrecorded, social costs, which directly or indirectly affected large segments of American society.

Opportunity Costs.   Opportunity costs are a major social cost of transportation. Wastes, diseconomies, and inefficiencies may be thought of as social opportunity losses brought about through excess competition.

It has been argued that transportation belongs outside the competitive calculus that provides the environmental backdrop for other U.S. industries.[4] Many countries of the world include transportation with other utilities classified as "natural monopolies" as part of the public ownership sector because: (1) Transportation requires heavy initial investments of capital and operates with high fixed-cost percentages. (2) Each transportation facility should be planned and operated as an integral of a larger national or international transportation system. (3) There is a predominantly social character to the benefits of most transportation facilities.[5]

In the United States, a mixed system of public and private transportation exists. This system has been characterized by a notable lack of integration and planning, which has diluted the potential efficiency of our transportation network. The increased costs associated with duplication of service and general diseconomies of operation are opportunity costs, which are spread throughout society in the form of higher prices and decreased personal mobility.

NOISE: A SOCIAL COST OF PASSENGER TRANSPORTATION

Transportation and transportation-related activities have been praised for providing services beneficial to virtually every segment of American society and condemned as polluters who debase the quality

---

[4] K. William Kapp, *The Social Cost of Private Enterprise* (Cambridge: Harvard University Press, 1950), pp. 197-206.

[5] Ibid., pp. 197-199.

of life throughout the United States. One example of this social benefit–social cost controversy is the noise generated by the operation of aircraft. This topic will be explored further as typical of the many transport-related social benefit-social cost trade-offs.

Airports: Social Benefits and Social Costs

A good deal of the noise problem is associated with airports. But airports have both positive and negative elements and in turn social benefits and social costs.

Social Benefits.   Although the public generally is inclined favorably toward air transportation, the air terminal itself is a point of controversy. In addition to the convenience of nearby air service, airports are acknowledged to have a significant positive impact on the economy of a community. For example, Los Angeles International Airport is the largest employer at a single location in Los Angeles County. Over 40,000 people are employed directly or indirectly by the LAX industry and another 61,000 secondary jobs are provided in services and trade. The annual payroll for all these employees is $1.4 billion.[6]

Another example of social benefits is the Honolulu International Airport. This airport is a major link between the islands and the mainland as well as the heart of the $1 billion Hawaiian tourism business. The economic impact of the airlines operating through Honolulu International during the 1972-1973 fiscal year was $238 million. Tax benefits derived from airport operations exceeded $44 million, and state and municipal tax revenues generated from tourism totaled $161 million.[7]

Further examples of the economic impact of airports are in the following data collected by Professor Lynagh on employment and payroll: New York-New Jersey—77,800 employed, $1 billion payroll; San Francisco International—23,000 employed, $400 million annual payroll; and Atlanta Airport—17,546 employed, $209 million payroll.[8]

[6] "LAX Industry Has Major Impact on Southern California Economy," *The Newsletter, Los Angeles Department of Airports,* February 1972, p. 1.

[7] "The Airport and You," *Honolulu Airlines Committee* in Cooperation with the Air Transportation Association of America, 1973.

[8] Peter M. Lynagh, "The Airport and the Environment," *High Speed Ground Transportation Journal* (Spring 1973), p. 56.

Social Costs.   There are two major social costs associated with airport operation: air pollution and noise pollution. Of the two, noise pollution tends to be regarded as the more serious problem. The Environmental Protection Agency estimates that perhaps 40 million people in the United States are exposed to sound levels potentially damaging to hearing or that could otherwise affect their health. Excessive noise may contribute to heart disease, ulcers, mental illness, nausea, headaches, sexual impotence, and general anxiety.[9]

The standard measure of sound is the decibel (dB), which is a logarithmic scale reflecting absolute sound pressure. The quiet of a library has been measured at about 35 decibels. An alarm clock may reach 80 decibels and the interior of a discoteque 117. The threshold of human pain is between 112 and 120 dB and exposure to noise over 140 dB can produce permanent hearing loss.[10]

Urban sound levels range from 40 dB in the early morning to 88 dB in the noisiest part of the day. In the contour surrounding the 20 major airports in the United States, the sound level averages 88 dB. In its landing approach, a 747 generates about 113 dB. It is expected that unless checked, aircraft will become the most pervasive and disturbing source of urban noise.[11]

Noise Reduction

Many programs and devices designed to reduce noise are available. All are expensive and some are controversial.

The Legal Issue.   If a person is damaged because of noise, who is legally responsible? The legal-liability issue is a most difficult one and something over which the courts have long pondered.[12] Suppose a person's property, say his home, becomes less valuable due to increases in noise at an adjacent airport: Who compensates the homeowner? Further, if the airport or the airline is liable, at what point geographically does this liability end? Property directly in a

[9]Marvin Zeldin, "Don't Shout About It, But a New Law May Lower the Decibel Din," *Audubon* (May 1973), pp. 104-105.

[10]Ibid., p. 103.

[11]Melville C. Branch, Jr., "Outdoor Noise, Transportation, and City Planning," *Traffic Quarterly*, XXVII, no. 2 (1973), pp. 169-176.

[12]John French, III, "Public Liability for Motor Vehicle Noise," *High Speed Ground Transportation Journal* (Spring 1973), pp. 1-16. Contains an excellent review of cases relative to both highway and airport noise.

guidepath into an airport may have a good case, but what of property some distance from the airport approaches? None of these questions can be easily answered but all of them are examples of what one well-known author has called "The Dilemma of Aircraft Noise."[13]

The Noise Control Act of 1972.   The Environmental Protection Agency has been given broad authority under the Noise Control Act to establish noise limits for new motors, engines, and other transportation equipment. After developing noise standards, the EPA then must suggest regulations governing airport noise to the Federal Aviation Administration for approval. Noise-emission standards relating to interstate railroads, trucks, and buses may be made only after consultation with the Department of Transportation.

Upon enactment and approval of noise regulations, enforcement powers will be vested with the Environmental Protection Agency. Under provisions of the Noise Control Act, private citizens will also have the right to bring action against any violator of federal noise control standards, including the Federal Government. Further, citizens may file suit against the EPA or against the FAA if these agencies fail to carry out provisions of the Act.

Noise Reduction Programs.   Noise from jet aircraft is being reduced slowly and in small increments. The problem is a complex one involving not only the matter of reducing sound but also of lowering sound pressure levels. Noise reduction efforts are proceeding along two basic lines: reducing noise at its source (i.e., quieter aircraft) and by using flight procedures that keep aircraft higher and, therefore, quieter.

Progress has been made in reducing noise at the source through a new generation of more powerful, quieter engines. The wide-bodied aircraft (747, DC-10, and L-1011) feature new high bypass ratio engines that are two and one-half times more powerful than those on earlier 707s and DC-8s, but are significantly quieter. Figure 16 illustrates the reduction of sound pressure levels, in decibels, emitted by this generation of wide-bodied aircraft during landing approaches. The older jet aircraft (707, DC-8, 727, etc.) may be made quieter. The cost of noise attenuation hardware is estimated at $500,000 per aircraft. Retrofitting the entire United States fleet would cost over one billion dollars.

Carriers have also altered flight procedures to reduce aircraft

[13] Donald V. Harper, "The Dilemma of Aircraft Noise at Major Airports," *Transportation Journal* (Spring 1971), pp. 5-28.

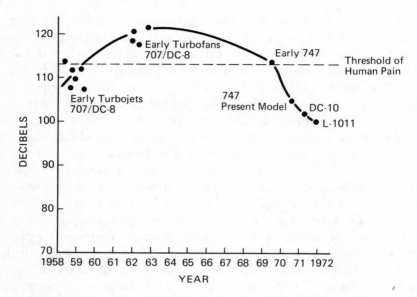

Figure 16.   Sound Pressure Levels of Various Jet Aircraft During Landing Approach. (Source: Air Transport, 1974. *Annual Report of the United States Scheduled Airline Industry (Washington, D.C.: Air Transportation Association of America, 1974), p. 13.)*

noise. Takeoff and landing methods designed to reduce low altitude flying over residential areas surrounding air terminals have been developed within Federal Aviation Administration Guidelines. On take-off, more power is used to get the aircraft higher as soon as possible. Figure 17 illustrates a jet takeoff procedure which minimizes noise.

On landing approaches a two-segment method is used to keep the aircraft at higher elevations longer. Figure 18 illustrates a landing procedure designed to minimize noise in the residential contours surrounding airports.

Even with these improvements in aircraft noise levels, this social cost of air service remains a matter of great concern for urban planners and city dwellers throughout the United States.

Airport Noise Reduction Programs: The Orange County case. The Orange County Airport is located in the high-income residential coast area of Orange County, California, about 40 miles south of Los Angeles. The county Department of Airports has been among the leaders in the United States in reducing its aircraft-noise impact areas.

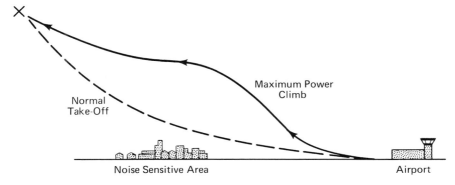

Figure 17.   Noise-Reducing Jet Takeoff Procedure.

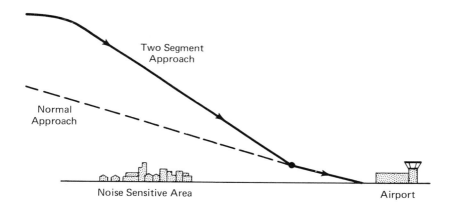

Figure 18.   Noise-Reducing Jet Landing Procedure.

The county has approved a 15-point master plan for noise abatement, which could become a model for similar programs at other airports. The 15 points include:[14]

Extension of the main runway by 750 feet to the north, so take-offs will begin further away from populated areas.

Changing landing and takeoff angle from 3 to 6 degrees.

Moving back landing curfew from 11 P.M. to 10 P.M.

Making it mandatory instead of voluntary for pilots to cut power at an altitude of 1000 feet.

[14]Orange County Master Plan of Noise Abatement.

Installation of sound-reducing kits on all jet engines of scheduled carriers at time of overhaul.

Licensing of all jet operators, with fees based on the level of noise created.

Regulating the schedules of carriers to prevent takeoffs and landings of aircraft in rapid succession.

Investigating means to convert land in the airport impact area from residential to industrial or other airport-compatible use.

The Orange County experience leans heavily on planning and is concerned primarily with operating procedures. As such, it is an interesting experiment in one area's attempt to come to grips with the social cost of noise.

Other approaches: Airport design, landscaping, zoning.   An approach with a somewhat longer time horizon concerns the initial design of the airport. Noise abatement can be readily designed into the airport plan when a new airport is constructed and sometimes when existing airports are expanded. Dulles International Airport in Washington and the Dallas-Fort Worth Regional Airports are two examples of facilities where noise considerations were one of the parameters in the original design. Both are larger in size than the typical airport (Dallas-Fort Worth is on 17,500 acres and the land area of Dulles is 15 square miles) and both have the resulting disadvantage of being at a considerable distance from the central business district.

In some instances, proper landscaping can assist in noise abatement. Over 1.5 million trees and shrubs were used to landscape Dulles Airport and cut down on noise pollution. Proper zoning is another approach and can be applied to existing airports as well as to future ones. The uses of land adjacent to the airport can be restricted by noise-sensitive zoning ordinances.

Existing airports may find it necessary to buy up property, not only because of expansion but also to minimize noise-pollution problems. Once more, a cost to the city (and society) is involved. Social costs in the form of displacement of householders, schools, and disruption of neighborhoods are involved. The decision once again must turn on balancing economic costs and social costs against economic benefits and social benefits.

(handwritten margin note: NO, NOISE IS REDUCED ONLY BY MASS.)

SOCIAL RESPONSIBILITY:
MEASUREMENT AND IMPLEMENTATION

It is clear that societal concern has become an increasingly important dimension of transportation decision making. Although acknowledged as significant, little data relating to the measurement of social performance (that is, the balance between the social benefits and the social costs of enterprise) are available. This is partly a reflection of the propensity of decision makers to treat the economic and social dimensions of their firms' operations as distinct and individual phenomena, assuming each has characteristics that are separate and only internally consistent. Further, an adequate system of accountability has been developed only for the economic aspects of operations. Because social accountability is an area of great subjectivity, few meaningful attempts to measure performance have been made.

Social benefits are also difficult to measure. It has been argued that actions taken by a business that in some degree help society achieve one or more of its objectives are socially responsible actions.[15] Unfortunately, many difficult questions arise when one applies this definition to the actions of passenger transportation carriers. First, what are the objectives of this society, or of any society, for that matter? Few societal objectives are clearly and precisely stated. Second, because our pluralistic society reflects divergence of views, many conflicting objectives are held by subsocietal groups. Which of these are to be given national priority? For example, during periods of severe energy shortages, are the objectives of society best met by firms stressing pollution reduction at the expense of increased fuel consumption, or by firms giving fuel economy top priority?

Under these conditions, it would seem that if firms are truly to be held socially responsible for their actions, it will be necessary for industry and society to agree on a system that would more precisely measure the social benefit–social cost ratios of corporate decisions. In short, what is needed is a system of social accounting that would parallel normal economic accounting procedures and be applicable to transportation carriers.

[15] George Steiner, "Social Policies for Business," *California Management Review,* XIV, no. 4 (1972), p. 19.

Measuring Social Performance

In the difficult area of measuring social performance, two relatively new devices are helpful. These are the social audit and social accounting.

The Social Audit. A major step toward the measurement of social performance is a controversial new concept termed the "social audit." Here the sectors of the social environment affected by transport activities would be identified and the impact of such action estimated.

Until recently, carrier management has had little incentive to report or even catalogue the social impact of its actions. Data relating to the social responsibility of firms were not generally regarded as relevant. Further, there would have been little motivation for executives to act on such information had it been available, since managerial performance generally is evaluated only on the basis of economic criteria.

As previously mentioned, current events have caused the attention of carrier management to focus on the need for data relating to social performance. It has been recognized that if carriers do not voluntarily move toward programs of social accountability, governmental action will impose such programs on them. In fact, such pressure has prompted some of the largest American corporations to seek measures of social performance.

An approach that could be used to obtain such information involves several steps. First, potential social-impact areas would be isolated and defined. Included here would be noise pollution, air pollution, land usage, energy consumption, employment policies, community service, and a variety of other categories. Second, an inventory of all carrier activities that have an impact in these social areas would be taken. Third, the circumstances surrounding these activities would be investigated and the rationale explored. Fourth, an informal evaluation of the acts, the rationale, and the social impact would be undertaken to estimate degrees of social responsibility. Finally, carrier management would assess the coordination of activities, stressing the interrelationships between the objectives of the firm and the well-being of society. These steps could be the foundation for a social audit. Evolving from a social audit would be sets of criteria that could be used to measure the social performance of a passenger transportation carrier.

Social Accounting: a macroeconomic approach.   A measure of the social performance of the economy as a whole has been proposed in the ninth edition of Nobel prize winner Paul Samuelson's classic introductory economics text.[16] Samuelson presents a quality-of-life indicator termed "net economic welfare" (NEW) as an alternative to the economically oriented gross national product (GNP) measure of national output. NEW corrects GNP by establishing value for leisure time, for household work, for pollution and its abatements, for commuting costs, for the "disamenities" of urban life, and for many other generally unmeasured social benefits and social costs of business enterprise. Growth of net economic welfare may be at the expense of the gross national product. The trade-off may be a lessening of the quantity of goods produced if an improvement in the quality of life is to be achieved.

In summary, it may be concluded that measures of social performance are rapidly becoming available. At the level of individual carriers, the transportation industry, or the national economy as a whole, social audits and broad systems of social accounting are emerging to provide a standard for the valuation of productivity in a social as well as in an economic context.

Social Responsibility Implementation

Two facets of social responsibility are involved in implementation: executive involvement and transportation legislation.

Executive Involvement.   Real changes in carrier performance, however measurable, will be accomplished only as a result of the actions of individual executives. In the areas of policy making and policy implementation, a requisite for social accountability is a formal acknowledgment of carrier commitment by key executives. This in itself has many positive dimensions of social value. Next, these executives must provide the leadership and guidance in developing positive plans for improving social performance, just as they do for improving performance in their economic ventures. In addition, there must be a systematic assessment of the present position of carriers with respect to the social impact of their previous activities. Has a carrier, for example, behaved in a socially responsible manner in years past? If not, programs to reverse the trend should be established.

[16]Paul A. Samuelson, *Economics: An Introductory Analysis,* 9th ed (New York: McGraw-Hill Book Company, Inc., 1973).

It is important to recognize that guidelines, measurement techniques, and control mechanisms that are established for a passenger transportation carrier must have parameters that apply to all carriers. Legislation in this area should be inclusive.

A systematic approach should be adopted for use in assessments of the ongoing operation to determine its probable future social impact. Substantially higher standards of social performance will quite likely be in effect during future years. In fact, the next decade may require the same degree of managerial creativity and dedication that were used to build America's vast corporate empires—for these same empires need to be directed toward an effective adaptation to the changing needs and demands of society. The survival of many of the freedoms so cherished by businessmen may well depend on their responses to these challenges.

Passenger Transportation Legislation.   The needs and demands of society have been interwoven with the functioning of passenger transportation carriers by the comprehensive regulatory system that influences most aspects of carrier operations. In Chap. 4, we noted that rates, market entry and exit, service, safety, ownership patterns, and many physical aspects of carrier operation are regulated by agencies representing all governmental levels.

The regulatory statutes affecting passenger transportation are heterogeneous and complex even though they share two basic objectives: (1) the protection of the public, and (2) the promotion of the best possible system of passenger transportation. In the implementation of the regulatory system, many basic conflicts between the needs of society and the economic requirements of carriers take place. The resolution of these conflicts has traditionally been accomplished through compromises and trade-offs between the countervailing forces involved in specific issues. Because of the close relationship between regulatory bodies and regulated industries, these accommodations have not always adequately considered the public interest. Many consider the result of almost 90 years of transportation regulation to be carrier inefficiency supported by distorted rate schedules. While the exact degree of inefficiency is hard to measure and is controversial, the result does seem to be that the two basic goals of regulation have not been accomplished: The public has not been completely protected, and the best possible system of passenger transportation has not been attained.

SUMMARY ON SOCIAL BENEFITS AND SOCIAL COSTS

In the past, there has been an almost total reliance on economic data as the basis for evaluating carrier performance. Even though social goals may have been outlined, only economic performance was measured. As a result, the criterion of dollar profitability has guided management action and little formal consideration has been given to actions that affect the public generally.

However, recent pressure from many groups has drawn the attention of carrier management, and businessmen generally, away from their preoccupation with economic issues and toward a broader social perspective. It is becoming apparent that firms are going to be held socially accountable and, as a result, the definition and measurement of the social performance of all passenger transportation carriers has become an important management concern.

ADDITIONAL READINGS

ANDERSON, THOMAS W. and WILLIAM CUNNINGHAM, "The Socially Conscious Consumer," *The Journal of Marketing*, XXXVI, no. 3 (1972), pp. 23-31.

BACON, K. H. and A. R. KARR, "The Regulators: Commissions Draw Increasing Fire, Called Inept and Costly," *The Wall Street Journal*, October 9, 1974, pp. 1, 25.

BRANCH, MELVILLE C., JR., "Outdoor Noise, Transportation, and City Planning," *Traffic Quarterly*, XXVII, no. 2 (1973), pp. 167-188.

CHANDLER, ALFRED D., *The Railroads* (New York: Harcourt, Brace, and World, Inc., 1965).

DAVIS, KEITH and ROBERT L. BLOMSTROM, *Business, Society, and Environment* (New York: McGraw-Hill Book Company, 1972).

DRUCKER, PETER F., "Business and the Quality of Life," *Sales Management*, CII, no. 3 (1969), pp.31-35.

DRUCKER, PETER, ed., *Preparing Tomorrow's Business Leaders Today* (Englewood Cliffs, N.J.: Prentice-Hall, Inc., 1969).

FRENCH, JOHN, III, "Public Liability for Motor Vehicle Noise," *High Speed Ground Transportation Journal*, VII (Spring 1973), pp. 1-16.

GAPAY, LES, "The Regulators: Agencies and Industries Show Persistent Signs of Cozy Relationships," *The Wall Street Journal*, November 1, 1974, pp. 1, 19.

HARPER, DONALD V., "The Dilemma of Aircraft Noise at Major Airports," *Transportation Journal*, X, no. 3 (1971), pp. 5-28.

HARDING, FORREST E. and RICHARD SPILLER eds., *Marketing Planning and Environmental Preservation*. Proceedings of the 1973 Southwest Marketing Educators Conference (Long Beach, California: Bureau of Business Services and Research, School of Business Administration, California State University, Long Beach, 1974).

HENDERSON, HAZEL, "Toward Managing Social Conflict," *Harvard Business Review*, XLIX, no. 3 (1971).

KAPP, WILLIAM K., *The Social Cost of Private Enterprise* (Cambridge: Harvard University Press, 1950).

KINNEAR, THOMAS C., JAMES R. TAYLOR, and SADRUDIN A. AHMED,"Ecologically Concerned Consumers: Who Are They?" *The Journal of Marketing*, XXXVIII, no. 2 (1974), pp. 20-24.

LAZER, WILLIAM and EUGENE J. KELLEY, eds., *Social Marketing* (Homewood, Illinois: Richard D. Irwin, 1973).

LIPSON, HARRY A., EUGENE J. KELLEY, and SEYMOUR MARSHAK, "Integrating Social Feedback and Social Audits into Corporate Planning," in *Social Marketing*, William Lazer and Eugene Kelley, eds. (Homewood, Illinois: Richard D. Irwin, 1973), pp. 174-191.

LYNAGH, PETER M., "The Airport and the Environment," *High Speed Ground Transportation Journal*, VII (Spring 1973), pp. 53-67.

MARSHALL, HOWARD D., *The Great Economists: A History of Economic Thought* (New York: Pitman Publishing Corporation, 1967).

National Bureau of Standards, Reports to the Environmental Protection Agency, *The Economic Impact of Noise*. NTID 300.14 (Washington, D.C.: Government Printing Office, 1971).

PIGOU, ARTHUR E., *The Economics of Welfare* (London: Macmillan and Company, 1924).

SAMUELSON, PAUL A., *Economics: An Introductory Analysis* (New York: McGraw-Hill Book Company, Inc., 1973).

SMERK, GEORGE M., "The Environment and Transportation," *Transportation Journal*, XII, no. 1, (Fall 1972), pp. 40-49.

STEINER, GEORGE, "Social Policies for Business," *California Management Review*, XIV, no. 4 (1972), pp. 15-22.

"The Expensive Sounds of Silence," *Business Week*, July 20, 1974, p. 28.

"The First Attempts at a Corporate Social Audit," *Business Week*, September 23, 1972, pp. 88-92.

U.S. Department of Commerce, *The Noise Around Us* (Washington, D.C.: Government Printing Office, 1970).

WEBBER, MELVIN M., "Societal Contexts of Transportation and Communication," Working Paper No. 220, Institute of Urban and Regional Development, University of California, Berkeley, November, 1973.

8

POLICY
PROBLEMS

It is probable that there is no area of discussion in this book that does not have policy implications and considerations. Policy problems are inherent in the very idea of systems, for there is always difficulty in integrating various components so that a total passenger transportation system emerges. But more specifically, each of the four component systems (physical, economic, pricing, and regulatory) has its inherent policy problems. Also very much evident are the policy implications and considerations arising from the prior discussion of the "problem" area of passenger transportation: marketing problems, urban transportation problems, and social benefits versus social cost problems. All in some way involve policy and recommend changes.

One might then ask, what is policy? While definitions vary, it is possible to think of policy at two levels in passenger transportation. First, policy may be thought of as specific goals and objectives dealing with operational patterns. Examples of specific policy might be the airline policy of reimbursing passengers up to a predetermined sum when tickets are oversold, or, the policy of overhauling the engine on an intercity bus every 100,000 miles, or, the policy of attaining 95 percent on-time performance in rail-commuter service between Long Island points and lower Manhattan. Any number of operational policies could be cited as examples of this level of approach.

A second level of approach is to consider general goals and objectives dealing with overall systems and concepts. Examples might be (1) a national policy to create the most reliable passenger transportation system at the least possible overall cost (both social and economic cost considered), (2) a metropolitan policy to create a passenger transportation system adequate for the needs of 1990, or

(3) a social policy to sustain a carefully balanced passenger transportation system that would give maximum choice to consumers while assuring the economic health of the carriers.

It is apparent that these examples of both specific and general policy are not mutually exclusive. Rather they blend into one another, and indeed, one may implement or supplement the other. It is also readily apparent that many of the operational policy problems are really managerial. As such, they will shift and change as new forces and events crop up that apply to the passenger transportation system. These policy considerations may also be technical and therefore there may be limitations to the choices that can be made at any one time due to the state of the art as well as mechanical and engineering factors.

Our concern here will be with the general level of policy considerations noted above. In a real sense, this will be "social," or overall, in that we will be discussing what society might do, acting through government as well as the marketplace, to improve the passenger transportation system. This is more in the way of an "approach" than a specific policy formulation. It would be presumptuous for us to dictate specifics of a passenger transportation system. However, it is quite permissible for us to suggest an "approach" or a way of looking at passenger transportation policy. Accordingly, we restate our policy problem as a question: "How can society approach problems arising from passenger transportation in such a way as to ensure an economical and adequate system of transporting people now and in the future?"

To answer this question, one needs to consider carefully how society presently or currently approaches passenger transportation, and then consider how society might approach passenger transportation in the future.

CURRENT POLICY APPROACH

In order to analyze and discuss the current policy approach in our nation, one must clearly identify national transportation policy as a first step.

Identification of Policy

The task of identifying national transportation policy is not as easy as it might first appear. First, there is no single statement of policy or national goals in relation to the total transportation system. One wishes, at times, that it were possible to refer to the national transportation policy for guidance, but no such exercise can be undertaken for no such policy exists. Second, there is no one group or agency charged with creating or setting policy. When the Department of Transportation was created in 1966, it was hoped that this agency might act as a policy-coordinating and recommending body. However, many levels of government are involved in policy determination. A number of states have created departments of transportation. Likewise, numerous committees or agencies at the local governmental level are charged with transportation policy considerations. Conflicting goals and policies are almost inherent in such a multiple-level system. Third, the interrelationship of freight and passenger service obscures the clear effect of actions or policies pertaining to either of the two services. A policy decision to improve freight transportation, say by reorganizing the Northeast railroads, will have a considerable effect on passenger transportation even though that is far from the intended result. Finally, there is a lack of a reliable means of communicating preferences. Governmental action is only one way in which policy and goals are established, and this approach is inexact at best. There is no good system for holding a referendum on various aspects of transportation policy. Even if a vote could be taken, it is really the actions of millions of individuals in their exercise of transportation choice that set the goals or policy involved. In some instances, referendums have been held only to reveal that the collective actions of interested users apparently do not follow the political sentiments of the votes cast.

In spite of the existence of these four hurdles to identifying policy (the lack of a single statement, multilevel systems of government and inherent conflicts, the interrelationship of freight and passenger service, lack of means of communicating preference), there are three types or bases of national policy that can be identified: statutory policy, informal policy, and consumer action.

Statutory Policy

In theory, Congress or the legislative branch establishes national transportation policy, the executive branch administers policy (including enforcement), and the judiciary interprets what is meant by the statutes as well as protecting the rights of individuals and other groups as enunciated by the Constitution. The same general framework is found for the states as the federal government and, with some modifications, for local governments as well. In theory, then, some statutory statement or declaration should exist that reflects the policy judgments of Congress, the state legislatures, and the duly elected local governing body. This policy ideally gives guidance to the executive and provides a basis for judicial interpretation, when it is necessary.

In actual practice, the statutory provisions that do exist are usually vague, often inconsistent and poorly defined, and sometimes out of date and applying to a prior age. At best they provide minimal policy guidance. At the national level, the most definitive statement of national transportation policy is found in the preamble of the Transportation Act of 1940. Here Congress stated:

> It is hereby declared to be the national transportation policy of the Congress to provide for fair and impartial regulation of all modes of transportation subject to the provisions of the Act, so administered as to recognize and preserve the inherent advantages of each; to promote safe, adequate, economical and efficient service and foster sound economic conditions in transportation and among the several carriers; to encourage the establishment and maintenance of reasonable charges for transportation service, without unjust discrimination, undue preferences, or advantages, or unfair or destructive competitive practices; to cooperate with the several States, and the duly authorized officials thereof; and to encourage fair wages, and equitable working conditions—all to the end of developing, coordinating, and preserving a national transportation system by water, highway, and rail as well as other means, adequate to meet the needs of the commerce of the United States, of the Postal Service, and, of the national defense. All of the provisions of this Act shall be administered and enforced with a view to carrying out the above declaration of policy.[1]

To its considerable credit, it should be noted that this declaration recognizes transportation *as a system* based on several modes, each of which has an *inherent advantage* of some role that it performs best.

[1] 54 *Stat.* 899 (1940).

The problem of interrelationship of freight and passenger service is apparent here. While in no place do the terms "passenger" or "freight" appear, it is apparent that the subject of this declaration is really freight transportation. It should be noted that air transportation, of primary importance to passenger service, is not directly included. Indeed, a separate declaration of policy for air transportation was drawn up by Congress a few years earlier. Likewise, the declaration obviously applies principally to for-hire transportation to the complete exclusion of private transportation. (The predominance of the private automobile in passenger transportation has been well established earlier in this book.) Additionally, since international transportation tends to be thought of as part of foreign relations, the declaration deals exclusively with domestic transportation to the exclusion of maritime and international air policy. Finally, the statement itself has been criticized on numerous occasions for its inconsistency, lack of clear meaning and definition, and difficulty of application.[2]

In spite of all these conflicts, omissions, and difficulties, the statutory declaration of national transportation policy by Congress and similar statutory statements by legislatures, city councils and the like, do provide a beginning for policy determination and sometimes importantly provide an overall philosophy of policy enactment.

Informal Policy

Action speaks louder than words and by examining what legislative groups have actually done in the past, it is possible to ascertain a type of informal transportation policy. Even though informal policy is less specific than statutory policy, it may actually be a broader and more comprehensive guide to the national passenger transportation policy than statutory declaration. By considering congressional practice and repetition of ideas and concepts in various actions at other level of government, it is possible to summarize informal policy into four groups or concepts: ownership patterns, investment concepts, modal orientation, and preference for choice.

---

[2] Martin T. Farris, "Definitional Inconsistencies in National Transportation Policy," *I.C.C. Practitioners' Journal* (Nov.-Dec. 1967), pp. 25-33; Martin T. Farris, "National Transportation Policy—Fact or Fiction?" *Quarterly Review of Economics and Business* (Summer 1970), pp. 7-14; John J. Coyle, "The Compatibility of the Rule of Rate-Making and the National Transportation Policy," *I.C.C. Practitioners' Journal* (March-April 1971), pp. 340-353.

Ownership Patterns.   It is apparent from our discussion in Chap. 2, Physical and Economic Systems, plus our analysis to this point, that the ownership pattern is a mixed one with a preference for public ways and private means. Some ways are privately owned (such as railways), but the vast majority are publicly provided. Some terminals are privately owned (such as rails and intercity bus), but the majority are publicly provided. Almost always the means of transportation (vehicle and carriers) are privately owned, although local transit and Amtrak provide exceptions. Social action by various levels of government not only established this preference for public ways and private means but has reinforced it over a period of time. Certainly one could conclude that the informal passenger transportation policy of the United States is built on the foundation idea that, where possible, the most desirable arrangement is private ownership of the means of transportation, public ownership of the ways and terminals.

Investment Concepts.   The foundation concept of public ways and private means is reinforced with the investment concept. However, once more the picture is a mixed one. All modes of passenger transportation have received public aid and support. The timing of this aid and support, however, has varied. It has been common for one mode of passenger transportation to receive public aid and support while a competitive mode does not receive the same support at the same time.

Further, public aid and support has more often than not been involved basically in providing the way. Thus, the public has been involved with supporting the development and provision of railways, highways and streets, airways, waterways and harbors, and urban mass-transit systems. This follows, of course, from the policy of public ways and private means.

Additionally, the extent of public aid and support has varied. In some instances (rail and highways, for example) it has mainly involved provision of the way; in other instances (airways, waterway-seaways, and mass transit) it has also included operation of the ways and provision of terminal. In some cases, such as with local-service airlines and mass-transit systems, subsidies to private firms have been involved.

Finally, reimbursement or repayment plans have varied with some, such as railroads reimbursing over time via reduced charges;

others, such as highways and airways, having user charges and trust funds; and still others, such as waterways-seaways and urban systems, not reimbursing at all.

Certainly, one could conclude that the nation's informal passenger transportation policy is based on public aid and support with a mixed pattern on timing, tendency to prefer aid for purposes of ways, a mixed pattern on extent, and a mixed pattern on reimbursement.

Modal Orientation.   In addition to ownership patterns and investment concepts, informal policy has certainly been modally oriented. Practically all public agencies created have been modal in approach. Hence, the Bureau of Public Roads, now under the Federal Highway Administration as part of the Department of Transportation, the Federal Aviation Administration (also part of DOT), the Office of High Speed Ground Transportation, now under the Federal Railroad Administration in DOT, and the Urban Mass Transportation Administration are concerned with highway transportation, air transportation, rail transportation, and urban transportation to the exclusion of the other means or modes. The same pattern has been repeated at the state level with a state highway department, a state department of aeronautics, and so forth.

This modal orientation has extended, at the federal level, to the point that such overall concepts as transportation safety are approached by mode. For example, in the Department of Transportation, the separate organizations of the National Highway Safety Administration, the National Traffic Safety Bureau, and the Bureau of Motor Carrier Safety (both part of the Federal Highway Administration), the Bureau of Railroad Safety (part of the Federal Railroad Administration), and the Bureau of Aviation Safety under the National Transportation Safety Board (a separate agency) are all concerned with safety. By considering an organizational chart, one would assume that no safety work done on highway or airway safety has any applicability to traffic safety or rail safety.[3]

But even on a broader issue, the modal orientation prevails. Congress acts on a separate highway bill, considers improvement of airways and airports, annually debates a rivers and harbors appropria-

[3] Grant M. Davis and Martin T. Farris, "Federal Transportation Safety Programs—Misdirected Emphasis and Wasted Resources, *Transportation Journal* (Summer 1972). pp. 5-17.

tion, on an emergency basis decides what to do about railway labor or the failing railroads of the Northeast, and establishes a massive program for mass-transit capital and operating grants, each independently considered. One would never guess that what takes place in the area of highways might somehow affect urban transportation, the airlines, or the railroads. The tendency to "modal thinking" about transportation prevails.

This preference for modal orientation may well reflect the national tendency to be "problem-oriented" or "results-oriented." Each area of concern is a crisis demanding immediate attention and an immediate solution. Once solved, it can be forgotten and new crises and problems attacked. The difficulty here is that some "crises" do not go away and are not solved by a specific legislative act or by the creation of a bureau or another agency. Further, the solution of one crisis may well create additional crises in other areas. Irrespective of these national propensities, it certainly can be concluded that the informal national passenger transportation policy has a marked tendency to be modally oriented.

Preference for Choice.   The final basis of informal passenger transportation policy is the informal desire to preserve the widest possible choice among our citizens relative to passenger transportation. Any action that would tend to limit consumer choice to one or two alternatives is avoided as being undesirable. The problem of urban congestion might logically call for the construction of a mass-transit system and bikeways to the exclusion of private automobile traffic during certain times and in certain places. This will be opposed on the basis that consumers should not be tied to a single means of passenger transportation but should be able to drive their own cars when they wish. The logic of resource use might dictate that air transportation should be exclusively used for intercity travel on distances over 500 miles. Yet this will be resisted and Amtrak will be publicly supported on the basis that consumer choice must always be available. The preference for the widest possible choice may lead to considerable duplication of facilities in local transit, in air transportation, highway transportation, and so forth, but it is also considered one of the costs that an affluent society is willing to pay. Irrespective of the rationale of such an approach, it is possible to conclude that preference for choice is one of the four bases of informal passenger transportation policy in the U.S.

Consumer Action

In addition to statutory policy and informal policy, the idea of reacting to the consumer seems to be an integral part of our national passenger transportation policy. That is to say, policy is determined not only by legislative declaration and collective legislative or governmental actions, but also by the populace itself in its own actions. By the way in which the user of passenger transportation acts and operates, passenger transportation policy is established.

While generalizations are difficult and many examples of consumer action could be cited, the three examples of convenience orientation, noneconomic behavior, and the individualistic approach will illustrate this type of policy.

Convenience Orientation.   As developed in Chap. 2, the consumer wants the convenience of the private automobile. He wants to have his own means of transportation available to go where he pleases and when. Further, he demands and expects highways and streets to be available to make it possible for him to go wherever his desire for convenience dictates. Designers of highways and streets are always especially cognizant of this strong desire for convenience—it becomes a "policy" within which they must operate.

As discussed under the regulation of entry and service in Chap. 4, the consumer also desires for-hire choices of passenger transportation to suit his convenience. The consumer wishes to have airline departures and arrivals available at a convenient time, surface transportation available to speedily and immediately whisk him to his ultimate destination, and airports available without a long drive or ride. Moreover, the consumer desires a choice between several for-hire carriers all competing to suit his convenience as noted above in informal policy.

As discussed under instantaneous demand, variability of demand, elasticities, and cyclical relationships in Chap. 3, if this desire for convenience is not served, it will shift elsewhere and when it is served, it causes many peak-service problems with resultant overinvestment and unused capacity on the part of carriers. Once more the orientation toward convenience is a policy factor, even though unmeasurable, which must be recognized by public or for-hire transportation executives alike.

Not only does this desire for convenience exist, but it demands

actions and reactions. The list of people and groups actively respond-
ing to this desire for convenience includes public planners, legislators,
bureaucrats, private operators, taxpayers, and others. The types of
actions and reactions are manifold but irrespective of the examples
that could be cited, the desire for convenience in passenger transportation is a consumer action that in effect establishes "policy."

Noneconomic Behavior.   In addition to helping set a policy of
catering to his convenience, the consumer is apparently quite willing
to pay for it. Payment here takes the form of fares, taxes (both
direct and indirect), operating bills such as gasoline and oil, and private investment (such as private automobiles). Payment itself is not
an example of noneconomic behavior, but when it takes place without comparisons or in spite of the existence of cheaper alternatives,
we can say it is noneconomic behavior.

As we have noted repeatedly, the cost per mile of private automobile operation is 15.8¢, whereas the fare per mile on for-hire
transportation modes are only a half to a third as much. In spite of
this, the consumer is willing to pay the added cost for the sake of his
convenience, perhaps because of his "love affair" with the private
automobile, as we have noted. Perhaps the consumer is willing to act
noneconomically because he makes his operating payments in small
and frequent purchases and his investments in capital either only
once every few years or spread out in small, "easy," monthly payments. These factors were suggested in an earlier chapter as reasons
for some noneconomic actions. Perhaps the consumer is willing to act
noneconomically because the purchase and use of a private automobile is more than a transportation expenditure and is an extension of
his personality or an expression of his ego. But regardless of the
reasons, the fact is that typically no cost comparisons are made and
we can call this noneconomic behavior a "policy" factor in that all
concerned must recognize this propensity when considering passenger
transportation.

Individualistic Approach.   Finally, it must be recognized that
consumer action is based on individualism. Obviously, convenience
orientation and the noneconomic behavior noted above are manifestations of individualism. But more than this, consumer action is
typically viewed in isolation with complete disregard for the problem
of aggregation.

As we noted in Chap. 6 and Chap 7, the consumer rarely perceives himself as adding to traffic congestion or air and noise pollu-

tion. As he drives along the crowded street, he looks about and asks himself: What are all these crazy people doing on the street at this hour? As he notes the air and noise pollution of the freeway, he says to himself: If we could only get rid of some of these vehicles, we could solve this problem. As he sits in the airplane impatiently awaiting his turn to take off, he muses: Why in the world do all these people travel at this time? The examples could go on and on but the point is that the consumer does not perceive that he is personally adding to the problem. It's always "the other guy" causing the difficulty. The consumer's view is completely individualistic and isolated in its frame of reference—it's "them" vs. "me"; rarely is it "us" or "we" causing the problem.

This widespread propensity to disregard the problem of aggregation must be recognized, for it is an important part of consumer action. The ramifications are many. The consumer may be perfectly willing to support restrictions on private automobile traffic in general but not to restrict his own use. The consumer as a taxpayer may be quite willing to support a tax to subsidize local transit but refuses to further support it with his patronage. The consumer may be quite willing to support an FAA policy of restricting takeoffs and landings at certain peak hours but writes his Congressman to complain of undue governmental interference when he cannot get airline service at eight in the morning. Many examples could be cited, but the point is that it is an immeasurable yet very real policy factor that in passenger transportation the consumer often acts with a completely individualistic approach. Splendid isolationalism and failure to recognize the problem of aggregation are very real factors, and transportation policy must react to them.

Summary on Current Policy Approach

Passenger transportation policy may be difficult to identify due to four hurdles: lack of a single policy statement, multiple levels of government and inherent conflicts, the interrelationship of freight and passenger service, and lack of means of communicating preference. Even so, we can ascertain three types or bases of current policy: one, statutory policy as contained in specific legislative declarations; two, informal policy as found in the repeated actions of governmental groups as to ownership patterns, investment concepts, modal orientation, and preference for choice; and three, consumer actions as exemplified by convenience-orientation, noneconomic behavior, and the individualistic approach. All of these add up to an immeasurable thing, hard to define and lacking logic and rationality, but which we call "current policy approach to passenger transportation."

FUTURE POLICY APPROACH

As noted above, it is inappropriate for us to attempt to dictate answers to these policy inconsistencies and inadequacies. However, we may suggest future approaches to policy problems. These can be summarized as the need for national goals, the need for budget goals, and the need for long-term planning.

Need for National Goals

The main element in a future approach to passenger transportation policy is the use of a "wholistic" approach. That is, we must begin to consider the "whole" of the problem and to conceive of a national goal for all of passenger transportation. Only by thinking wholistically will answers be possible to the broad goal contained in the question posed above: "How can society approach problems arising from passenger transportation in such a way as to ensure an economical and adequate system of transporting people now and in the future?"

Several elements are involved in the wholistic approach. First, we must consider national transportation policy as a national problem. While this seems self-evident, we have noted the conflicts between national, state, and local policy. Somehow these conflicts must be resolved—perhaps by better communication and coordination—and a total overall and truly national passenger transportation policy must emerge. This implies less regional thinking and more national thinking, less local thinking and more overall approach. The overall costs and benefits of a national transportation policy must be allowed to take precedence over regional and local preferences.

More important, perhaps, to the wholistic approach is the second element of thinking in terms of passenger transportation rather than the modal approach. Certainly it is time to abandon consideration of highways, railways, airways, waterways, and local transit as separate and distinct entities. They are all part of the system of passenger transportation and what happens in one area affects the others as well. Once we can abandon the approach of selectively considering airline transportation, street transportation, intercity bus transportation, international air transportation, and so forth, and begin to consider the whole of passenger transportation, the solutions to many problems will become clear. This is not to say that these specific elements disappear, but as an *approach,* society must consider passenger transportation as a *whole* rather than as modal parts.

The wholistic approach is easy to state but hard to implement. It means that the federal government, for example, must rethink the modal organization of its bureaus and departments. People involved in policy consideration must be willing to see that action on highways affects air transportation, that action on local transit affects automobile transportation, that action on the rail commuter problem affects street use, that action on international air transportation affects maritime passenger transportation. Indeed, the idea of a "system" has been repeatedly stressed in this book. We would stress once more that the approach must be to consider the passenger transportation system as a system, as a whole, and not as so many individual parts.

Once the wholistic approach and systems thinking are adopted, and once conflicts between governmental levels are overcome, then a truly national goal can emerge. The goal we have stated may or may not be an achievable one. Yet it is a goal, and a goal is needed. It is national, and national thinking is needed. Finally, it is wholistic and systems-oriented, and assuredly wholistic thinking and systems thinking are badly needed.

Need for Budget Goals

The second element in a future policy approach is to translate wholistic thinking about the passenger transportation system into dollars-and-cents terms. At present, the social budget for passenger transportation is uneven and mixed. Subsidy is given to some modes and not to others. Investment is made in one area and not in another. Of course, budget priorities must exist and some problems demand more attention than others. But the modal approach noted above is presently reinforced, perpetuated, and strengthened by a modal budget approach. Hence, there is a highway budget, an urban transportation budget, an airways and airport budget, and so forth—but no passenger transportation budget! The agencies involved, being restricted in their view to a modal world, work hard to justify their own needs for their own mode—be it highways, waterways, urban streets, or what have you. But as noted above, the wholistic approach and systems thinking demand that the interrelations between the parts be given primary consideration. The plea here is to translate this wholistic approach into budgetary terms.[4]

Need for Long-Term Planning

When society considers passenger transportation from the wholistic approach and as a system, and when this wholistic approach becomes translated into wholistic budgeting, the third factor of long-term planning is mandatory.

It is imperative that we begin to be future-oriented. To a considerable degree, previous passenger transportation policy has been oriented toward current problem solving ("putting out fires," as it were), correcting the mistakes of the past, or assisting one mode that has "fallen behind."[5] All too often, little or no consideration is given to the effects of present actions on the future. Decisions on urban transportation are made with an eye to solving a current problem with too little concern for what the future effects of these decisions will be on either urban development or intercity transportation. Intercity highway construction continues as an attempt to "catch up" by building an interstate system with practically no consideration given as to how this system will itself shape the future of passenger transportation. An Amtrak is established with the explicit goal of "preserving" intercity rail passenger transportation with precious little

---

[4] One small but unsuccessful attempt at this budgeting on a wholistic basis was the proposal by former Secretary of Transportation John Volpe for a "*transportation* trust fund" rather than a *highway* trust fund and an *aviation* trust fund, etc. For reasons of its own, Congress failed to adopt this approach and continues its modal thinking. However, in 1973, Congress did allow a portion of the highway trust fund to be diverted to urban transportation.

[5] It has been suggested that this tendency to enter into crash programs designed to "put out fires" or help one area of transportation "catch up," has actually become our national transportation policy since 1958. See Roy J. Sampson and Martin T. Farris, *Domestic Transportation: Practice, Theory, and Policy*, 3rd ed. (Boston: Houghton Mifflin Co., 1975), Chapter 23: "National Transportation Planning: A New Era," pp. 368-383.

consideration as to whether this service will be needed in the future. Freeways are constructed through cities without an adequate consideration of their future effects on the city and its neighborhoods. International air travel is stimulated to the detriment of maritime passenger transportation with practically no consideration of the future effects of increased international travel. Rarely are the effects of improved intercity transportation on urban systems given consideration. Other examples could be cited. Obviously, a future orientation must be assumed.

Two elements are involved in future orientation—the matter of goals and the matter of ramifications. It is imperative that we ask ourselves where we will be 10 years hence, 20 years hence, 30 years hence. Once we establish some idea of what conditions might exist in the future, the next question is what do we *want* the situation to look like 10 years, 20 years, or 30 years from now. In a word, what will the future be like and what is our goal for facing that situation or future condition?

Second, it is important that we realize that present action will have future ramifications. It is entirely possible that a type or mode of passenger transportation should be currently maintained because it is apparent that it will be needed in the future. In effect, society spends today so that it will not have to spend tomorrow. This may be much more logical than having to start over again at a later period. Many cities are finding today that it was a mistake to abandon local transit and that the ramifications of decisions made in the 1940s are acutely apparent in the 1970s. The abandonment of the Pacific Electric Suburban Rail System in Los Angeles in the 1940s and attempts to establish a new urban rail system in the 1970s provide a good example. We must realize that policy decisions to solve today's problems will have ramifications in tomorrow's world.

All of this is not to say that a "czar" will exist, a "big brother" who directs our transportation lives. Long-term planning does not imply coercion. But it does imply thinking about the future, establishing future alternatives, pointing out the future ramifications of current actions, and so forth.

Actually many governmental agencies at all levels are cognizant of the need for long-term planning, and many attempt to provide it. But two concluding comments should be made. First, too much of present long-term planning is modally oriented (for example, highway planning, airline planning, urban planning), and too little is wholistic and systems-oriented. If the systems approach is adopted and passenger transportation is considered as a whole, this modal orientation of long-term planning would disappear. Second, there is altogether too little long-term planning or future orientation on the part of the general public or society as a whole. Long-term planning is left to the long-term planners (and their efforts may be belittled or considered with amusement) while the general populace continues in its splendid isolation, concerned for the immediate and reluctant to think beyond its daily transportation requirements.

Society must learn to live with the future. The future means change. Change is sometimes distasteful and always uncertain. But the only certainty in life is that the future will not look like the past—that change will take place. Learning to live with change, be it the passenger transportation firm or the individual providing his own passenger transportation, is probably the biggest single task involved and certainly the biggest single problem of passenger transportation policy.

ADDITIONAL READINGS

DAVIS, GRANT M., "Significant Changes Derived from Establishing the U.S. Department of Transportation: An Evaluation," *Nebraska Journal of Economics and Business,* IX, no. 3 (Summer 1970), pp. 53-68.

FAIR, MARVIN L. and ERNEST W. WILLIAMS, Jr., *Economics of Transportation and Logistics.* (Dallas, Texas: Business Publications, Inc., 1975).
    Chap. 26: "National Transportation Policy," pp. 518-535.

FARRIS, MARTIN T., "National Transportation Policy: Fact or Fiction?" *Quarterly Review of Economics and Business,* X, no. 2 (Summer 1970), pp. 7-14.

MERTINS, HERMAN, JR., *National Transportation Policy in Transition* (Lexington, Mass.: D.C. Health Co., 1972).

NORTON, HUGH S., *National Transportation Policy: Formation and Implementation* (Berkeley, California: McCutchan Publishing Company, 1966).

PEGRUM, DUDLEY F., *Transportation: Economics and Public Policy,* 3rd ed. (Homewood, Illinois: Richard D. Irwin, Inc., 1973).
    Chap. 23: "The Urban Transportation Problem," pp. 534-568.

SAMPSON, ROY J. and MARTIN T. FARRIS, *Domestic Transportation: Practice, Theory and Policy,* 3rd ed (Boston: Houghton Mifflin Co., 1973).

    Chap. 23: "National Transportation Planning: A New Era," pp. 368-383.

    Chap. 28: "Passenger Transportation Policy Problems," pp. 455-472.

    Chap. 29: "Conflicts in National Transportation Policy," pp. 474-487.

SMERK, GEORGE M., "An Evaluation of Ten Years of Federal Policy in Urban Mass Transportation," *Transportation Journal,* vol II, no. 2 (Winter 1971), pp. 45-57.

WILSON, GEORGE W., "The Goals of Transportation Policy," *The Future of American Transportation,* Ernest W. Williams, Jr., ed. (Englewood Cliffs, N.J.: Prentice-Hall, Inc., 1971), pp. 9-40.

PART THREE

The
Future
Of
Passenger
Transportation

We have noted that one of the five problems flowing from passenger transportation systems is the problem of the future. Additionally, our last chapter ended with the thought that learning to live with change is a major problem in passenger transportation. It is obvious that we hope to be future-oriented in our approach and we hope our readers will likewise adopt such an approach.

Simply because of this orientation and hope, we end our analysis of passenger transportation with a separate division composed of a single chapter dedicated to the proposition that change and the future *are manageable*—and that management of the future is probably the most important single problem affecting passenger transportation.

9

MANAGING CHANGE AND THE FUTURE

Nothing is permanent except change. This premise, a challenge during the 1960s, has become an accepted reality in the 1970s. Contemporary man has been confronted with change of great magnitude, change that has permeated his society, his business, and even his home. The pace of change has become both a source of widespread promise and of lingering dread. Decision makers, living in these unsettled days, cannot avoid dealing with the unfamiliar. Consequently, they must recognize change, interpret its implications, and manage its direction within their firm or industry. This is the challenge of the times.

The major premise of this chapter is that broad and interrelated external environmental forces (and we use the term "environmental" in its broadest connotation) exert a major influence on the demand for and delivery of passenger transportation services. It is suggested, further, that there is a time lapse between change in one or more of the dynamic external environmental areas and its impact on problems relating to the movement of people. The external environment, therefore, is a potential lead indicator for persons and planners that may be useful in their attempts to anticipate, understand, and manage change.

Just as each biological organism exists within a broad environmental setting, so it is that industries, business firms, and individuals are also part of a larger environment. More specifically, industries and firms exist within both a market environment and an extended external environment. The market environment may be perceived as people—people with wants, money, and the willingness to spend. The external environment may be defined as those social, economic, political, technical, international, and competitive forces that affect the firm directly or indirectly. Both the market and the external environment are beyond the direct control of the individual, business firm, or industry. That is, although environmental conditions may be *influenced* through promotion, political activity, research and development, and other means, these environments are *not controllable* by anyone. As environmental changes occur, executives and planners must first recognize them and then adapt to them.

This approach may be analogous to the relationship between seeing a distant flash of lightning and hearing, several seconds later, the thunder. If one is looking for the lightning, he will be more prepared for the subsequent thunder. In this context, it is suggested that the focus of passenger transportation decision makers be directed toward the broad external environmental forces that may foretell change.

To lend support to these thoughts, we will seek certain direct and indirect relationships between changes in each of the external environmental areas (social, economic, political, technical, international, and competitive) and the means and ends of moving people. Then, in conclusion, we will utilize this environmentalist perspective to peer into the murky future of passenger transportation for the remainder of the twentieth century.

THE EXTERNAL ENVIRONMENT AND THE MANAGEMENT OF CHANGE

The external environment is made up of six separate "environments": the social, the economic, the political, the technological, the international, and the competitive. Each should be analyzed in turn in order for us to understand the whole external environment.

The Social Environment

It is clear that the movement of people has many broad social implications. Many aspects of group interaction, neighborhood character, and the geographic structure of society are involved. Further, the means of transportation (highways and streets, railroad right-of-ways, airports and airways, and bus routes) have been identified as often counterproductive to their intended end: the unification of people.

In recent years, the American social environment has evolved more rapidly than it has during perhaps any other period in our history. We have seen minority groups gain a sense of ethnic awareness and demand their full share of societal privileges. We continue to observe a younger generation that challenges many traditional values. We have witnessed the erosion of confidence in the future of our major cities take the form of massive migrations to the suburbs. The pollution and misuse of our natural resources, once accepted as the price of economic progress, has become repugnant to many Americans. Further, we have experienced a loss of trust in our political and business institutions. Although these represent only a few of the social environmental changes that have occurred during the last decade, each has profound and long-range transportation implications.

Minority-group spokesmen and other urban leaders have pointed to transportation networks as forces contributing to the continuation of sharply defined ghetto areas. Railroad tracks and freeways are cited as barriers between population segments that retard, rather than enhance, societal mobility. Limited public transportation facilities have been blamed for unemployment and underemployment as well as for the higher prices that are said to be charged by merchants catering to immobile consumers. These problems interact with other evidence of massive urban decay and threaten the very survival of certain cities. Although improved transportation is no panacea for these social ills, improved mass transportation facilities can play a role in improving the quality of urban life.

Young Americans are on the forefront of those contributing to social environmental change. They have been articulate in their emphasis on the need to alter aspects of our social structure and they have been successful in changing many of the attitudes that underlie societal values.

Young Americans have been among the leaders in condemning industry for its contribution to the pollution of our physical surroundings as well as for providing goods and services of questionable quality and merit. These attitudes, too, probably will endure.

Passenger transportation planners must take cognizance of the values represented by this generation. Its views have already altered the social environment of this country. And for many years to come, the setting in which all business endeavors, including transportation, exist will be shaped and defined by representatives of this group. The outcome may be a significant reordering of our national priorities.

The Economic Environment

The economic environment may be best perceived as an enabling force, which influences both the demand for passenger transportation services and the means for the delivery of those services. Changes in the economic environment, therefore, have an impact on both the demand and supply sides of the industry.

Events during the mid-1970s have induced some economists to postulate a period of economic stagnation and resource shortages for the United States and other industrialized nations. This change in the economic environment would have an effect on both business and pleasure travel. In the business sector, trips may be eliminated or postponed and coach class will often replace first-class accommodations as standard fare under such conditions. On the other hand, limitations on the use of private carriage could result in increased revenues for the carriers.

Just as business travel is affected by the ability of firms to pay, so is the pleasure market similarly tied to the economic expectations of individual consumers. The demand for pleasure travel, however, is much more elastic. Vacation trips, perceived as a luxury expense, are among the first consumption casualties during a period of economic uncertainty. In the past, it was the carriers who first felt the "pinch" as consumers who did not eliminate vacation trips altogether, revised their travel plans in favor of shorter journeys in which the family automobile was the dominant mode of transportation. This pattern of behavior was evident during the 1970 winter season. Caribbean or Hawaiian vacations were rejected in favor of the Florida beaches. However, at the same time that hotel occupancy rates were increasing, the traffic of air carriers serving Florida was declining. Vacationers were economizing by driving rather than flying. In the future, gasoline price increases and shortages may eliminate even this alternative during periods of economic downturn. If so, major dislocations could take place throughout the travel industry.

On the supply side, the impact of economic conditions is equally significant. The operation of those providing passenger transportation is characterized by extensive capital investments in technologically sophisticated equipment. Accompanying what is seemingly a capital-intensive industry are high labor costs that further increase the total cost of providing service. The cost of carrier operation, therefore, is most sensitive to the kind of inflationary pressures that have characterized the early 1970s. Revenues, however, are dependent not only on demand, but also on rate decisions made by regulatory agencies.

During periods of inflation, the costs of operation sharply increase, and during periods of economic uncertainty, the demand for service is eroded. Since the carriers ordinarily cannot rapidly alter route structures, schedules, or rates to meet increased operating costs, profit margins tend to decrease when either of the above conditions is present. Recently, they occurred simultaneously. As a result, the sharp cutbacks in service frequency that were required of the carriers in response to critical fuel shortages were often welcomed by airline management. Unprofitable routes were eliminated at the same time labor overhead was reduced. However, the initially favorable effects on carrier profits must be tempered by the costs associated with fleets of aircraft that are underutilized, and by continued sharp increases in the price of fuel.

If economic change is to be managed by transportation planners, it is essential that the myriad of economic data that are currently available be utilized more effectively to provide insights into what may await us in the future. This is a profound and complex task. Here the development and use of a management intelligence system could be of great value. More will subsequently be said about management intelligence systems.

The Political Environment

Those who provide passenger transportation services, or any industry deemed "affected with the public interest," have an intimate operating relationship with the political environment. Historically, national health and well-being have been greatly affected by transportation capabilities. As a result, participation by the "body politic" has been necessary even in a country where private forms of enterprise have prevailed. Change in the political environment has a substantial and unique impact, therefore, on the ways and means by which passengers are transported and on the internal policies of the carriers.

A legacy of the changing political conditions in the United States is the web of transportation-related laws, statutes, and ordinances that have evolved since this country's inception. To assure that the intent of such legislation is carried out, regulatory agencies have been created to oversee the day-to-day operation of all transportation carriers. Therefore, the operational milieu of the carriers has changed in response to the philosophical alterations that are brought about through political transitions. Legislation relating to both the direct operation of passenger transportation carriers and to the agencies of regulation has been affected.

Changes in the political environment have a direct bearing on the nature of the interface between government and the transportation industry. Among the most important implications of such change would be: (1) new legislation affecting the nature and scope of operations; (2) alterations in the amount and administration of public aid (government investment and subsidies); (3) new appointments to regulatory agencies, which could alter the philosophical makeup of these bodies; (4) long-range statements of national transportation policy that could shape the industry's future.

Further, it should be noted that inherent in the system of regulation are certain limitations on the prerogatives of passenger transportation management. The dual role of regulation (protecting society and promoting the industry) limits executive action in regard to market entry and exit, price determination, and the standards of service offered. Consequently, the marketing of transportation services, as well as their delivery, are substantially influenced by the political environment.

The Technological Environment

Transportation has always been directly connected to the technological environment. Advancing technology has influenced both the development and the maturation of the physical means through which both people and goods are moved.

Effect of Technological Change.   While there are many effects, we can note four specific results of technological change that involve the many dimensions of passenger transportation. First, technology has greatly altered the dominant type of vehicles utilized. Since the turn of the century, we have seen horse-drawn coaches give way to the automobile as the primary form of private carriage. Public inter-city transportation, once the realm of the railroads, is now dominated by air carriers. Second, technological progress has brought higher levels of passenger safety. Aircraft are routed, monitored, and con-trolled by electronic devices. Surveillance of railroad operations and public transportation services has been improved through the use of highly sophisticated automated systems. Research continues toward a goal of lessening the hazards of highway travel. New urban systems such as BART have safety features not even dreamed about two decades ago. Third, technology has helped carriers increase and im-prove the services provided to their customers. The automation of travel information and reservation services, previously developed by the air carriers, has now been adopted by Amtrak. Air-ground com-munication is available to passengers on many flights. Dial-a-bus systems, using computers to route vehicles to passengers' doorsteps, are in use. Fourth, the efficiency of operation has been enhanced through applications of technology. One example, of special signifi-cance during periods of fuel shortages, is related to the availability of a new generation of wide-bodied aircraft (Boeing 747s, DC-10s, Lockheed Tri-stars). Utilization of the "jumbo jets" enables carriers to reduce service frequency without significantly lessening capacity. The continued substitution of these larger aircraft into a contracted schedule could result in lower total operating costs, maintained capacity levels, and improved load factors.

We cannot discuss the technological environment without ref-erence to the computer. No postwar development has had more implications for American business, both in its current effect on day-to-day functions and in its potential for future applications.

Some uses and potential uses of computers in passenger trans-portation are: research and problem solving, operations, weather information, reservations, in-flight control, handling clerical detail, purchasing and procurement of supplies, maintenance, highway monitoring and control, the operation of urban transportation sys-tems such as BART, determining fuel use and energy requirements, matching originations and destinations in car pools, and many other important activities. However, in the context of this chapter, the most relevant computer application may be its potential in the crucial and complex task of managing change.

It was previously mentioned that management intelligence sys-tems show great promise as a tool that may be utilized in the management of change. The computer, as a processing device, lies at the heart of these systems.

Management Intelligence Systems.   The management intelligence system (MIS) is an interacting structure of people, equipment, methods, and controls designed to create an information flow. The distinguishing features, compared to traditional data sources, are the quantity of diverse, interrelated, and relevant data it can provide; the speed with which these data can be collected, processed, and transmitted; and the continuous flows (rather than intermittent statements) of information to the *appropriate* decision makers.

There are many potential advantages of an MIS in transportation planning. First, it can provide inputs of information from other internal and external environmental sources. Second, it can permit quicker recognition of trends in these environmental areas. Third, it can become a coordinating agent. In this capacity it would enable management to integrate data from many academic disciplines and thus assist corporate planners in the anticipation, recognition, and handling of external environmental change. Fourth, it can make data available within the time constraints involved in contemporary decision making. Finally, utilization of a management intelligence system can enhance the control management exerts over its entire operation.

The inputs to a management intelligence system utilized in passenger transportation could come from: top management, marketing research, accounting and finance, operations, sales, systems analysts, operations researchers, statisticians, programmers, transportation planners, computer equipment experts, suppliers, and company or public employees. Further, and more directly related to our discussion of the management of change, inputs from experts in each of the external environmental areas highlighted in this chapter could be included in the system.

The outputs of a transportation-oriented management intelligence system are integrated flows of information, presented in usable form and rapidly directed to appropriate decision makers. The result could be to make a change a much more manageable phenomenon.

The International Environment

With a suddenness that startled executives and planners throughout the world, an energy shortage of severe proportions emerged in late 1973 to signal the end of an illusion of endless natural-resource abundance. The shortages of energy that, in reality, had been unfolding for over a decade attained crisis levels when Middle Eastern oil producers began to restrict shipments to most industrialized nations. The potential economic impact of this action is grave. Economists in Japan, where 90 percent of all oil products are imported from Arab nations, sharply revised downward their predictions of a 10 percent real economic growth figure for 1974. Economic spokesmen for European countries, dependent on the Arab states for about 70 percent of their oil, expressed deep concern about the economic well-being of their community of nations. Even though much less dependent on foreign energy, the United States imposed strict conservation requirements on its citizens.

Although virtually every American industry will be affected in some degree by energy shortages, for the transportation and travel industries, the problem is crucial. They simply cannot operate without fuel.

The airline industry was one of the first to react to fuel shortages. Flight cutbacks, personnel layoffs, lower operating speeds, and airport tie-ups characterized the initial problems faced by airline management. Travelers, long accustomed to capacity surpluses, found themselves faced with a new set of circumstances. Printed schedules suddenly were badly out-of-date. Seat shortages and advance booking requirements made last minute travel difficult for both businessmen and pleasure travelers. Airport congestion caused massive check-in and baggage snarls. On the other hand, even though the airlines were badly pinched for fuel, the energy crisis proved to be a convenient excuse for gracefully eliminating much of their unprofitable service and at the same time enabled them to trim payrolls. In fact, the overall effect of the energy crisis on carrier profitability, as reflected in early 1974 data, was generally rather favorable.

Other passenger carriers also felt the glow of windfall traffic increases. Travel by bus increased by 10 percent as gasoline restrictions prompted motorists to seek reliable public transportation. The larger interstate bus lines are seeking to expand their capacity with new equipment designed to handle anticipated demand increases. Bicycle and motorcycle sales spurted.

Paralleling this experience, Amtrak also realized dramatic increases in passengers carried in the twilight of 1973. Reservations and service inquiries increased by 25 percent as both motorists and air travelers sought transportation alternatives. To meet the increased demand, Amtrak management utilized all available equipment and shifted railroad cars from sparsely traveled routes to key points. Major new increases in capacity will be limited by the one- to four-year lead time required for the construction of new equipment.

Throughout the vacation and travel industry, concern is being expressed over the potential impact of energy shortages and higher prices on revenues and profits. The initial impact of reduced weekend and other leisure-time motoring plus the cutbacks in scheduled and private air service is magnified by pessimistic short-term economic forecasts. During periods of economic downturn, travel is one of the items most quickly trimmed from business and family budgets.

The impact of sharply higher oil prices on the economies of industrialized nations throughout the world makes the international environment a focal point for all business forecasters. The availability and the price of imported oil will define the nature and the scope of their operations for the foreseeable future.

The Competitive Environment

The competitive environment in passenger transportation extends beyond the usual intermodal or intramodal comparisons. Intermodal competition, once reduced to the private automobile versus "the field," has been stimulated by recent shortages of energy. A revival of passenger interest in rail intercity bus, mass transit, and bicycle transportation has been discussed. Even transoceanic steamships may experience an upsurge in popularity.

Intramodal competition, especially among air carriers, remains intense. In fact, much of what previously has been said about the marketing of passenger transportation services applies directly to competition between the airlines. However, as important as successful intramodal and intermodal competition are to the survival of individual carriers and to the overall quality of service offered, it is only after other aspects of the competitive environment are considered that such competition becomes a matter of relevance.

For the pleasure traveler, transportation is part of a larger system that includes hotel accommodations, food service, automobile rentals, and other related services. This larger system may be termed the tourist industry. Tourism is generally considered a luxury expense by consumers. In affluent societies, there are many products and services that compete for an individual's discretionary dollars. Clothing, jewelry, motorcars, appliances, furs, various kinds of entertainment, private education, and travel are all competitive in this market. For example, one may choose between a new sports car and a trip to Europe. A husband can select a mink stole or a Hawaiian vacation as a gift for his wife. In any case, however, the primary consideration for the passenger transportation carriers is that travel be chosen from among the multitude of competing goods and services. It is only then that competition between modes of transport, individual carriers, and classes of service comes into focus.

Other aspects of the total system of tourism are included in the decision matrix of consumers, and should be considered by those providing transportation services. In deciding between various geographic areas, the potential traveler may consider comparative aesthetics, the relative costs of travel, the dependability and availability of hotel accommodations, the quality of food service, and a host of other issues. Since individual carriers are limited in the number of geographic areas they serve, they should be vitally concerned that travelers choose to visit areas covered by *their* route structure. In other words, if a carrier has routes to Hawaii but not to Mexico or Europe, management of that carrier should work to assure that Hawaii maintains its competitive position as a tourism center. Geographic competition, then, is another dimension of the travel market. Since both the preference for various types of luxury goods and services and the relative attractiveness and novelty of geographic areas are subject to change, the competitive environment becomes another dynamic external area toward which managerial attention must be focused. It is suggested that not only must the transportation executives remain attuned to competitive environmental change but, further, they must form closer associations with those providing other tourism services. Cooperative efforts between those in the hotel, food, auto rental, and transportation industries have recently been undertaken. They are to be encouraged.

THE MANAGEMENT OF CHANGE: IMPLICATIONS FOR ACTION FOR CARRIERS AND DECISION MAKERS

It has been said that to manage a business or a public enterprise is to manage its future. The management of the future is the management of information. Managing information entails obtaining and interpreting data relating to the external, as well as to the internal, environments of business. The essence of the management of change is to be found in an external environmental orientation on the part of passenger transportation planners. We have, in this chapter, pointed to external environmental variables as important lead indicators of relevant future events. The recognition and utilization of such indicators are important in the complex task of managing the challenges and opportunities brought by change.

In order to optimize the management of change through utilization of some of the ideas presented in this discussion, three recommended actions are suggested. They are: (1) a focus on environmental variables, (2) the use of specialists, and (3) the use of management intelligence systems.

Focus on Environmental Variables

Executive and decision-maker focus should include both internal and external environmental variables. Executives within and outside the transportation industry traditionally have been oriented not to the external environment but internally, toward the functional areas within their operations. Attention has been focused on a much narrower range of finance, marketing, or production issues. Businessmen and planners have become skilled in interpreting accounting reports, sales information, production schedules, and a host of other intrafirm or industry data. This perspective is necessary but insufficient.

Looking at dynamic market conditions with an internal environmental perspective is, by definition, to focus on the past and not on the future. That which is observable (and reportable) is already part of the past. Planning based solely on such information contains much obsolescence. In effect, such planning is simply a reaction to change rather than the management of change. To *manage* change is to *anticipate* change.

Use of Specialists

External environmental specialists should be included with those staff specialists who now advise passenger transportation executives and planners. The anticipation of external environmental change is a complex and specialized task. Executives and decision makers, trained to handle problems in a business environment, are often simply not equipped to suddenly become experts in an environment containing social, economic, political, technical, international, and competitive dimensions.

Some firms and political entities have recognized this problem and taken steps to solve it. They have hired specialists to help them gain insight into specific aspects of their operations from an external environmental perspective. For example, economists currently play an important role in interpreting and predicting economic environmental changes and in suggesting appropriate courses of adaptive action. In the area of technology, leaders in various technical fields have been called together to render their predictions of forthcoming technological advances. These predictions are then refined and converted into implications for corporate and public action. Management also relies on the opinions of statisticians, engineers, psychologists, attorneys, and others to provide the expertise upon which complex decisions may be based. Key members of the corporate staff or the planning staff assume the role of synthesists, bringing together and evaluating the ideas of specialists. Their insights then become important inputs in the decision-making process.

It is suggested that there also be other specialists, with expertise that could be of significant value in the identification, prediction, and interpretation of external environmental variations. Political scientists, geographers, foreign affairs specialists, physicians, ecologists, urban planners, sociologists, cultural anthropologists, and assorted "futurists"—all have specialized knowledge that could make a measurable contribution to the attempts of passenger transportation executives to manage change.

Use of Management Intelligence Systems

Management intelligence systems should be recognized as an important executive and planning tool in the process of managing change. While advice of outside consultants is not a panacea for those attempting to manage change, their expertise would provide decision makers with a substantial range of information previously not available to them. In the management of change, executives and decision makers can use available flows of data that parallel fluid external environmental conditions. Such a system would enable them to have a moving view of their operations against a dynamic environmental backdrop. The use of management intelligence systems is *mandatory*.

PASSENGER TRANSPORTATION AND THE FUTURE

The past is history, interesting for what it can explain about the present or lead us to expect about the future. The present is only an instant of time, a transition between past and future, which disappears as we contemplate it. Our focus must be on the future.

As a conclusion to this chapter, let us peer into the somewhat murky future of passenger transportation. If we consider the capabilities of today against the challenges of tomorrow, somewhere between the two should be found that which will constitute the future of passenger transportation.

Society

The future of our society is clouded by questions relating to the availability of energy and other natural resources. In these projections, it is assumed that these resources will continue to be available, but in lesser quantities and at higher prices than was the case in previous decades. Societal concern for conservation will cause products to be designed for easy repair, recycling, and longer life. The quest for continually higher productivity will shift to an emphasis on efficiency in the utilization of materials and energy. The concept of limitless resources will be laid to rest along with other remnants from our frontier days.

The urbanization of America will continue, but the geographic growth of metropolitan areas will level off. Our population will grow older as a result of both increased life-spans and declining birth rates. People will have more leisure time because of four-day workweeks, longer vacations, and earlier retirements. The population will be more educated, and mobility in employment will become even more common. There will be greater equality in the distribution of wealth among the citizens of tomorrow.

Technology

Projections of technology should avoid the popular "Sunday supplement" kind of forecasting. Although technological advances will take place at a steady pace, it is not realistic to expect our pressing transportation problems to be solved simply by some vague future technological breakthrough. It is more likely that solutions will come through step-by-step technological progress and through more ingenious applications of what we currently know.

The major technological thrust of the future will be toward the development of alternative sources of energy. Energy from nuclear, tidal, wind, geothermic, and solar origins will become available in varying degrees. Nuclear power will emerge to provide more of our electrical energy.

Speed may be de-emphasized in favor of increased fuel economy. Supersonic air travel probably will not make inroads in the service plans of international passenger carriers. However, high-speed rail service will become more common.

Improved travel safety will continue to be an important objective. Automation in all modes of passenger transportation will reduce collision hazards. The air and rail carriers will improve their already enviable safety records. The everyday security of the citizens of tomorrow will be enhanced through the use of helicopters and other technological advances by those providing police and fire protection and ambulance service.

Air Transportation

Safety and efficiency of operation will characterize the operations of air carriers. The facilities of those providing air service will be decentralized to reduce ground time. Feeder and outlying airports will be utilized more extensively. New types of vehicles, including aircraft with vertical takeoff and landing capabilities, may be utilized to expand and speed service. The price structures of interstate and intercontinental air service may achieve some stability, reflecting the productivity increases brought about by improved load factors and larger aircraft. Carrier profitability, however, will be tempered by significant investments in new capital equipment and by increased fuel costs.

Adequate supplies of energy will be available, but there will be limitations on supply allocations. The streamlining of carrier route structures will continue, with efficiency of operations replacing frequency as the prime carrier objective. Third-level, or commuter, airlines, will emerge to serve many of the routes dropped by the major carriers. Their impact will be positive, reducing fuel consumption by utilizing smaller aircraft and by providing service to outlying areas previously only accessible by automobile.

Railroads

The revival of rail passenger service, which has seemed just around the corner during recent years, will finally arrive as part of a larger energy-conservation program. Railroad planners will probably resist the temptation of across-the-board competition with air carriers and concentrate their passenger resources in high-yield geographic areas. The megalopolises of Southern California, the Eastern Seaboard, and the Great Lakes region constitute the most important passenger markets. Railroads probably will become the major regional carriers of people. Their operations will reflect the service styles and standards of the airlines.

Intercity Highway Transportation

Highways will continue as the backbone of intercity travel where densities of movement are light, between smaller cities, as interconnections to long-distance systems, and for vacation travel. While development of economical and efficient long-distance systems will decrease our dependence on automobiles, we foresee no demise of the private car. Highways will continue to exist, although continued freeway development will probably diminish. Highways to serve intercity buses and motor freight carriers will continue to be available to the commercial and pleasure traveler and his car.

We foresee more built-in safety in the highways of the future with more divided lanes, less hazardous curves and grades, and more safety devices to decrease the appalling human suffering caused by today's highway accidents. Perhaps even automatic guidance systems will come about.

Since energy, along with environmental concerns, will be a major consideration, highway vehicles will cease to be a major source of pollution—either as a result of increased efficiency in the internal combustion engine or through new power sources. The automobile of the future will tend to be less of a status symbol, and functional performance will be stressed. Fuel economy and reliability will be the most important purchase considerations.

Urban Transportation

The focus of transportation will increasingly be on the movement of people in urban areas. New systems, perhaps modeled on the Bay Area Rapid Transit format or the Morgantown Personal Rapid Transit System will be developed by urban planners where densities permit. The increased use of bicycles seems inevitable. Where densities are low, applications of the "Dial-A-Bus" experiment will be utilized. The integration of all modes of urban transport into one operational system will be an important outgrowth of energy-related research and experimentation. The emerging systems will have freight- as well as passenger-carrying capacity, thus reducing the total number of vehicles on city streets.

Downtown and other central city areas may regain much of their former glow as massive redevelopment projects are completed. Malls with trees, flowers, shrubbery, and walkways could replace crowded city streets. Bicycle paths will become part of the urban transportation network. Vehicle traffic will be routed around or below urban centers. And, to the delight of downtown retailers, this park-like atmosphere will draw shoppers.

Energy shortages will spark a migration back into the central cities and contribute to a reconstruction of many homes in formerly decaying neighborhoods. High-rise buildings will be constructed to combine residential, commercial, and office facilities in one location. Employees will be able to take an elevator a few floors to their offices instead of facing the commuter rush twice a day.

Parking in the downtown areas will be a less crucial problem in the future, as it will have long been unfashionable, impractical, or unlawful to drive private vehicles in these areas.

Regulation

Governmental agencies regulating all aspects of transportation will be restructured under congressional guidelines designed to refocus the activities of regulators toward protection of the public rather than toward the sheltering of individual carriers.

As a result of energy concerns, political institutions will become more responsive to current transportation needs. There will be philosophical changes in transportation regulation that will encourage intermodal and intercarrier cooperation. Unification, integration, and coordination of the entire system will be stressed.

Finally, a national transportation policy will have emerged to establish clear objectives for the industry. The tangled web of legislation that had developed over the previous 100 years will have been reviewed and rewritten into one piece of omnibus legislation.

SUMMARY ON MANAGING CHANGE AND THE FUTURE

These comments reveal our optimism about the ability of this nation to solve its problems, energy-related and otherwise, and in its future ability to transport people in an efficient and pleasant way. But all of these future developments turn on the management of change and the related ability to meet the challenges of the years ahead. We hope that the challenge of change and the promise of tomorrow will become an inspiration to those of our readers who will be involved in shaping a better transportation system in a more livable environment. It is our expectation that their actions will contribute to a more satisfying life for us all.

ADDITIONAL READINGS

BUEL, RONALD A., *The Automobile in Mass Transportation* (Englewood Cliffs, N.J.: Prentice-Hall, Inc., 1972).

CAPOZZA, DENNIS R., *The Economic Impact of Declining Population in Los Angeles* (Los Angeles: Center for Futures Research, University of Southern California, 1973).

CHINOY, ELY, *The Urban Future* (New York: Leiber-Atherton, 1973).

CLAWSON, MARION and PETER HALL, *Planning and Urban Growth: An Anglo-American Comparison* (Baltimore: John Hopkins University Press, 1973).

CREIGHTON, ROGER L., *Urban Transportation Planning* (Urbana: University of Illinois Press, 1970).

DOUGLAS, LATHRUP, "Tomorrow: Omnicenters on the Landscape?" *Harvard Business Review*, LII, no. 2 (1974), 8-12.

FREEMAN, S. DAVID, *Energy, The New Era* (New York: Walker and Company, 1974).

HEBERT, RICHARD, *Highways to Nowhere: The Politics of City Transportation* (Indianapolis: The Bobbs-Merrill Company, Inc., 1972).

HELLMAN, HAL, *Transportation in the World of the Future* (New York: M. Evans and Company, Inc., 1968).

HELLMAN, HAL, *Transportation in the World of the Future* (New York: M. Evans and Company, Inc., 1968.)

HOLLANDER, STANLEY, *Passenger Transportation* (East Lansing, Michigan: Michigan State University Business Studies, 1968). See especially pt. VIII, pp. 598-650.

NORTON, H. S., *National Transportation Policy: Formulation and Implementation* (Berkeley: McCutchan Publishing Company, 1967).

ORLEANS, PETER, *Social Structure and Social Process* (Boston: Allyn and Bacon, 1969).

SOBIN, DENNIS, P., *The Future of the American Suburbs: Survival or Extinction* (Port Washington, N.Y.: National University Publications, Kennikat Press, 1971).

STONE, TABOR, *Beyond the Automobile* (Englewood Cliffs, N.J.: Prentice-Hall, Inc., 1971).

THOMSON, GEORGE, *The Foreseeable Future* (London: Cambridge University Press, 1965).

WILLIAMS, E. W., *The Future of American Transportation* (Englewood Cliffs, N.J.: Prentice-Hall, Inc., 1971).

INDEX

Date Due

Due	Returned	Due	Returned
FEB 12 '79	FEB 1 4 '79		
APR 25 '79	MAY 3 '79		
MAY 24 '79	MAY 2 9 '79		
JUL 28 79	OCT 1 79		
DEC 14 '79	DEC 14 '79		
JUL 2 3 1980	AUG 1 5 '80		
OCT 2 6 1990	OCT 2 1 90		
APR 1 6 1984	APR 1 9 1984		
MAR 1 9 1987	MAR 2 4 1997		
SEP 2 1 1988	SEP 1 9 1988		
OCT 1 0 1988	OCT 1 2 1988		
NOV 0 6 1988	NOV 0 9 1988		
APR 1 3 1989			
JUN 0 9 1989			
AUG 0 7 1989	AUG 1 5 1989		
APR 3 0 1990	APR 1 3 1990		
JAN 0 7 1991	NOV 0 7 1990		